M & E HANDBOOKS

M & E Handbooks are recommended reading for examination syllabuses all over the world. Because each Handbook covers its subject clearly and concisely books in the series form a vital part of many college, university, school and home study courses.

Handbooks contain detailed information stripped of unnecessary padding, making each title a comprehensive self-tuition course. They are amplified with numerous self-testing questions in the form of Progress Tests at the end of each chapter, each text-referenced for easy checking. Every Handbook closes with an appendix which advises on examination technique. For all these reasons, Handbooks are ideal for pre-examination revision.

The handy pocket-book size and competitive price make Handbooks the perfect choice for anyone who wants to grasp the essentials of a subject quickly and easily.

THE M & E HANDBOOK SERIES

Human Resources Management

H. T. Graham
DPA, Dip Soc Stud, FIPM, MBIM
Principal Lecturer in Personnel Management,
Croydon College

FOURTH EDITION

18/5/85

MACDONALD AND EVANS

Macdonald & Evans Ltd
Estover, Plymouth PL6 7PZ

First published 1974
Reprinted 1976, 1977
Second edition 1978
Reprinted with amendments 1979
Third edition 1980
Reprinted 1981
Fourth edition 1983

British Library Cataloguing in Publication Data

Graham, H. T.
  Human resources management.—4th ed.—(The
M & E HANDBOOK series)
  1. Personnel management
  I. Title II. Series
  658.3   HF5549

ISBN 0–7121–0822–X

Printed in Great Britain by
Richard Clay (The Chaucer Press) Ltd,
Bungay, Suffolk

Preface to the Fourth Edition

Human resources management is a subject which under various titles appears to an increasing extent in many professional and technical courses. It combines elements of industrial psychology, personnel management, training and industrial relations, therefore raising difficulties for the student because he is referred to a large number of textbooks, nearly all including much more detail than he needs and some not easily available or accessible. This HANDBOOK brings together in concise form the essential points he requires and relates the various parts of the subject to each other by cross-references between chapters and sections. The book therefore provides a framework for the study of the subject and an aid to examination revision. In addition it may also be useful to managers who wish to have a convenient reference book covering the human aspects of their work.

In this fourth edition, changes have been made in Chapter XXV, on industrial relations, to take account of the provisions of the Employment Act 1982, though at the time of writing not all the provisions of the Act are in force. Some other sections of the book have also been revised, particularly those dealing with motivation, personnel records and the general approach to personnel management. The bibliography and specimen examination questions (Appendixes VII and VIII) have also been updated.

The reader is reminded that employment law is very complex and this book can only summarise its main provisions; for full details the statutes themselves or specialist textbooks should be consulted.

For convenience, the term company has been used to denote any kind of employer, public or private, large or small, in preference to such words as undertaking, enterprise or organisation. The words employee or worker refer to any employed person, whether paid by wage or salary.

Further reading on this subject is, of course, essential and Appendix VI lists books which, at the time of writing, are easy to obtain and comparatively inexpensive.

Some of the examinations for which this book should be found useful are:

Diploma and Certificate in Management Studies;
Fellowship of the Chartered Insurance Institute;
Institute of Management Services;
London Chamber of Commerce and Industry, private secretary's certificate;
National Examination Board for Supervisory Studies (NEBSS);
Institute of Administrative Management;
Institute of Personnel Management;
Institute of Chartered Secretaries and Administrators;
BEC national and higher diplomas.

1983   HTG

Contents

INDUSTRIAL PSYCHOLOGY

CHAPTER I

Elementary Individual Psychology

INTRODUCTION

1. Definition. The purpose of human resources management is to ensure that the employees of a company, i.e. its human resources, are used in such a way that the employer obtains the greatest possible benefit from their abilities and the employees obtain both material and psychological rewards from their work. It is based on the findings of industrial psychology summarised in the first part of this book and uses the techniques and procedures known collectively as personnel management which are described in the second part. Everyone who has control over others shares in human resources management; it is not a function which he can avoid and leave to specialists. Human resources are much more difficult to manage than material resources, partly because conflict often occurs between the employer's and the employees' wishes and partly because to an increasing extent employees try to share in making decisions about their working environment.

2. Psychology and the manager. The above definition implies that the manager, to be successful, must understand and be able to use personnel management techniques and in addition have some knowledge of the principles of industrial psychology on which they are based. He must be aware of the results of psychological studies of the employee as an individual, as a member of a working group and as a person whose behaviour is influenced to some extent by his technological environment. No one can lay down precise laws of psychology; we have to be content with tendencies, principles or theories rather than laws. It is possible to predict how the majority of people will behave in certain circumstances but almost impossible to foresee whether an individual will belong to the majority or the minority. The reason for this is the nature of psychology itself.

3. Psychology as a science. In their investigations into natural phenomena, scientists try to follow accepted rules in order to reach well-founded conclusions. Scientific method, as these rules are called, requires the following.

(*a*) *Facts which are impersonal*, i.e. independent of any particular observer. Impressions or opinions should be avoided.

(*b*) *Objective observations*, i.e. separate observers will agree when observing the same phenomenon simultaneously, or when it is repeated on different occasions. Subjective observations, i.e. those which depend on interpretation, surmise or judgment by an individual, should not be used.

(*c*) *Investigation into all aspects of the problem*, rather than making assumptions. Every possible fact should be collected and considered.

(*d*) *Experimental controls*, so that changes in one factor (the subject of the experiment) are observed while other factors are kept unchanged.

(*e*) *Quantitative measurements and descriptions*. The need to provide measurements improve the design of an experiment, and numerical results can be classified and analysed, if necessary by statistical methods.

A study of these rules of scientific method will show how difficult it is to carry out truly scientific investigations into human behaviour.

(*a*) *Behaviour is very often interpreted* according to an observer's *own* experience and personality (*see* **10**).

(*b*) Human behaviour has a quality which on any occasion *may please some judges and displease others*, or the same observer may form a different opinion of the same behaviour when it is repeated. Completely identical judgments rarely occur.

(*c*) Investigation of all aspects would include, for example, *complete knowledge of a person's heredity and environment* (*see* IV, **2**). This is never possible with human beings.

(*d*) *It is very difficult to control experiments with human beings* because it is impossible to know that all factors (except the one being investigated) are really stable. There may be unknown influences at work (e.g. dislike of the experimenter) and interference by various factors in the environment cannot in practice be eliminated.

(*e*) *Many aspects of human behaviour cannot be measured*, for example personality traits (*see* IV, **9–15**).

4. Improving the quality of experiments. Psychological investigations can never therefore be truly scientific, though every effort should be made to follow scientific method as far as possible. The following methods are often used to improve the quality of experiments.

(*a*) *Animals instead of humans* are sometimes the subjects of experiments, because their heredity and environment can be closely controlled and because they are available in large numbers. Obviously, it should not be assumed that animal behaviour is necessarily a true guide to human behaviour.

(*b*) *Large groups of experimental subjects* are used instead of individuals or small groups. Results from large groups will indicate a statistical probability of certain behaviour. For example, an experiment regarding a selection test might show that out of every 100 people reaching a score of X, about seventy-five will be successful in a certain occupation—but the identities of the successful and unsuccessful candidates in any group cannot be shown.

(*c*) As far as possible, people are studied in their *normal environment* and not in a laboratory or some other artificial situation which would make their behaviour untypical.

Psychology therefore does not give us infallible laws of behaviour, but instead suggests a series of principles, theories or tendencies which predict with a fair degree of accuracy how most people will behave in various situations, and can explain behaviour after it has occurred. In this and the following chapters the principles of psychology most relevant to industry and commerce will be considered.

ATTENTION AND PERCEPTION

5. Sensation. People, like the police, act on the basis of information received. The information coming from a person's environment reaches him through his *senses*, by messages called *sensations*. The following are the most important senses, nearly all of which need no explanation.

(*a*) Sight.
(*b*) Hearing.
(*c*) Smell.
(*d*) Taste.
(*e*) Skin (pressure, heat, cold, pain, etc.).
(*f*) Balance.
(*g*) Kinaesthesis (means of knowing the position and movement of limbs by messages received from muscles and tendons).

Therefore at any time a variety of information regarding the outside world is reaching a person's brain through his senses. The amount of information would be overwhelming and baffling unless some arrangement, called *attention*, was made to deal with the relevant and necessary part of it, discarding the rest.

6. Attention. The selection of certain sensations to be dealt with by the conscious mind may be either deliberate or involuntary.

(*a*) *Deliberate*—by an effort of will irrelevant, useless or distracting sensations are shut out. A student may in time develop the power of reading a textbook in a room where others are watching television, or a worker may concentrate on a job disregarding conversation going on round him. Certain sensations are only recognised if they are searched for deliberately, for example the ticking of a clock.

(*b*) *Involuntary*—a person, even though he is attempting to concentrate, may find that certain sensations are forced on his attention by the subject matter of the information, or the form in which it is presented. The factors which govern involuntary attention are divided into two groups: subjective and objective.

7. Subjective and objective factors of attention. Subjective factors of attention are the elements in sensations which carry a personal message; the sound of a long-awaited bus, or one's name mentioned in a conversation at the other side of a crowded room. Sensations which have a personal interest, or comply with current moods and needs, are likely to take precedence for our conscious attention over sensations which are impersonal, neutral or relevant to others rather than ourselves.

Objective factors of attention are those which lie outside the personality of the receiver; they are likely to have the same effect on everyone. They chiefly concern the form in which the sensation is presented rather than its subject matter. The objective factors are as follows.

(*a*) *Intensity*—the loudness, brightness or size of the sensation. Shouted words are more likely to receive attention than a whisper, vivid colours more than pastel shades, a stench more than a faint odour.

(*b*) *Change or movement*—constant variety in the shape, size or position of an object will cause it to be noticed. This factor applies particularly to the sense of sight.

(*c*) *Repetition*—something seen, heard, etc., over and over again is likely to receive conscious attention providing the repetition does not become monotonous and accepted as customary, like the lamp-posts along a road.

(*d*) *Systematic arrangement into patterns*—sensations presented in an orderly way, for example a notice set out with headings and sections, is more likely to receive attention than an untidy and confused arrangement. The completion of a pattern is also significant; for example after a flash of lightning people usually listen to see if a clap of thunder will follow, or a speaker may hold the attention of his audience by saying he will make five points and delaying his exposition of the fifth until the end of his speech.

(*e*) *Novelty*—the unusual or unexpected event is always likely to receive more attention than the familiar. A person normally dressed quietly and conventionally will be noticed if he wears bright-coloured bizarre clothes; a speaker, to obtain his audience's attention, may begin with an outrageous assertion which he then knocks down.

8. The relevance of attention in management. The advertising profession makes use of the subjective and objective factors of attention when devising advertisements and publicity campaigns (see *Marketing* by G. B. Giles, M & E HANDBOOK series). Managers should also bear these factors in mind when communicating with employees (*see* IX). Some of the factors are less relevant than others to managers (for example, change or movement), and at work subjective factors tend to be more important than objective, but the use of the appropriate principles of attention is vital if communications within an organisation are to be effective.

9. Perception. Sensations are by themselves no more than colours, shapes, sounds, pains, pressures, etc. Something must be added to them before they have meaning and their source is identified. The mental function of giving significance to sensations is called *perception*; for example, one *perceives* black marks on white paper as words and sentences. The process of perception appears to follow the following principles.

(*a*) *The brain relates incoming sensations to its store of past experiences* and associates them with events or objects which in the past have provided the same or similar sensations.

(*b*) *A meaning is then perceived*; for example, a sound may be recognised as a train, another as a bus (perhaps mistakenly—it may be a lorry).

(*c*) *If the sensation does not appear to provide evidence*, confirmation may be sought by looking for other sensations to support the first. For example, if someone is not sure whether the sound he hears represents a bus or not, he may look among the approaching traffic to see if a bus is there.

(*d*) *Perception may be made confidently and sometimes wrongly* on the basis of little sensory information. A slight change of facial expression is sometimes perceived as meaning approval, disapproval, interest, indifference, etc.

(*e*) *Perception may be influenced by suggestion*. It is difficult for one individual to perceive a sensation in a different way from a group or an influential person, because a certain perception is suggested to him. Pre-conceptions can affect perception by suggestion; for example in a firm where industrial relations are poor, practically any action or statement by management may be perceived as hostile to the employees. Sometimes one sense may influence the perception of another sense; for example, a voice may seem to emerge from a ventriloquist's dummy.

(*f*) Perception is also influenced by a person's *motives* (*see* II) and attitudes (*see* VII, **12**). He tends to perceive sensations in ways which conform to his general outlook, are welcome rather than unwelcome, and are familiar rather than unfamiliar.

10. The importance of perception. Since every individual is different, it is possible for one set of sensations to be perceived in different ways by different people, because they all interpret sensations through their own experiences, motives and attitudes. In the management of people, differences in perception can be the source of many difficulties and conflicts.

(*a*) *Communication*—a quite sincere and well-meaning communication from management to employees, or vice versa, may be perceived as a threat or a deprivation. Before the communication is made it may be necessary to reduce suspicion and allay fears so that the message may be correctly perceived (*see* IX).

(*b*) *Judgment of people*—the assessment of candidates for employment (*see* V) or the appraisal of subordinates (*see* XVIII) is affected by the assessor's own preferences and prejudices. An interviewer tends to perceive a candidate favourably whose background is similar to his own. Manager A, when appraising a subordinate who frequently comes to him with suggestions for changing work procedures, may rate him as outstanding in initiative. Manager B might rate the same sort of person as uncooperative. It is much easier to gain agreement on the perception of a *ranking* of some quality (i.e. in what order individuals in a group should be placed for their possession of that quality—height, initiative, co-operation, etc.) than on the perception of the absolute degree to which one individual shows that quality. If several managers who knew a group of employees well were asked to rank them in order of dependability quite close agreement would be obtained between the rank-orders, but if the managers were asked to say how dependable one person was there would be considerable disagreement between them.

(*c*) *Training*—in manual tasks particularly, the object of a large part of the training is to teach the trainee to perceive certain cues or signals in the process to which he must make an appropriate response (*see* XX, **6**). The training officer will not be successful unless he first identifies these "perceptual cues" and devises exercises to facilitate their recognition.

(*d*) *Motivation*—people with the same need to satisfy may not perceive the same means of satisfaction (*see* II). There may be different perceptions as to what motives are likely to be pre-eminent in a particular situation; management may expect employees to be motivated towards increased production by an incentive scheme, but find that the employees do not respond, as they put the unity of the group first (*see* VII).

(*e*) *Performance criteria*—it may be necessary to compare the actual performance of an employee with the standards of performance that the manager perceives to be reasonable. Unless performance can be objectively measured (for example, by quantity produced), differences in perception are almost bound to occur; managers will disagree as to which parts of a job are the most important and how quality of work can be judged, and the employees may well disagree with the managers.

PROGRESS TEST 1

1. Why is it impossible to formulate scientific laws of human behaviour? **(2, 3)**

2. What are the subjective and objective factors of attention? **(7)**

3. What is the relationship between sensation and perception? **(9)**

4. In what ways can differences in perception cause difficulties for managers? **(10)**

CHAPTER II

Motivation in Work

NEEDS AND THEIR SATISFACTION

The study of motivation—the reasons why people behave as they do—is of fundamental importance in the management of human resources.

1. Human needs. Psychologists make these basic assumptions when interpreting human behaviour.

(*a*) All human behaviour has a *cause*, which itself is the consequence of the combined effects of heredity and environment.

(*b*) At the root of human behaviour are needs, or wants or motives. Need is the term usually employed in this connection.

(*c*) Human behaviour is *goal-seeking*; people try to achieve objectives or goals which, when reached, will satisfy their needs. For example, food will satisfy the hunger need.

2. The hierarchy of needs. The American psychologist, A. H. Maslow, has divided human needs into the following classes.

(*a*) *Physiological or basic needs*—people must satisfy these needs just to keep alive. They include, for example, hunger, thirst and sleep. In the work environment, the fundamental purpose of a wage or salary is to provide the means of satisfying basic needs.

(*b*) *Security or safety needs*—these are concerned with self-protection, with the avoidance of harm and, to some extent, with provision for the future. Examples are the needs for shelter, warmth and self-defence. At work the wish for security of tenure, the existence of restrictive practices, and many aspects of trade unionism show how employees try to satisfy needs of this kind.

(*c*) *Belonging or affection needs*—everyone, in various degrees, wishes to give and receive friendship. Companionship and association with others for recreational purposes are examples of these needs. Note that, for example, people may join with others partly to satisfy affection needs and partly for greater security.

(*d*) *Esteem or ego needs*—these include the needs to become independent, to receive the esteem of others, to dominate and to acquire possessions. As it is possible for needs of this kind to be satisfied through social activity, there is again overlapping between needs of groups (c) and (d). At work a position of authority, a company car, an office carpet or a special type of overall are means by which these needs are satisfied.

(e) *Self-actualisation needs*—this final group comprises the needs to make the fullest use of one's capabilities, to develop oneself and to be creative. In the working environment the majority of employees find few opportunities to satisfy needs in this class; skilled men, professional workers and managers are the most likely to be satisfied in this way.

Maslow has suggested that the classes of needs, in the order shown, form a hierarchy; people tend to satisfy their needs in a certain order of precedence. In general, when physiological and security needs have been satisfied, the higher needs (belonging, esteem and self-actualisation) become important, usually, according to Maslow, in the order of the hierarchy. For example, a manager who receives a substantial salary, and thus adequately satisfies his lower needs, regards status symbols like a well-furnished office as important, but a former manager who has been unemployed for a long time will eventually take any available job that brings him a reasonable income, even though it is of low status.

3. Modifications to Maslow's theory. Maslow's theory is widely accepted, easy to understand and can be used to explain much, but not all, behaviour at work. Alderfer has proposed instead a modification of the theory, consisting of three levels of need.

(a) *Existence needs*—approximately equivalent to Maslow's physiological and security needs.

(b) *Relatedness needs*—including affection needs and that part of esteem needs which is concerned with personal relationships.

(c) *Growth needs*—including self-actualisation needs and that part of esteem needs which is concerned with individual effort.

The theory (often known as the ERG theory) agrees with Maslow in saying that as one level becomes satisfied the level above becomes important, but adds a further proposition that if one level is not sufficiently satisfied the level below becomes more important, e.g. a disappointment in promotion (growth needs) may produce a greater wish for social involvement (relatedness needs). Alderfer claims that his theory provides a more comprehensive explanation of behaviour than Maslow's.

4. Individual differences in need-satisfaction. People differ in the way they satisfy their needs in a variety of ways.

(*a*) *Cultural*—the manner in which for example hunger and sex needs are satisfied is surrounded by many customs and laws.

(*b*) *Perceptual*—in general, people perceive the world in terms of their least-satisfied needs; their perceptions tend to recognise goals which will help satisfy their needs (*see* I, **9–10**). A starving man perceives an apple orchard as a source of food rather than an attractive feature of the countryside.

(*c*) *Individual*—people have different physical and intellectual capabilities and aptitudes; they also have different personalities. These are reflected in the various ways in which needs are satisfied; one man might achieve self-actualisation by an intellectual feat, another by sporting prowess.

5. Conflict of needs. A person may find that he wishes to satisfy two needs simultaneously, but that they are mutually exclusive; if he satisfies one he cannot satisfy the other. For example, if he wishes to retain his job he may have to carry out his work in a way he dislikes, or his boss may expect him to stay late frequently although this has adverse effects on his family life. A situation of this kind, where an individual is pulled in two ways at once, is called a *conflict of needs*. Until it is resolved it may show itself in anxiety and irritability, or sometimes in what appear to be physical disorders like headaches or stomach complaints.

When an individual resolves his conflict, that is by accepting the situation into which he has been forced or finally making his choice between the needs he wishes to satisfy, he usually attempts to justify the decision he has made. He may, for example, explain to everyone he meets the great benefits he will now gain and exaggerate the disadvantages of the choice he has rejected.

At work, management should try to avoid putting employees into situations where conflict may occur; for instance, an employee should not be promoted unless it is certain that he would welcome the promotion. A man promoted to take charge of a branch in a part of the country he and his wife dislike would be torn between the wish to advance his career in the company and the wish to remain in a district he likes. The resulting conflict might be difficult to resolve, and its effects might not be beneficial to the company or the employee.

6. Achievement of goals. The assumptions regarding human behaviour set out in **1** may be shown in diagrammatic form as shown below.

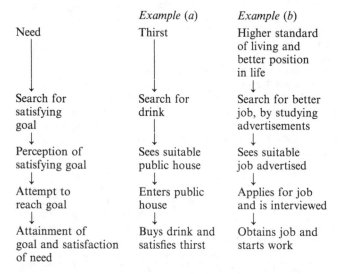

	Example (a)	*Example (b)*
Need	Thirst	Higher standard of living and better position in life
↓	↓	↓
Search for satisfying goal	Search for drink	Search for better job, by studying advertisements
↓	↓	↓
Perception of satisfying goal	Sees suitable public house	Sees suitable job advertised
↓	↓	↓
Attempt to reach goal	Enters public house	Applies for job and is interviewed
↓	↓	↓
Attainment of goal and satisfaction of need	Buys drink and satisfies thirst	Obtains job and starts work

The left-hand column shows the need–path–goal hypothesis in general terms. The other two columns show the ways in which actual needs might be satisfied.

The importance of *perception* (*see* I, **9–10**) should be noted. Although people are in many cases motivated by the same needs, their perceptions of need-satisfying goals are different. A tee-totaller, for example, would not perceive a public house as a means of satisfying thirst, and job-seekers do not all apply for the same job. Need-satisfaction is usually complex; a new job, if well chosen, can satisfy needs ranging over the whole of Maslow's hierarchy.

7. Frustration. A goal which is attempted may not always be reached; the individual may be *frustrated* in his attempt to reach it. The *positive reaction* to frustration is to try to solve the problem, perhaps by finding a way round the obstacle that prevents him from reaching his goal, perhaps by perceiving an alternative goal which will satisfy the need—though probably not to the same extent. The perception and achievement of an alternative goal is sometimes called *deprivation*, because the individual is deprived of the extra satisfaction he would have gained if he had been able to reach his original goal.

Frustration may also produce various forms of *negative reactions*—exceptions to the general rule that all behaviour is purposeful and goal-seeking. A negative reaction may occur for various reasons.

(*a*) The goal being attempted seems unique and there appears to be no practicable alternative, e.g. there is no other public house for miles, and this one has just closed.

(*b*) There is a strong emotional attachment to the goal, e.g. the candidate has boasted to everyone that he is certain to get the job he has applied for, and then hears that he has been turned down.

(*c*) The individual is by his personality prone to react negatively.

Negative reactions can take several forms; the four found most often are as follows.

(*a*) *Aggression*—a physical or verbal attack on some person or object, e.g. abuse of the landlord of the public house.

(*b*) *Regression*—a reversion to childish behaviour, e.g. pouting or tears.

(*c*) *Resignation*—giving up, apathy, withdrawal, e.g. a man disappointed in promotion may come late, leave early and avoid making decisions.

(*d*) *Fixation*—persistence in useless behaviour, e.g. pushing on the public house door long after it is apparent that it is locked.

8. Frustration at work. Frustration may frequently occur among the employees of an organisation, for the following reasons.

(*a*) Their methods and speed of work may be closely controlled, and not what they themselves would choose.

(*b*) Their work may appear meaningless.

(*c*) Their grievances and problems may not be dealt with speedily or adequately by management.

(*d*) They may not be told, or cannot understand, the reasons for many management decisions which affect them.

When employees are frustrated at work they may react negatively, their behaviour taking the following forms:

(*a*) lateness, absence or eventually leaving the company;

(*b*) poor-quality work;

(c) unwillingness to take responsibility;

(d) quarrels with colleagues, disputes with management;

(e) accidents, damage to equipment and products.

9. Reducing frustration. Because frustration can have such serious consequences, every effort should be made to reduce it. A case may be made that the work situation is inherently frustrating because it implies that, for monetary payment, one person is putting himself under the instructions of another; however, the possibility of frustration at work can be reduced in the following ways.

(a) Designing jobs to give them greater meaning.

(b) Improving selection and training; a person will be more satisfied in a job for which he is suitable and for which he has been trained.

(c) Recognising effort and merit, thus providing satisfaction of higher needs.

(d) Improving communications, consultation and disputes procedures so that potential causes of frustration may be identified and removed as far as possible.

10. Expectancy theory. The motivational process may also be explained in another way. *Expectancy theory* states that effort to satisfy needs will depend on the person's perception that he can expect the effort to be followed by a certain outcome which will bring desirable rewards.

To illustrate this, suppose there are three employees who wish to obtain promotion in order to satisfy self-actualisation needs (Maslow) or growth needs (Alderfer). The first employee perceives prominence in the firm's social club as the best route and spends much of his spare time there, confident that he will be voted into honorary office. The second employee perceives a professional qualification as the best way and works hard in the evenings to achieve one. The third also perceives the professional qualification as the best way, but does not make the effort to study because he does not believe he would be able to pass the examinations; neither does he try to become an honorary officer of the social club because, unlike the first employee, he does not perceive this as a way of getting promotion.

WORK AND NEED-SATISFACTION

11. Definition of work. Work may be defined as an activity which is directed by others as regards purpose, methods, materials, time and space. Its usual aim is to contribute towards the production of goods and services. In contrast to leisure, which is primarily concerned with the satisfaction of one's own needs, work is concerned with things that others require and are willing to pay for.

12. Satisfaction of needs at work. Although the above definition implies the opposite, it is still possible for needs to be satisfied at work to some degree.

(a) *The definition implies a passive acceptance of work* by an employee and does not indicate to what extent, if any, he will derive benefit from it. However, it must be assumed that since the great majority of people in western society are employees of some kind they must obtain some satisfaction of their needs from this arrangement. The normal contract of employment (*see* XIV, **20**) states that in return for an employee's services given during a specified part of the employee's time, the employer will make a monetary payment and sometimes provide fringe benefits also (*see* XXIII, **14–19**). He is also expected by law to provide reasonable working conditions (*see* XXIII, **9–13**). Physiological and security needs may thus be satisfied.

(b) Some employers, particularly in the public sector, offer their employees a *steady wage or salary*, often with guaranteed increases according to length of service, generous fringe benefits and the prospect of almost complete security of tenure. Employees are expected to take the view that they have entered a family, and in return for the privileges and protection they receive are to fulfil the duties expected by the head of the family. This approach by an employer is usually termed "paternalistic"; it emphasises above all the satisfaction of security needs.

(c) Another philosophy of employment is to attempt *to vary the employee's need-satisfaction* according to his merit and performance in the job. Additions to his basic wage or salary are made according to management's assessment of these qualities, and employees who fail to reach certain standards of conduct or output are penalised by warnings, official reprimands, fines or dismissal. This approach, combined with particular attention to work study and specialisation of task, is usually known as scientific management, the name given to it by F. W. Taylor in 1910. Once more, it is concerned only with the satisfaction of physiological and security needs.

(d) More recently, influenced above all by Maslow's hierarchy of needs (*see* **2**), industrial psychologists have shown how work can be made more satisfying by giving greater attention to affection, ego and self-actualisation needs. The job is looked at not simply as a means of efficiently carrying out a specified function but as something which could be intrinsically satisfying to the worker. The rewards for work can go beyond pay or fringe benefits. This approach has also influenced thinking about leadership (*see* VIII, **1–10**), participation (*see* VIII, **11–18**), management by objectives (*see* XVIII, **7–12**) and job design (*see* IV, **1**).

(*e*) Using Maslow's hierarchy, it can be seen that paternalism and scientific management can only satisfy physiological and security needs, except that under scientific management a high-performance worker whose efforts were recognised by high pay might get some satisfaction of ego needs. The following table shows for each class of need the chief ways in which satisfaction may be obtained at work.

Needs	*Method of satisfaction at work*
Basic	Money, physical working conditions.
Security	Money, physical working conditions, pension and sick pay schemes, restrictive practices, trade union membership, company policy regarding security of tenure.
Affection	Companionship of fellow employees, group norms of production (*see* VII, **8**), trade union membership, company social activities.
Ego	Job title, possession of a certain skill or expertise, position of authority, status symbols—carpet in office, own parking space, etc., money as a sign of status.
Self-actualisation	A job that is satisfying for its own sake, self-regulation, the opportunity to be creative—to use all one's abilities and special talents, knowledge of results of one's work.

13. Herzberg's theory of motivational hygiene. The American psychologist Frederick Herzberg has propounded a theory of motivation at work which divides the factors of the work environment into two classes: motivators or satisfiers on the one hand; and hygiene factors or maintenance factors on the other.

Herzberg developed his theory by analysing the answers to two basic questions he and his collaborators put to engineers and accountants.

(*a*) What events at work have resulted in a marked increase in your job satisfaction?

(*b*) What events at work have resulted in a marked reduction in your job satisfaction?

The replies showed that, in general, the experiences which were regarded as exceptionally satisfying were not the opposite of those which were exceptionally dissatisfying. For example, someone might say that he disliked a job because of poor working conditions, but very rarely would he say that he liked a job because of good working conditions.

From his analysis, Herzberg concluded that the elements in a job which produced *satisfaction* were:

(*a*) achievement;
(*b*) recognition;
(*c*) responsibility;
(*d*) promotion prospects;
(*e*) work itself.

He called these the motivators or satisfiers.

The elements whose absence or inadequacy in a job produced *dissatisfaction* were:

(*a*) pay;
(*b*) relations with others;
(*c*) type of supervision;
(*d*) company policy;
(*e*) physical working conditions;
(*f*) fringe benefits.

Herzberg called these hygiene factors (because, using the analogy of drains and refuse collection, they made the job environment fit to occupy), or maintenance factors (because they tended to maintain an employee in his job). He said that an employee might leave a firm because he disliked its working conditions or thought the pension scheme inadequate, but he would not be motivated to work harder or better if working conditions or the pension scheme were improved (provided they were already reasonably adequate).

On the other hand, the absence of achievement or responsibility, for example, would be unlikely to cause an employee to leave, but if these could be increased the employee would be more motivated in his work. Herzberg recognised that individuals varied in the relative importance they attached to motivators or hygiene factors; some were very concerned to seek achievement, recognition, etc., in their jobs, while others were interested particularly in pay, personal relationships, etc.

14. Discussion of Herzberg's theory. When Herzberg's enquiries have been repeated using his methods, his findings have been confirmed to a large extent. However, when other methods have been used, for example questionnaires, different results have emerged. Very few enquiries appear to have been conducted with manual workers. Herzberg's method of investigation, which may be described as anecdotal self-report, is likely to produce answers of a certain type. Someone will probably describe his good work experiences in terms which reflect credit on himself—success, greater responsibility or recognition. He will always be tempted to attribute bad work experiences to things beyond his own control—uncongenial colleagues, an unpleasant boss or poor working conditions. Thus he will take the credit for the good experiences and blame others for the bad experiences.

The main application of the theory has been in the enlarging or enriching of the jobs of non-manual workers (*see* **15**). It would be possible to find theoretical justification for this in the hierarchy of needs without postulating a two-factor theory. Herzberg does, however, emphasise that improving fringe benefits or other conditions of work will not motivate employees; again the hierarchy of needs would explain this because working conditions are relevant to the lower needs (*see* **12** (*e*)), which in modern industry and commerce are usually adequately satisfied.

JOB EXTENSION

15. Job enlargement and job enrichment—definitions. A job is enlarged when the employee carries out a wider range of tasks of approximately the same level of difficulty and responsibility as before.

A job is enriched (or vertically enlarged) when the employee is given greater responsibilities and scope to make decisions, and is expected to use skills he has not used before. Both are examples of *job extension*.

16. Effects of job enlargement and enrichment. Both are attempts to build opportunities into the employee's job for the satisfaction of ego and self-actualisation needs (*see* **2** (*e*)). A greater range of tasks or decisions will, it is thought, make the employee feel more important, give him a sense of achievement and make more use of his abilities. He will therefore receive satisfaction from the job itself (intrinsic satisfaction) as well as money and fringe benefits (extrinsic satisfaction).

Many companies have introduced either job enlargement or job enrichment and increased the job satisfaction of their employees. In most cases it appears that non-manual workers (often managers) rather than manual workers are concerned. It is easier to extend the job of a non-manual worker, whose responsibilities and actions are very often not precisely described, than to change the job of a manual worker whose tasks may be highly specialised and precisely defined because they are part of a complex production process. There may be a conflict between specialisation and development of specific skills required for efficient operation of the process and the construction of a job sufficiently enlarged or enriched to give greater satisfaction to the employee. In order to make the job significant to the worker it may have to be extended so much that productivity is seriously affected. The result may be a compromise between efficiency and job satisfaction in which the worker, instead of doing one meaningless task, is now expected to do several meaningless tasks.

Extension of jobs may meet with trade union opposition because demarcation lines between skills are eroded. It will almost certainly necessitate increases in pay; wider or deeper responsibilities must be recognised by an increase in the monetary worth of the job, as measured by job evaluation (see XXI). An employer might hesitate, therefore, before introducing job extension because the benefits to him would be somewhat uncertain, whereas the costs might be considerable.

17. Job rotation. Some of the difficulties the employer finds in job extension can be avoided if *job rotation* is used instead. Employees are trained in several minor skills and exchange jobs with each other at intervals. Greater satisfaction is obtained because the employee has a greater understanding of the work process through experiencing several jobs within it, and the increased versatility of the workers is useful to management when sickness absence is high. It is not necessary to redesign production methods, and rises in pay, if any, are small.

Not all individuals respond favourably to job enlargement, enrichment or rotation. Some do not appear to be motivated very strongly by the higher needs, or do not expect to satisfy them at work (*see* X, **7**). Others resist any attempt to give them decision-making functions; they say that managers are there for that purpose.

JOB SATISFACTION

18. The measurement of job satisfaction. Job satisfaction questionnaires are used to find out to what extent employees are satisfied at work. They may take several forms, some of which are described below.

(*a*) A series of questions covering different aspects of the job and working conditions. Against each question there are usually five possible answers; the employee is asked to indicate the answer he agrees with.

I feel that my job is:
  (*i*) extremely boring;
  (*ii*) rather boring;
  (*iii*) fairly interesting;
  (*iv*) interesting;
  (*v*) extremely interesting.

It is possible to give a numerical score to this type of questionnaire by giving one point to answer (*i*), two points to answer (*ii*) and so on.

(*b*) A list of factors in job satisfaction which the employee is asked to rank in order of importance to him. This type of questionnaire is not directly linked to the conditions in which the employee works, or to the nature of his job, but its results may be used as a guide to future company policies.

Consider the following factors in a job and put the figure 1 against the factor you think is the most important, 2 against the next most important and so on.

  Security
  Pleasant colleagues
  Pay
  Good boss
  Efficient organisation
  Fringe benefits (pension, sick pay, etc.)
  Interesting job
  Authority over others
  Promotion prospects
  Responsibility; freedom from close supervision
  Pleasant working conditions

In such surveys pay is usually placed about fifth in rank order, behind such things as promotion prospects, responsibility, interesting job and security. When employees are asked instead to put the factors in the order in which the average man would place them, pay usually comes first (compare with the comment on Herzberg's questions, in **14**).

(c) A free expression questionnaire, in which the employee is asked to write an essay on what he likes and dislikes about his job and his employer. Sometimes the employee is interviewed and asked to reply orally instead of in writing.

19. The advantages of free expression questionnaires.

(a) The employee can use his own words instead of those chosen for him by someone else.

(b) The employee can discuss topics which might not have occurred to the designer of a questionnaire of type (a) in **18**.

20. The disadvantages of free expression questionnaires.

(a) Unless the employee is quite sure that his remarks will be treated in complete confidence, he will not be frank.

(b) The analysis of a large number of completed questionnaires of this type is difficult and often subjective.

(c) Some employees find great difficulty in expressing themselves clearly, particularly in writing.

21. Comments on job satisfaction questionnaires. Although the results of questionnaires, especially of the type described in **18** (a), often correspond with actual behaviour, there must always be some doubt regarding their reliability. They are open to objection on the following grounds.

(a) The questions asked may be interpreted in various ways by different people.

(b) The form of the questions may call for a misleadingly definite answer, omitting conditions and qualifications.

(c) An individual's self-perception may lead him to give replies which he thinks are true, but which do not in fact represent his actual behaviour—a form of innocent self-deception.

(d) When responding to questions, people often give the answer they think will be most acceptable, or will show themselves to the best advantage.

The following conclusions regarding job satisfaction seem to be generally accepted, because they are confirmed by large numbers of questionnaires given to a wide variety of employees.

(a) Women are usually more satisfied than men, even when their jobs are lower in status, authority and income.

(b) Job satisfaction usually increases with age.

(c) Higher social class and status are related to greater satisfaction but, among those doing the same job, better education is associated with lower satisfaction.

(d) The less secure the job, the less the satisfaction.

(e) There is no firm relationship between job satisfaction and productivity (see 23).

22. Behavioural evidence of job satisfaction. A more reliable way of assessing job satisfaction should be through behaviour at work rather than replies to questions. Unfortunately, the interpretation of much working behaviour is highly subjective, e.g. whether the employees seem "happy". The most objective measures seem to be the extent of absence from work and the rate at which employees leave the company; it is logical to assume that if people are satisfied in their jobs they will tend to remain in that employment and have little avoidable time off. Of course, job satisfaction is not the only influence on leaving or absence; for example, suitable alternative jobs may not be easily found, or the employee may lose pay for absence.

When statistical correlations (see *Statistics* by W. M. Harper, M & E HANDBOOK) are calculated between scores of job satisfaction and avoidable absence a definite, though not high, negative correlation is found, i.e. the greater the satisfaction the less the absence. The correlation between job satisfaction and the rate of leaving is also negative, but lower.

23. The relationship between job satisfaction and productivity. Although common sense might lead us to expect that a worker who found his job satisfying would produce more than one who was not satisfied, many investigations have shown that, generally speaking, productivity and job satisfaction are not related. It is possible for any degree of job satisfaction to be associated with any degree of productivity, i.e. a satisfied worker may have low productivity or a dissatisfied worker may have high productivity, or vice versa. Closer analysis may provide at least a partial explanation of this apparently irrational effect.

The expectation that a satisfied employee will work hard is basically a paternalistic attitude on the part of the employer. It implies either that the employee, grateful for being given a satisfying job, shows his gratitude by complying with the employer's wishes, or that because he is satisfied he is inevitably enthusiastic, conscientious and persistent and therefore produces at a high rate. However, a more realistic assumption is that the employee may not have any feelings of gratitude towards his employer and that his enthusiasm may either show itself in a form unwelcome to the employer, for example an overemphasis on accuracy, or may be tempered by other considerations, for example a wish to adhere to group norms of production (*see* VII, **8**). The interests of the employer and the employee do not always coincide.

From the employee's point of view, work brings many kinds of rewards: money, friendship, status and achievement among others. In some circumstances working harder may increase these rewards, in others it may reduce them. Status and achievement, which might be expected to favour higher productivity, are needs which have little appeal to some employees, or are needs which they do not expect to satisfy at work. It is quite possible also for employees to work hard in jobs they dislike because they fear dismissal, are attracted by a high level of pay, or simply find hard work the best way of making the time go quickly. On the other hand, many employees, in particular professional and skilled workers and those who have a moral involvement in their jobs, combine high job satisfaction with high productivity, perhaps because they are motivated by loyalty towards a profession, craft or ideal rather than towards an employer. The relationship between productivity and the motivation of employees is extremely complex, and much research remains to be done.

24. Job satisfaction and costs. Although a manager who is successful in increasing the job satisfaction of his employees may or may not benefit from an increase in their productivity, he will probably find that the costs of running his department are reduced. Labour turnover and absence (*see* **22** above and also XVII) can be extremely expensive to the company and may well be reduced if jobs are made more satisfying. The manager should, however, be sure that the cost of re-designing jobs (which may include less efficiency in working methods and higher pay rates) does not outweigh the expected saving.

25. The concept of total rewards. An employee may receive extrinsic rewards (pay and fringe benefits) or intrinsic rewards (friendship, status and self-fulfilment) from his work. The total reward is the employee's *perception* of the total value of all these.

For example, individuals differ in the value they attach to achievement as compared with pay, or promotion opportunities as compared with security. For their part, employers recognise that some rewards compensate for the absence of others; a job which requires a strong moral involvement, e.g. social work, is often accompanied by a low level of pay, and a company which traditionally offers its employees almost complete security of tenure may have lower wage rates than a company with a "hire and fire" reputation.

Employers and employees may have different perceptions of the rewards to be obtained from various jobs. Changes in working conditions regarded by the employer as improvements may not appear to be such to the employees, for example a new open-plan office instead of the small separate offices. Sometimes the way in which the decision is reached and the change introduced is more significant than the change itself (*see* VIII and IX).

PROGRESS TEST 2

1. What are the three basic assumptions underlying the study of motivation? **(1)**

2. What is the hierarchy of needs? **(2)**

3. Give an example of conflict of needs. **(5)**

4. Define frustration, and illustrate how it may produce either positive or negative reactions. **(7)**

5. How may needs be satisfied at work? **(12, 13)**

6. Define, and give examples of, job enlargement and job enrichment. **(15, 16)**

7. How may job satisfaction be measured, and what is its relationship with (*a*) productivity and (*b*) costs? **(18–21, 23, 24)**

CHAPTER III

Learning

INTRODUCTION

1. Definition. Learning is a relatively permanent change in the repertoire of behaviour occurring as a result of experience.

This definition implies that learning can only be said to occur when a person shows different behaviour, for example when he can prove knowledge of new facts or do something he was not able to do before. Changes in behaviour due solely to ageing or injury would not be examples of learning. If, however, an injured person had found ways of adapting himself to his disability, this new behaviour would then have been learned.

EXPERIMENTS WITH ANIMALS

2. Experiments in animal learning. Our knowledge of the psychology of learning is drawn partly from experiments with animals and humans, and partly from general observations of the human learning process. Experiments with animals, which have made a great contribution to psychological knowledge, have the following *advantages*.

(*a*) *Close control*—extraneous influences can be avoided, and the environment of the animals can be precisely supervised from birth. Even their heredity can be controlled. Thus any change in behaviour is due solely to the experimental situation and not to any other factors.

(*b*) *Large numbers*—laboratory animals can be readily obtained so that results can be seen not from a few but from many subjects. The reliability of experiments is therefore increased.

(*c*) *Freedom of action*—experiments with animals may be repeated many times or changes made in their environment at the wish of the experimenter. He is not concerned about the psychological or social after-effects on the animals, nor does he have to obtain their consent.

(*d*) *No communication*—the animal (presumably) is unable to deduce from the experimenter's words, facial expression, gestures or tone of voice what particular action is expected or desired. Any change in behaviour must therefore be due to the conditions the experimenter has contrived and not to his personal influence.

The *disadvantages* of animal experiments are as follows.

(*a*) *Limited motivation*—the motivation of animals is (very probably) limited in comparison with humans. We assume, for instance, that animals have no conception of ego and achievement needs. When humans learn, the higher needs are frequently very potent.

(*b*) *No verbal communication*—much human learning occurs through verbal communication. It is impossible to simulate this in animal experiments because animals cannot work from spoken or written instructions (apart from the monosyllabic words of command which a dog obeys), nor can they express their difficulties.

(*c*) *Lack of insight*—much human learning requires insight, the ability to see the connection between events or objects and from them mentally construct a significant pattern. As insight is probably possessed by the higher mammals only, e.g. chimpanzees, the value of experiments with most animals is limited to a certain extent.

(*d*) Limited range of rewards—humans respond to a variety of non-material rewards, like praise or the sense of achievement, when they are learning. Rewards of this kind cannot be introduced into animal experiments.

Using the results of animal experiments, and making due allowance for the differences between humans and animals, a great deal has been learned about the principles of human learning.

CONDITIONING

3. Important terms in learning. In studying the psychology of learning it is necessary to understand the meanings of four important terms—drive, stimulus, response and reinforcement. In the following definitions the word organism will be used to denote either a human being or an animal.

(*a*) *Drive*—the necessary condition of arousal or readiness for action or behaviour to begin. It is a condition in which the organism wishes to satisfy a need.

(b) *Stimulus*—the cue or signal which initiates a response. It is usually conveyed by sight, hearing, smell or touch. For example the ringing of the telephone is the stimulus to pick it up, or the change of colour of the material is the stimulus to alter the application of paint.

(c) *Response*—the behaviour which is the result of stimulation (even though it may not be possible to identify the stimulus). Often a particular response becomes associated with a particular stimulus so that one almost automatically follows the other, for example changing gear when approaching a corner. The object of much industrial training is to establish these associations.

(d) *Reinforcement*—any event or object which strengthens a response, either by causing it to continue or increase, by providing the organism with some kind of reward. A dog after performing a trick may be rewarded either with food or with a pat and a friendly word. A learner-driver when he changes gear smoothly may be rewarded with the instructor's approval.

4. Classical conditioning. Experiments with animals have shown two important learning processes: classical conditioning and operant (or instrumental) conditioning.

Classical conditioning is associated above all with the Russian psychologist Pavlov. A typical experiment in this field would proceed as follows.

(a) *First stage*—a dog which is hungry (drive) is shown some food (stimulus). Its mouth waters (response). Eventually it is allowed to eat the food (reinforcement).

(b) *Second stage*—as before, but when the food is shown a bell is also rung.

(c) *Third stage*—the food is not shown, only the bell being rung. The dog's mouth waters at the sound of the bell.

The dog has now been *conditioned* to respond to a new stimulus. Since this response (watering of the mouth) is a reflex action, i.e. not consciously controlled, it is called a *conditioned reflex*.

By elaboration of this procedure Pavlov was able to show that dogs were colour-blind and that they could distinguish between a circle and an ellipse.

It is possible that certain superstitions and fears in humans may be due to a classical conditioning process. For example, an American psychologist was able to produce in his infant son terror of a teddy bear by making a loud noise whenever the child was shown the bear. Later he de-conditioned his son by associating the bear with a favourite fruit jelly. Although classical conditioning may contribute to the development of certain personality traits, it is of only minor importance in learning within commerce or industry.

5. Operant (or instrumental) conditioning. This process, which is much more relevant to human learning, is associated with the American psychologist B. F. Skinner. A typical experiment would proceed as follows.

(*a*) A special cage is constructed which contains a lever on one side and a food receptacle on the other. Whenever the lever is depressed a piece of food is released from a container into the receptacle.

(*b*) An animal (very often a pigeon), which is hungry (drive) is placed in the cage. Eventually, during the course of random behaviour, it touches the lever with some part of its body and depresses it. This releases the food, which the pigeon eats. After some accidental repetitions of this sequence, the pigeon learns the connection between the lever and the food. The sight of the lever (stimulus) leads to the response of pressing it. The food is then eaten (reinforcement). This is an example of learning, because through experience the pigeon now behaves in a new way.

(*c*) Once behaviour is established in this way, the occasional reinforcement gets better results than the reinforcement of every response (compare a person who is told continually while he is learning that he is doing very well).

(*d*) Behaviour can be *shaped* by operant conditioning, that is, gradually made more precise and less general. For example, pigeons have been trained to play table-tennis with each other, to play simple tunes on a toy piano, and even to reject misshapen tablets in a pharmaceutical factory by pressing levers with their beaks as the tablets go past on a moving belt.

Operant conditioning is *different* from classical conditioning in the following respects.

(*a*) The animal is not passive but active (hence operant).

(*b*) Its behaviour is *instrumental* in obtaining a reward or reinforcement; in classical conditioning the reward is not important.

(*c*) It learns new behaviour instead of providing an existing response to a new stimulus.

(*d*) Its behaviour is consciously controlled, not a reflex action.

ANIMAL AND HUMAN LEARNING

6. The application of animal experiments to human learning. Classical conditioning is not appropriate to learning in commerce and industry since it does not deal with consciously determined responses. Operant conditioning has had one very specific human application, programmed learning (*see* XX, **16**), but it has been valuable above all in emphasising the patterns which must be followed if any human learning is to be successful, though it must be borne in mind that operant conditioning with animals as subjects is a form of trial and error learning, whereas most human learning occurs by copying and by receiving explanations in words or diagrams. Taking training in a manual skill as an example:

(*a*) The trainee must be motivated (cf. drive) to complete the course. He must see some benefit from it, for example an increase in pay, a different job title, the satisfaction of possessing a skill that few have.

(*b*) His motivation must be maintained during training by various methods.

(*i*) Intermediate goal-setting—dividing the whole task into self-contained units or elements, each with a given standard of performance the trainee tries to achieve.

(*ii*) Competition—though it should not be carried too far, competition between trainees is frequently motivating.

(*iii*) Indicating relevance—the purpose of any theoretical knowledge or exercises that are given should be explained.

(*iv*) Factors of attention—the subjective and objective factors of attention (*see* I, **7**) are relevant in maintaining motivation.

(*c*) In designing the programme, the stimulus and response must be made very clear. Recognition of the appropriate stimulus among many incoming sensations, or the appropriate response to a particular stimulus, can be very difficult for a trainee to learn unless the training programme is carefully designed to help him.

(*d*) At frequent intervals during the training programme the trainee's responses should be reinforced, not of course by pieces of food but by much less tangible rewards.

(*i*) Knowledge of results is an extremely powerful reinforcement for humans. A trainee should very frequently receive reports of the progress he is making, either from his instructor or by feedback of a score against a target. The Cambridge psychologist, F. C. Bartlett, said: "That practice makes perfect is not true. But it is true to say that it is practice, the results of which are known, which makes perfect."

(*ii*) Praise by the instructor is strongly reinforcing. Strong criticism or penalties for incorrect responses should be avoided; they tend to emphasise wrong methods unduly, encourage un-adventurous behaviour and may cause the trainee to dislike the instructor and the task.

The principles of operant conditioning, therefore, indicate how the best results can be obtained from training in industry and commerce. Other important factors in human learning, not derived from animal experiments, are described in the next para-graph.

7. Other factors in human learning. The principles described below are generalisations and tendencies rather than scientific laws; their truth varies according to the qualities of the learner and to the type of subject-matter which is being learned.

(*a*) *Whole* v. *part learning*—a task to be learned is usually taught in parts if it involves difficult perceptions or unusual stimulus-response associations. Motivation is stronger when the whole, rather than parts, is taught, particularly when the learners have relatively high intelligence. Whole methods are also prefer-able where the task loses much of its meaning unless it is dealt with as a complete unit. The teacher must therefore decide which method to follow by weighing difficulty against motivation. If a task is learned in parts (A, B, C, etc.), the following procedure has been found to give the best results:

Learn A, then practise A.
Learn B, then practise A + B.
Learn C, then practise A + B + C, etc.

In this way the early parts are not forgotten when the later parts are learned, and the task has more meaning as it is gradually built up.

(*b*) *Distribution of practice*—continuous learning should be avoided; either rest periods should be given or practical training alternated with theoretical training. In general, training sessions should be shorter at the beginning of a training programme and longer towards the end. Another generalisation is that complex or difficult material requires shorter sessions than straightforward and simple material.

(*c*) *The learning plateau*—graphs showing the relationship between performance and training time are called *learning curves*. Figures 1 and 2 show learning curves for easy and difficult tasks respectively. The curves can, of course, be interpreted in terms of the learner's ability or motivation. Figure 3 shows that during weeks two and three the learner has apparently been at a standstill; from week four onwards he again makes progress. The horizontal part of the curve (in weeks two and three) is called the *learning plateau*; it can be found in many learning situations where the learner appears to mark time for a period after the programme has started. The learning plateau has been explained as follows.

FIG. 1 *Learning curve—easy task.*

FIG. 2 *Learning curve—difficult task.*

FIG. 3   *Learning curve showing plateau.*

(*i*) The trainee is temporarily discouraged by the increasing difficulty of the task; he has lost motivation.

(*ii*) He has acquired some incorrect responses during the first part of his learning programme which he must lose if he is to make further progress.

(*iii*) He wishes to look back over the material he has learned so far and discover its significance.

(*iv*) In the case of manual training, the task may include some difficult perceptions or stimulus/response associations. Up to a point the trainee can make progress simply by copying, but beyond this point he must understand and mentally organise these difficulties; he must see the significance of the various cues and responses and realise how one movement is co-ordinated with another. When he has reached this level of understanding he is able to make progress once more.

The learning plateau can be shortened or removed altogether if the material to be learned is carefully analysed and a method devised which anticipates the learner's difficulties instead of leaving him to solve them. Skills analysis (*see* XX, **6**) is an example of this approach.

TRANSFER OF LEARNING

8. Transfer of learning. If someone learns task A and then task B, which is somewhat similar, to what extent will his learning of task B be affected? If it is made easier, then it is said that there is *positive transfer of learning*; if it is made more difficult there is *negative transfer*. There are two theories regarding transfer of learning—*identical elements* and *transfer through principles*.

(*a*) *Identical elements*—this theory states that if parts of task A are the same as parts of task B there will be positive transfer of learning for those parts of task B. For example two office jobs may be different from each other except that they both include telephoning and alphabetical filing. A clerk who has been transferred from the first job to train for the second job will have an advantage over someone who has been transferred from a completely different job, because he will benefit from a carry-over of his learned skills in telephoning and filing.

Unfortunately this theory, although apparently attractive, has difficulties in practice. The elements may not in fact be as identical as they appear at first sight. There are, for example, differences between telephoning to collect debts and to give advice, and between alphabetical filing by company name and by name of town. The clerk may therefore not learn the new job as quickly as was hoped, possibly even more slowly than someone whose previous job contained no identical elements. Quite possibly, perception is again important; an operation which outwardly looks the same within two jobs may be perceived differently by the worker because it occurs in different contexts.

(*b*) *Transfer through principles*—according to this theory, transfer of learning is facilitated not because identical elements are present but because the learner applies to the new task general principles he has derived from experience in the previous task. Thus a clerk is likely to learn a different clerical job more easily than, for example, a manual worker because he can bring to the new job his experience of organising documents in an orderly manner.

There is some common ground between the two theories, especially at the point where an element becomes a principle. The second theory, however, encourages an approach to industrial training which is more in accordance with other trends in industrial psychology. It suggests that instead of a rigid training programme run authoritatively, training methods which enable the employee to understand the purpose of the task and its context will help him to adapt in the future to new jobs more easily. The principles discussed in II, **23** also suggest that such methods will increase the employee's motivation during training and subsequently.

Negative transfer, that is increased difficulty in learning a new task because of knowledge of a previous task, is frequently found. Drivers often report difficulty when first driving a car with an automatic gearbox; quite possibly a novice driver would have much less trouble with it. A typist who has taught herself to type using two fingers finds a course in touch-typing more difficult than someone who has never used a typewriter before. On the other hand a touch-typist who is used to copying from documents has little difficulty in learning to type from a dictating machine.

The general rule seems to be that negative transfer between tasks is particularly probable where the same stimulus occurring in both tasks is followed by a different response in each case, e.g. for the same driving conditions one action is required for a manual gearbox, another action for an automatic. Where the stimuli are different, but the responses are the same, there will probably be some degree of positive transfer, e.g. a driver who has learned to stop suddenly to avoid a pedestrian will just as easily be able to stop when he sees a red light.

9. The importance of transfer of learning. The possibility of negative transfer makes it very important for new employees to be taught correct methods of work from the very beginning, rather than be allowed to pick up incorrect methods which they might find difficult to lose.

Positive or negative transfer may occur when an employee moves to another job, depending on the similarities and differences between the two jobs. Transfer may also be significant when an employee leaves a training environment and begins productive work. The ex-trainee often finds adjustment very difficult; he may have been taught methods which are different from those others round him are using, or the equipment he has been trained on may not be similar. The social atmosphere and working conditions in a training school do not usually resemble those in a productive workshop or office, again giving the trainee problems of adjustment. For this reason on-the-job training is sometimes held to be preferable to off-the-job (*see* XIX), but the difficulties can be reduced by continually reviewing training methods and equipment, emphasising principles as well as methods, and introducing the trainee gradually to the training environment instead of giving him the sudden plunge.

PROGRESS TEST 3

1. What are the advantages and disadvantages of using experiments with animals as a guide to human behaviour? **(2)**

2. Define and show the connection between drive, stimulus, response and reinforcement. **(3)**

3. What are the differences between classical and operant conditioning? **(4, 5)**

4. Describe how the results of experiments in animal learning can be applied to human learning. **(6)**

5. What is the learning plateau? **(7)**

6. Define and give an example of transfer of learning. **(8, 9)**

CHAPTER IV

Individual Differences

INTRODUCTION

1. Fitting the man to the job. In I reference was made to the importance of achieving a good fit between worker and job; one of the aims of human resources management is to see that employees are working in jobs which are suitable for them and that their jobs are designed with due regard to the abilities and limitations of the employee. The design of jobs is dealt with elsewhere in this book under the following headings.

Physical conditions of work—VI
Satisfaction of human needs—II
Job analysis and job specifications—XIII

The methods by which employers try to make the best use of their employees and satisfy their needs are covered under the following headings.

Recruitment and selection—XIV
Transfer and promotion—XV
Development—XVIII to XX
Pay—XXI and XXII

A manager must have some understanding of the important differences that exist between individual employees. He must know how these differences can be identified, to what extent they can be measured, and how they can be related to job performance.

2. Heredity and environment. In the preceding chapters the psychological principles of perception, motivation and learning have been discussed on the assumption that they have universal application, that everyone's behaviour is influenced by them. However, although in one sense people are alike in following the same psychological rules, they are different in the way they put these rules into practice. These variations in behaviour are due to differences between individuals, which in turn derive from differences in heredity and environment. Since there are countless possible combinations of these two factors, the differences between individuals are infinite in number and degree—a fact which makes life interesting, though sometimes difficult, and presents the manager with the opportunity to use these differences in a productive way. When they are thoughtfully used they can help to increase productivity and job satisfaction; badly used, or ignored, they can reduce efficiency and bring about unhappy relationships at work.

It is usual to deal with individual differences under three headings—physique, intelligence and personality.

PHYSIQUE

3. Physique. This can be defined as the attributes of the body; its size and shape, its speed and strength of movement, the efficiency of its senses. Physical qualities are basically determined by heredity, though they can be developed or suppressed by upbringing or training. For example, there are inherited tendencies to be short or tall, fast or slow, but a poor diet will cause a person to be shorter than he might have been, and appropriate training will enable an athlete to run longer and faster than he could before.

It is easy to measure most physical characteristics objectively, i.e. measurements of height, weight, eyesight, reaction speed, etc., can be quickly and simply made, independent observers producing identical results. Rather tantalisingly, under modern conditions physical differences are not very important in placing individuals in appropriate jobs. The advance of technology has greatly reduced the number of jobs in which great physical endurance or strength is required, and instrumentation often decreases the need to rely on the senses of touch, hearing, etc.

Eyesight is the most important physical factor in the employment field; in some manual jobs it is necessary for employees to have above-average eyesight or perfect colour vision. In other jobs, co-ordination of limb movements or speed of reaction may be important. Tests are available to measure these qualities.

A small number of candidates for jobs have disabilities which exclude them from certain occupations or compel them to work only in sheltered conditions. The Disabled Persons (Employment) Acts 1944 and 1958 place obligations on employers in this respect (*see* XIV, **19**).

Ideally, an employer should arrange for every candidate to have a medical examination before an offer of a job is made so that no one is asked to do work for which he is physically unsuited. In practice, medical examinations are given only in a minority of cases because employers assume that physical unfitness for work is so rare that the expense of examining all candidates is not justified. This matter is discussed later in XIV, **18**.

INTELLIGENCE

4. Definition. Intelligence is the capacity to make effective use of the intellect, which is the sum total of the mental functions of understanding, thinking, learning, observing, problem-solving and perceptual relationships. It is sometimes called mental ability.

The structure of intelligence is still the subject of intense controversy among psychologists. It is not necessary to recount the various theories that have been put forward; in simple terms, most British psychologists believe that there is a general factor of intelligence which enters into all functioning of the intellect and influences the performance of all tasks. Subordinate to general intelligence are a number of specific mental abilities which enter into the performance of some tasks but not others, e.g. verbal fluency, spatial ability, mechanical aptitude, numerical ability.

5. Intelligence tests. Since the early years of this century tests of intelligence have been developed to the stage when they are both *reliable* and *valid*.

(*a*) *Reliable* means that the test gives consistent results when repeated.

(*b*) *Valid* means that the test measures what it claims to measure, i.e. intelligence and not general knowledge.

Most intelligence tests used in commerce and industry are group written tests, i.e. they may be given if necessary to several candidates simultaneously, and consist of a number of printed questions to which the candidates must give a written reply. The test is then scored with the use of a key.

Publishers of tests usually restrict their sale to people who have been trained in their use. They must be given in precisely the manner described in the test manual, and the results interpreted by a qualified person.

6. Types of questions. Some intelligence tests contain questions of only one kind, e.g. verbal, numerical or spatial (i.e. diagrammatic) questions. Most tests used in industry contain a mixture of all three types, the candidate being asked questions along the following lines.

(*a*) Identify a word or phrase which has the same or opposite meaning as the one given.

(*b*) Solve anagrams or decode words.

(*c*) Perform addition, subtraction, multiplication and division.

(*d*) Identify one or more shapes which match or complete others.

(*e*) Write down the next number in a series.

(*f*) Solve a problem in logic.

Intelligence tests have a time limit (usually between twenty and sixty minutes), and very few candidates indeed complete a test within the limit.

7. Intelligence quotient. The early work on intelligence testing was done with children, and it was found convenient to introduce the concept of *mental age*. If a child was able to accomplish tasks which were considered appropriate to a child of average intelligence aged x, he was said to have a mental age of x which could, of course, be higher or lower than his chronological age, or the same. An easy measure of intelligence was then possible by expressing a mathematical relationship between mental age and chronological age, as follows:

$$\frac{\text{Mental age}}{\text{Chronological age}} \times 100$$

This formula is known as the intelligence quotient, usually abbreviated to IQ. A person of average intelligence will obviously have intelligence quotient of 100.

It is found that the mental age shown by intelligence test scores does not increase beyond a certain point; for some people the maximum mental age is as low as thirteen, for others as high as twenty. Therefore, in order to avoid an apparent steady decrease in intelligence with age, chronological age in the IQ formula never exceeds fifteen. Although mental age may not increase, adults may perform many tasks better as they get older because they have learned from experience.

Intelligence test manuals contain tables converting test scores, i.e. number of questions answered correctly within the time limit, into intelligence quotients. Because of the rather unsatisfactory device of giving an adult a chronological age of fifteen, another method of scoring, the percentile ranking, is sometimes used. A percentile rank is the number showing the percentage of the population attaining a score equal to or below the score in question. Thus if a given intelligence score is at the sixtieth percentile, then 60 per cent of the population would attain lower or equal scores; or alternatively the individual is more intelligent than 60 per cent of the population.

The meaning of the word population can be restricted to adult, graduate, manual worker and so on, enabling different ranges of percentiles to be quoted.

8. Intelligence tests in industry. By studying large numbers of people in a certain occupation it is possible to say that to be successful a candidate for that kind of job must have a certain minimum IQ. When selecting candidates, therefore, an employer may give them an intelligence test and use it to eliminate those who fail to reach this score.

Those who exceed the score will *not* automatically be successful in the occupation concerned because other factors, particularly motivation and previous experience, are extremely important. In many cases, however, there is a strong probability that the higher the score the greater the success in the job.

Occupations in which intelligence test scores have been found to be good predictors of success are:

(*a*) managers;
(*b*) supervisors;
(*c*) clerks;
(*d*) electrical workers;
(*e*) inspectors;
(*f*) complex process workers.

It is quite possible for people who achieve a high test score to be unsuccessful in a job because there is too great a discrepancy between their intelligence and the mental demands of the job. This lack of success, which may often include a liability to fatigue or accidents, is probably due to insufficient motivation.

Intelligence tests are neither expensive nor time-consuming, but employers frequently do not give them to candidates for jobs. They maintain that in most cases intelligence can be estimated accurately on the evidence of academic qualifications and past achievements and from the candidate's behaviour at an interview. On the other hand, although copious evidence of intelligence is often available from these sources, it may be interpreted in a highly subjective way by the selector, whereas tests can be objectively scored and may often be a better predictor of success than a poorly-conducted interview.

PERSONALITY

9. Definition. Personality may be defined as the sum total of the various qualities that are shown in behaviour. Although this definition taken literally includes intelligence and physique the term personality is usually taken to include above all emotions, motivation, interests and social qualities. It is incorrect to use the word personality as a synonym for charm or dominance; everyone has a personality, just as everyone has weight, height and intelligence.

10. Personality judgments. We assess the personality of someone we know well by recalling their behaviour in different circumstances, usually describing it in terms of traits, e.g. they are judged to be sociable, enterprising, tolerant, etc. As an individual passes through adolescence into adulthood, the personality becomes more consistent in the sense that behaviour in various circumstances becomes more predictable.

It is dangerous, however, to describe personality in terms of traits because they are affected so much by the situation at the time, as well as by personality. A man may be dominant when dealing with his subordinates but submissive when speaking to his boss. Co-operation and honesty are other traits which are often highly dependent on the situation at the time.

11. Self-report personality tests. Most personality tests are written questionnaires of the self-report type, asking for the subject's views about his behaviour in various hypothetical situations or his opinions about other people. Although tests of this kind are used as one of the tools of personnel selection by a few consultants and large companies, the general opinion in this country is that personality questionnaires are unlikely to be useful and reliable in industry, for various reasons.

(*a*) Self-report is inherently unreliable when the person answering the questions has a strong reason for presenting himself in the best light. The prospective employer can never be sure which answers are genuine and which have been faked.

(*b*) Even when the candidate tries to answer the questions sincerely he may give a misleading impression because his self-image, his personality as he sees it himself, may not correspond with his personality as seen by others.

(*c*) Experience has shown that personality questionnaires are not reliable predictors of success in a given job and that the scores are unstable—when a test is repeated with the same candidates, different scores are obtained.

12. Projective tests of personality. These tests are based on the assumption that given a rather generalised stimulus an individual will react in a way which will express his personality—he will project revealing behaviour. Two types of test are used.

(*a*) *Rorschach ink blot*—the candidate is shown a set of ten standard ink blots, some in monochrome and some coloured, and asked to say what he sees in each blot and what it makes him think of.

(*b*) *Thematic apperception test* (*TAT*)—the candidate is shown a standard set of pictures which depict in a rather vague way situations involving someone of the same age and sex as the candidate. He is asked to say what is happening, how it happened and what will happen next.

Psychologists who use these tests must undergo prolonged training in interpreting candidates' responses, but even then intuition and subjective judgment must play a large part. Because of the scarcity of psychologists trained in these techniques, and above all the techniques' proven unreliability in personnel selection, they are very rarely used in industry and commerce.

13. Physical indications. The traditional belief that plump people are jolly and sociable while thin people are quiet and solitary has been confirmed to a certain extent by modern research, but exceptions and intermediate types are so numerous that little reliance can be placed on body-build as a way of assessing personality. Other physical attributes which have been claimed to be significant are handwriting, gesture, palmistry and facial features. Although these may be related to personality, no one has yet found a way of analysing and classifying them into a reliable system.

Many people when selecting employees are influenced by intuitive first impressions, based perhaps on an interpretation of body-build, manner and speech and affected by prejudices about dress and hair style and by the mood of the moment. Some claim to be able to judge a person as soon as he enters a room. Occasionally such judgments have turned out to be surprisingly accurate; usually they are not. In some jobs the first impression a person makes is very important, e.g. sales representative, but in most jobs it is irrelevant. In any case, training can often greatly improve the first impression a person makes.

14. Situational tests of personality. In tests of this type, the personality of the candidate is not judged indirectly from answers to questions or interpretation of appearance but more directly from the observation of actual behaviour under controlled conditions.

The armed forces were the pioneers of situational testing during the 1939–45 war. Candidates for commissions were formed into groups and asked to cross ditches with apparently inadequate means, or to transport heavy objects across obstacles. Sometimes a leader was appointed for the group, and his abilities as an organiser and leader assessed. Sometimes no leader would be appointed, and the observers would watch to see if any natural leader or leaders emerged.

This method is still used in officer selection, and in modified form has been taken up by the Civil Service and by some industrial and commercial employers. In its civilian applications, the candidates are still dealt with as a group (usually from five to ten in number), but their task is intellectual rather than practical. They are asked to discuss a topic of current interest for about thirty to forty-five minutes without a chairman; hence its title "leaderless group discussion". Several observers are able to watch and listen, but they do not intervene except to bring the discussion to an end or introduce a new subject.

It is remarkable how with a little training observers can agree easily on their assessment of such attributes as quality of contributions, influence over others or positive/negative behaviour. Candidates for their part usually regard the methods as acceptable and fair because all of them are quite obviously competing on equal terms. Following its original use for officer candidates, leaderless group discussion is primarily used for the selection of management trainees and sometimes for trainee sales representatives.

Leaderless group discussion is acceptable both to the employer and to the candidate, and it has high face validity, i.e. it appears to provide the means of assessing some facets of personality. Its true validity has not yet been proved; in all probability it can give information about personality which would be difficult to obtain in any other way, and it is almost certainly preferable to any other personality test at present available for selection purposes.

Misleading results can, however, sometimes occur. Some candidates, normally quiet and retiring, can for the day of the test successfully act the part of the self-assertive leader; and frequently the performance of individuals is affected by the composition of the group—if it contains one or two uncongenial members the remainder may behave out of character. For this reason it is wise to change the seating arrangements of the group after every discussion.

15. Interviewing. In spite of its drawbacks, the interview (which will be discussed in V) is by far the most used method of personality assessment. Even when a personality test is given to a candidate its results are regarded as supplementary to the interviewer's judgment of personality.

APTITUDE AND ACHIEVEMENT TESTS

16. Aptitude tests. Quite frequently a candidate applies for a job in which he has had no previous experience. The employer accepts that training will be necessary, but wants to ensure as far as possible that the candidate is suitable for training. He wishes to know whether the candidate possesses an aptitude for the job, i.e. the basix mental and physical qualities which can be developed into the specific skill.

An aptitude seems to be made up of several components: general intelligence, one or more specific mental abilities, physical attributes (such as muscular coordination), experience in a related activity and possibly personality factors like interests and motivation.

Some aptitudes, e.g. managerial or selling aptitudes, are so complex and controversial that no satisfactory way of testing for them has yet been discovered.

Some of the simpler aptitudes, for which tests have been shown to give worth-while results, are as follows.

(*a*) *Verbal aptitude*—a good command of written or spoken English.

(*b*) *Arithmetical aptitude*—ability in addition, subtraction, multiplication and division.

(*c*) *Spatial aptitude*—facility in judging shapes and dimensions, important in e.g. drawing, packing or driving.

(*d*) *Mechanical aptitude*—understanding of mechanical principles.

(*e*) *Manual dexterity*—more accurately called psychomotor dexterity.

Tests are available for these aptitudes, but their construction and interpretation is a skilled task, only to be carried out by psychologists or under their guidance.

17. Achievement tests. In contrast to aptitude tests (which measure potential ability after training), achievement tests measure the skill and knowledge that the candidate already has. They are the most common of all tests; every candidate during his interview is asked at least one question about his previous experience.

Construction of achievement tests is usually quite simple; generally they are either *work-sample* or *symbolic*.

(*a*) *Work-sample tests* consist of a carefully-chosen part of the actual job. If the candidate fails to reach the required standard of performance in this part it is assumed that his performance in the whole job will be inadequate. Examples are the shorthand and typing test nearly always given to candidates applying for secretarial posts, the vehicle handling test for road transport drivers and the test piece of work for engineering craftsmen.

(*b*) *Symbolic tests* are used when a work sample would be impracticable; they represent aspects of the job in symbolic, usually verbal, terms. They may consist of questions to probe the candidate's knowledge, circuit diagrams or technical specifications to be interpreted, or occasionally in-tray exercises in which the candidate is confronted with a batch of incoming letters and memoranda to be answered.

VALIDATING TESTS

18. Methods of validation. All tests used to measure individual differences should be validated, i.e. an investigation made to see if the test measures what it is claimed to measure, or predicts what it is claimed to predict. During this investigation the text may also be standardised, i.e. a cut-off score decided, below which a candidate is to be rejected.

There are four types of validity, the last two being particularly relevant for personnel selection.

(*a*) *Content validity*—an inspection is made of the subject-matter of the test to see if it is relevant to the quality being measured.

(*b*) *Construct validity*—the results of the test are compared with the results obtained by the same group of candidates who have taken another test, the validity of which has already been established.

(*c*) *Predictive validity*—a group of candidates is given the test. They are all engaged, and their subsequent job performance compared with their test scores. If there is a reasonable relationship, the test is valid and it can be standardised, i.e. a score identified which will cut off the unsuitable and admit the suitable candidates. There are possible disadvantages with this method.

(*i*) Job performance may be difficult to assess objectively.

(*ii*) The process of validation may be lengthy; adequate assessment of performance may not be possible until a long time after the test has been given and a large number of results will be necessary before validation is complete.

(*iii*) In practice it is rarely possible to engage *all* candidates, but if the results of the test are compared with the performance of a selected group only it is not completely validated.

(*d*) *Concurrent validity*—the test is given to present employees in the job in question. If the test is valid, then the more proficient the employee, the higher the score. This method is quick, but has the following disadvantages.

(*i*) Standardisation is difficult.

(*ii*) The test is validated against a non-typical group, i.e. present employees rather than candidates for employment.

(*iii*) The employees may not behave normally when they do the test. They may be suspicious and deliberately give a poor performance, or they may be anxious to excel themselves and give an unusually good performance.

A common method of validation is to combine predictive with concurrent validity. The test is first tried out on present employees, after reassuring them that it is not in their interests to falsify their performance. Prima facie validity can be established and standards approximately found. The test is then used on candidates for the job concerned, their subsequent progress being compared with their test scores. Validity can therefore be confirmed and the standard fixed more precisely. It is in any case good practice to make a continual review of test scores and proficiency because many jobs gradually change in character, thus reducing the validity of the test.

PROGRESS TEST 4

1. In what way is the measurement of physique different from the measurement of intelligence or personality? (**3**)

2. Define "intelligence". (**4**)

3. What is the most common type of intelligence test used in commerce and industry? (**5**)

4. What does "IQ" stand for? Define the term. (**7**)

5. Why is a high intelligence test score not a guarantee of success in a job? (**8**)

6. Define "personality". (**9**)

7. What are "self-report" personality tests? What is their value in personnel selection? (**11**)

8. Should personality be judged by first impressions? (**13**)

9. What is "leaderless group discussion"? (**14**)

10. What is the difference between an aptitude test and an achievement test? (**16, 17**)

11. Describe one way in which a test may be validated. (**18**)

CHAPTER V

Interviewing

THE SELECTION INTERVIEW

1. Description. A selection interview is an extension and development of the inevitable meeting which takes place between an employer and a prospective employee. It includes questions designed to test achievement or aptitude, and is at present the most commonly used method of personality assessment.

2. Reliability and validity of the selection interview. There is much conflicting evidence here. Some studies have shown how easily interviewers can disagree about a candidate, and how predictions made on the basis of an interview are often not fulfilled. Other studies, however, provide evidence of agreement between interviewers, and of predictions coming true (see *Employment Interviewing* by J. Munro Fraser, Macdonald & Evans, Plymouth). The majority opinion is that the selection interview is in any case unavoidable, so the best possible use should be made of it. Reliability and validity can be greatly improved if the following conditions are observed.

(*a*) The interviewer is not rigid or authoritarian in his views and is reasonably sensitive to other people.
(*b*) The job is thoroughly studied and described.
(*c*) The interviewer plans his questions in advance.
(*d*) He is trained in interviewing.

3. The philosophy of the selection interview. There are two schools of thought regarding the way a selection interview should be conducted.

The first makes the assumption that an individual's general behaviour has become stable by the time he has reached adulthood, i.e. his personality has now become established. At the interview, therefore, questions should be asked about his past behaviour, in particular his motivation, how he dealt with crises and his social adjustment. The pattern that emerges from the candidate's answers will be a reliable guide to his future behaviour, after making allowances for a different environment. In order to obtain this information the interviewer must establish a good personal relationship with the candidate (establish rapport, as it is sometimes called) and encourage him to speak freely and frankly. This is the approach favoured by most employers.

The second view is that a candidate attending a selection interview will intentionally or unintentionally distort his answers, exaggerating points in his favour and minimising others. Since none of the information he gives about his past life can be relied on, the interviewer must draw conclusions based on the candidate's present behaviour only, i.e. the way he reacts to situations contrived and controlled by the interviewer. Testing is, of course, a special example of this attitude with which no one would quarrel; a test taken away by the candidate to be done at home and unsupervised would be valueless. Leaderless group discussion (*see* IV, **14**) is another example where candidates are observed in a controlled social setting. When this philosophy is applied to the interview its outcome is usually a situation where mental stress is applied; for example, the candidate may not be invited to sit down, his answers may be ridiculed or the interviewer may remain silent and expressionless for long periods.

The stress interview is intended to provoke the candidate into displaying his true personality rather than the facade he is trying to maintain to impress the prospective employer. Though superficially attractive, this approach is rarely used by reputable employers for the following reasons.

(*a*) Behaviour under the created stress conditions will probably not be typical of the candidate's behaviour under genuine stress. All the interviewer will learn is how the candidate behaves when he encounters some rather foolish and annoying events at a selection interview. His responses will largely depend on how badly he wants the job.

(*b*) The employer's good name will suffer and candidates may withdraw their applications.

(*c*) A stress interview, by concentrating entirely on personality, is incomplete. It makes the candidate unwilling to talk freely about his experience.

4. Purposes of the selection interview. A well-conducted selection interview fulfils three functions.

(*a*) To elicit information about the candidate's motives and behaviour in order to assess personality.

(*b*) To check the factual information the candidate has already given about himself, to examine the value and relevance of his experience and qualifications, and often to give an achievement test in symbolic terms (*see* IV, **17**).

(*c*) To give information to the candidate about the job and company. This part of the interview is very often omitted or skimped, but it is quite essential. Selection is mutual; the employer selects the candidate, and the candidate must be given the information he needs to select the employer.

5. Preparing for the interview. It is impossible for an interview to be done well unless thorough preparations have been made.

(*a*) The job is analysed and described (*see* XIII). If a job specification already exists, it should be brought up to date. It is impossible to say if a candidate is suitable for a job unless the job is thoroughly known.

(*b*) Written information about the candidate is obtained (*see* XIV, **14**).

(*c*) The candidate's written statement is compared with the job specification so that the interviewer can decide where clarification or further information is needed. He makes a note of the key questions he must ask.

(*d*) An appointment is made to allow ample time for the interview and for any tests it is decided to give. If the candidate is a young person applying for training, it may be wise to invite his parents to attend.

(*e*) The interviewer makes sure that during the interview he will not be interrupted by visitors or telephone calls.

(*f*) Interviewing across a desk which is cluttered up with filing trays, telephones, ornaments and other objects is avoided, because a physical barrier between two people seems to create a psychological barrier. The candidate is placed at the side of the desk, or better still the interview takes place away from a desk, using perhaps two chairs with a low table between them to carry an ashtray and any necessary papers.

6. Conduct of the interview. Most experienced interviewers begin the interview with a few remarks and questions designed to welcome the candidate and set him at his ease. For example, a question about the candidate's journey to the place of the interview not only breaks the ice but provides the interviewer with useful information.

It is often easier to get the candidate to talk freely if the early questions are about his present job rather than about his schooldays followed by a laborious plod in strict chronological order. The order in which topics are dealt with is not important as long as they are all covered. Maintaining an easy conversational tone should have precedence over a rigid programme of questions.

The object of the questions is to get the candidate to talk about his experience and reveal his motivation, social adjustment and the way in which he has dealt with any difficult episodes in his private or working life. These rules should be followed when framing questions.

(a) *Questions should not suggest their own answers* (e.g. "I'm sure you have had experience in stocktaking, haven't you?") or be answerable in a very few words (e.g. "I see from your form that you've passed GCE in four subjects"). Open-ended questions are best; they suggest no particular answer and encourage the candidate to talk at some length. Examples are: "Tell me about any stocktaking experience you have had?", or "What were your best subjects at school?"

(b) *The meaning of questions should be clear* and they should be expressed in a way appropriate to the candidate's experience and education. The interviewer must try to adapt his manner and choice of words to suit the candidate, though not to a ludicrous degree.

(c) *Probing questions should be used.* If a candidate says he was responsible for a certain activity this must not be taken at its face value—further questioning may show that his responsibility was confined to keeping records about it. Similarly a candidate's impressive list of hobbies and interests may be merely things he has done once or watched others do.

(d) *The interviewer should unobtrusively guide* the course and subject-matter of the interview by questions which introduce new topics, linking them to what has been dealt with before. The candidate should do most of the talking, but on subjects which have been chosen and introduced by the interviewer.

(e) *A very large number of questions* should begin with the words how or why. The reasons behind the candidate's actions and the way he goes about getting things done are invaluable clues to his personality.

During the interview the job, company and working conditions, e.g. hours, holidays, pension scheme, etc., should be briefly described, and the candidate if possible be shown the place where he would work. He should be given plenty of opportunity to ask questions.

The interviewer should indicate clearly to the candidate when the interview is at an end, and what the next step will be, e.g. he will receive a letter or should telephone the company on a certain day.

ASSESSMENT

7. Recording the interview. Note-taking during the interview should be avoided because it seems to inhibit the candidate from speaking freely; exceptions may be made, however, for information which must be recorded exactly, such as a change of address or the candidate's present salary. A full note should be taken *immediately after* the interview and certainly before the next candidate is seen.

It is essential for the record to be made in a systematic way to be sure that comments have been made on all important points and to enable comparisons with other candidates to be made more easily. There are many systems for describing candidates, two of which are as follows.

(*a*) *The seven-point plan of the National Institute of Industrial Psychology*, which suggests that the candidate should be assessed under the following headings.

(*i*) Physical make-up.

(*ii*) Attainments.

(*iii*) General intelligence.

(*iv*) Special aptitudes.

(*v*) Interests.

(*vi*) Disposition.

(*vii*) Circumstances.

(*b*) *The five-fold grading*, devised by John Munro Fraser, which uses the following classification.

(*i*) First impressions and physical make-up.

(*ii*) Qualifications.

(*iii*) Brains and abilities.

(*iv*) Motivation.

(*v*) Adjustment.

The second scheme is perhaps more realistic for adult candidates, particularly as it draws attention to the main fields an interview should cover. It is usually advisable to add a sixth heading, circumstances, since a candidate's domestic life, travelling problems, etc., are sometimes relevant to his suitability.

Many experienced interviewers evolve their own systems, often because they deal almost exclusively with a particular type of candidate, e.g. university graduates or manual workers, and wish to give attention to some points rather than others. Either of the two systems described above may be used as the basis of one's own scheme.

8. Assessing the candidate. The information given by the candidate and recorded by the interviewer must now be interpreted so that suitability for the job can be assessed. It is comparatively easy to make an objective judgment about the candidate's experience and qualifications, particularly if questions on these subjects have been carefully thought out in advance. It is often possible, in addition, to give an achievement test (*see* IV, **17**).

Assessment of personality is much less reliable. The candidate's replies are interpreted by the interviewer, who has his own prejudices and preferences, and will be guided by his own perceptions. It is impossible to eliminate the effects of bias on the part of the interviewer, but he may reduce them and improve the quality of his assessment by the following means.

(*a*) He should keep an open mind until the end of the interview; first impressions, though important in some jobs, can be extremely misleading.

(*b*) He must try to become aware of his prejudices, and allow for them.

(*c*) The candidate's statements are analysed to look for recurring patterns of behaviour, e.g. constant rebelliousness against authority or a tendency to avoid decision-making. Any conclusions reached about personality are justified by reference to incidents the candidate has described, so that no personality assessment is made without evidence.

(*d*) Doubts about a candidate's personality can often be resolved by deferring a decision for twenty-four hours or by asking him to return for a second interview.

(*e*) Several experienced interviewers are more likely to make a reliable assessment than one alone. There are, however, some practical difficulties in arranging this (*see* **10–13**).

(*f*) The interview is validated by following-up the successful candidate's progress and behaviour after he has been working in the job for some time (*see* XIV, **22**). Unfortunately it is not possible to follow-up the candidates who are judged unsuitable, so that interview validation will always be incomplete.

9. Final rating. It is useful to conclude the written assessment of the candidate with a final rating, particularly if a number of candidates are to be seen over a period. Selection is then made easier by comparing the final ratings. A five-point scale can be used:

A—Outstanding candidate.
B—Very good candidate but . . .
C—Good candidate but . . .
D—Needs further consideration because . . .
E—Unacceptable because . . .

The "buts" in grades B and C indicate that the candidate may need some special training or that the job may have to be modified in some way for him. The "becauses" in grades D and E are important in that they show the quality of candidates coming forward and the reason for rejection; the latter may sometimes be required by some outside body, e.g. an industrial tribunal.

MULTIPLE INTERVIEWS

10. The use of several interviewers. In most organisations it is unusual for employees to be engaged on the authority of one person, e.g. a personnel manager, a departmental manager and his deputy might wish to be involved. The use of several interviewers enables a wider and more expert range of questions to be asked, and reduces the effects of personal bias. On the other hand a single interviewer is more likely to establish rapport and develop a connected line of questioning to explore motivation and social adjustment.

There are three ways of arranging for a candidate to be seen by several selectors: successive interviews; panel interviews; and board interviews.

11. Successive interviews. In this method the candidate is seen by one interviewer, then by a second and then by a third (rarely more). This method preserves the one-to-one relationship but has disadvantages.

(*a*) The candidate often finds the procedure very tedious, particularly when he is asked the same questions by all the interviewers.

(*b*) An inexpert interviewer can cause damage.

(*c*) The candidate's responses change as he goes from one interview to the next because he learns to expect certain questions and becomes more adept at giving acceptable answers to them.

12. Panel interviews. These are interviews in which the candidate is seen by a comparatively small number of people simultaneously. The usual membership of a panel is three or four; anything larger than this would best be described as a board.

(*a*) A panel interview has the following *advantages*.

(*i*) The candidate's time is saved as compared with successive interviews.

(*ii*) Each interviewer can specialise in asking questions in which he is expert.

(*iii*) There is time for each interviewer to ask several questions.

(*iv*) All the interviewers are able to take part in the joint assessment of the candidate and express their own views.

(*v*) Inexperienced interviewers can be trained by including them in panels.

(*b*) The *disadvantages* of the panel interview are as follows.

(*i*) It is less easy to establish rapport with the candidate than it is in a one-to-one interview.

(*ii*) The questioning may be disorganised and repetitive.

(*iii*) Occasionally, the interviewers transact company business during the interview.

These disadvantages can be overcome with some forethought. The interviewers should agree among themselves which one of them is to carry out the main part of the interview—the biography, the exploration of motivation, etc. The other interviewers arrange to join in later with prepared questions in their particular fields. The principal interviewer acts as chairman, controlling and directing the proceedings. It is preferable to have the interviewers and the candidate sitting round a table rather than the common arrangement in which the interviewers sit on one side of a table and the candidate on the other.

13. Board interview. In this method the candidate is seen by a comparatively large number of selectors simultaneously, i.e. five or more. The board interview is used above all in the public sector of employment, where boards of thirty or more members are not unknown.

(*a*) *Advantages.*

(*i*) It enables many people to see the candidate on one occasion.

(*ii*) It shows the candidate's behaviour under stress.

(*b*) *Disadvantages.*

(*i*) Rapport between the board and the candidate is impossible.

(*ii*) The candidate's behaviour may not be typical of his conduct under more normal kinds of stress.

(*iii*) When so many wish to ask questions, any connected line of enquiry is impossible.

(*iv*) The interviewers are seldom expert.

(*v*) With such large numbers, it is very difficult for the chairman to agree and control an interviewing plan.

(*vi*) Rivalries and disagreements among members of the board often appear, putting the candidate in an awkward position.

(*vii*) It is difficult for a board to have adequate knowledge of the requirements of the job.

(*viii*) The final assessment of candidates is very difficult.

As a means of selection there is very little to commend in the board interview. It has been suggested that if a large group wishes to be involved in selection it should delegate the actual interviewing to a panel drawn from the group, the rest observing the interview by closed circuit television. This would be an improvement, but it would still not avoid the difficulties caused by lack of knowledge of the job and by the large number from whom agreement must be reached.

THE COUNSELLING INTERVIEW

14. When counselling is used. In general, counselling interviews are used for present employees of the company rather than candidates for employment. They are not primarily intended to obtain information, like the selection interview, but instead they are used to give advice and information and to discuss problems. Compared with a selection interview a counselling interview is unstructured, little preparatory work being necessary or possible because the interviewer's role is mainly to react to the interviewee.

Sometimes, particularly in appraisal or grievance interviews, the manager who conducts the interview makes up his mind to some extent to follow a particular line before he has seen the employee and then conducts a telling interview, rather than a problem-solving interview, in which he listens and responds to the employee's statements and attitudes. When the manager is highly respected and very knowledgeable a telling interview may be successful because the employee learns clearly what his manager thinks of him and what he now expects of him, but in this type of interview the telling is one-sided; the manager is told very little about his subordinates.

15. Problem-solving interviews. Although many managers find such an approach inconsistent with their usual management style (*see* VIII), the problem-solving method is much more likely than any other to increase an employee's satisfaction in his work. Whether the purpose of the interview is to appraise the employee or to deal with his complaints, an approach which encourages the employee to state his own point of view and, with the manager's prompting, work out his own plan of action is more likely to have a satisfactory sequel than an interview where the manager attempts to dictate to the employee a course of action based on insufficient information.

Problem-solving interviews are often difficult because the normal manager-subordinate relationship may inhibit frank speaking. The best way to overcome this is to remove the physical signs of this relationship, e.g. to conduct the interview in chairs side by side rather than across the manager's imposing desk.

The manager should try not to express his own point of view during the early part of the discussion; if he does, the subordinate will tend to say things which conform with this point of view instead of what is really in his mind. In extreme cases the grunting technique may be used; in order to encourage the subordinate to talk the manager merely grunts or murmurs to show he is listening, with occasional remarks encouraging the subordinate to continue or summing up what has already been said.

THE DISCIPLINARY INTERVIEW

16. Definition. A disciplinary interview enquires into a complaint made about the work or conduct of an employee in order to see if he should be reproved, warned or threatened. The dividing line between a disciplinary and a counselling interview is not always clear; an investigation into a complaint may end with the employee being given advice rather than a warning. Some counselling interviews may contain a veiled threat from the manager that he does not want the problem in question to occur again.

17. Conduct of the disciplinary interview. This is best illustrated by assuming that a manager has learned that an employee's work has become unsatisfactory. He should not automatically take disciplinary action but follow this procedure.

(a) Check the facts; on what basis and by whose judgment is it said that the employee's work has deteriorated?

(b) When interviewing the subordinate tell him what he is accused of and the source of the manager's information.

(c) Give the employee every opportunity to reply; in some firms it is customary for his shop steward to assist him in stating his case.

(d) At this point it may be apparent that the information is not as reliable as appeared at first, or that there are extenuating circumstances. The manager may then in the first case promise to investigate further, or in the second case continue the interview on a counselling basis.

(e) If the manager considers the employee has been at fault he tells him so, giving his reasons (if possible) in objective, quantitative terms, e.g. "Your output is x per cent below the average for the department."

(f) The manager then tells the employee what he proposes to do, e.g. give a warning that an improvement must occur within one month. This warning is recorded in writing.

(g) After a month the employee is seen again, whether or not his work has improved.

This procedure may seem cumbersome but it follows the rules of justice and obviates the awkward situation in which disciplinary action has to be withdrawn because the employee's case has not been properly heard. It should also improve industrial relations within the organisation.

PROGRESS TEST 5

1. How can the reliability and validity of the selection interview be improved? **(2)**

2. What is a stress interview? **(3)**

3. What are the purposes of a selection interview? **(4)**

4. What kinds of questions should be avoided in a selection interview? **(6)**

5. How should an interviewer assess personality? **(8)**

6. What are the advantages and disadvantages of panel interviews? **(12)**

7. What is a problem-solving interview, and what is it used for? **(14, 15)**

8. State the procedure to be followed in a disciplinary interview. **(17)**

CHAPTER VI

Physical Conditions of Work

FATIGUE

1. Definition. Because it is used rather loosely in industrial psychology the term fatigue is difficult to define. The most satisfactory definition appears to be "a reduction in the energy available to perform a task". Fatigue is used to explain physical changes occurring in the body as a result of effort, the subjective feeling of tiredness and the cause of an otherwise unexplained reduction of output during a working spell.

2. Physical fatigue. Towards the end of the nineteenth century the Italian scientist Mosso, using a device known as the ergograph, formulated some laws of physical fatigue, i.e. the fatigue occurring as the result of muscular effort. The most important of his laws are:

(*a*) light loads lifted frequently cause less fatigue than heavy loads lifted infrequently;

(*b*) rest pauses can give complete recovery from fatigue.

To illustrate the first law, moving a heap of sand by 100 movements of a large shovel will be more fatiguing than moving the same amount by 200 movements of a shovel half the size. Jobs which involve lifting should therefore be designed in such a way that heavy loads are avoided and lighter loads used instead.

The second law has been verified in industry many times, particularly by the work of the Industrial Health Research Board in the 1914–18 war. It is found that the output of employees engaged on manual work gradually rises at the beginning of an uninterrupted working spell until it reaches a steady amount; after a time output begins to decrease until the spell is over. The periods when output is increasing, stable or decreasing vary in their length according to the characteristics of the job and the workers, but the pattern remains the same.

If a rest pause is introduced before production begins to fall, the period of stable production will usually continue after the pause, and the period of decreasing production will be shorter. The more physically taxing the job, the more frequent the rest pauses that are required.

Physical fatigue shows itself in ways other than reduced output and a feeling of tiredness. Evidence of an objective kind can be found in the changed chemical composition of body fluids and in the accumulation of waste products of muscular exertion, particularly lactic acid. The physiological effect of a rest pause is to allow the body fluids to return to their normal state and for the waste products to be removed from the vicinity of the muscles, but the recovery will take longer if the rest pause occurs after the physiological changes have started.

Experiments can be made to determine the number and timing of rest pauses which give the best results; it is not advisable to allow the worker to rest when he feels tired, because by then fatigue will be well established and a comparatively long rest pause will be necessary before he feels refreshed and is able to put out his normal amount of energy. To obtain the greatest benefit, therefore, the rest pauses should be compulsory and occur before the worker begins to feel tired. Study of the rate of output will show a decrease or irregularity occurring before the feeling of tiredness arrives; the rest pause should be taken at the average time of this change in output.

3. Psychological fatigue. Modern technology has greatly reduced the number of physically tiring jobs, and physical fatigue is therefore not so important as it was. However, symptoms very similar to those of physical fatigue still occur in people doing work which is not physically tiring—a reduction or irregularity of output and the subjective feeling of tiredness, but without any chemical changes in the body.

The symptoms occur when an employee has been working for a period on a job such as light assembly, inspection, machine operating or clerical work of many kinds. Because the physical effort required in these jobs is very small, and no other explanation can be found, it is said that *psychological fatigue* must have occurred.

People differ in their susceptibility to psychological fatigue, but the introduction of rest pauses has been found to alleviate it in nearly every case. As with physical fatigue, they should be given when output begins to deteriorate; this will occur before the worker feels tired.

In relatively unstructured jobs, like many kinds of office work, it may not be possible to fix rest pauses by reference to output. Office workers in fact take many informal rest pauses (often without realising it), and an office manager who tried to insist on un-interrupted work without intervals for chats or meditation would find that the quality and quantity of work produced had suffered.

Because psychological fatigue seems to depend above all on motivation and suitability for the job it may be reduced in ways other than rest pauses.

(*a*) Variety—a change to another job, a visit to another de-partment to obtain materials or occasional (not continuous) music.

(*b*) Good initial selection—unsuitable employees become bored sooner.

(*c*) Adequate training—an employee who understands his job and feels confident in it will feel fatigue less.

(*d*) Adequate motivation—a sense of achievement, competi-tion with other employees, rewards of money or time off.

4. Fatigue and the design of jobs. It is in the interests of both employers and employees to reduce fatigue. Rest pauses have been shown to be very effective in this, ten minutes away from the job bringing large dividends in increased production. (It is strange that when the benefits of rest pauses are well-established they are so frequently used as bargaining counters; employees often agree to give up their rest pauses in exchange for a pay increase, as though management were buying back a troublesome conces-sion.)

Besides introducing rest pauses managers may find it possible to adopt one of the measures described in II, **16–17**, in the hope that it may increase motivation. Another approach is to apply ergonomics to the design of jobs (*see* **7–8**); fatigue can be reduced by attention to illumination, noise, position of controls, etc.

ACCIDENTS AT WORK

5. Definition. An accident at work is an unplanned event which occurs within a planned programme and is actually or potentially harmful to the worker.

6. Accident proneness. During the 1914–18 war, studies in muni-tions factories produced the concept of accident proneness—that certain employees are inherently likely to be involved in accidents to a greater degree than others, irrespective of the job or working environment. The original research showed that a large proportion of the accidents suffered by a group of workers happened in fact to a very small minority; the members of this small minority were then called accident prone.

Later research has not always confirmed the findings. It has often been found, for example, that workers who appear to be accident prone during one period are safe workers during another period, their places being taken by workers who previously had low accident records. As an illustration of this, it was found in a study of nearly 30,000 bus drivers in America that the unsafe drivers in a three-year period became the safe drivers over the next three years. Conversely, the safe drivers in the first period, i.e. those who had one accident or none, became unsafe in the second, causing no less than 96.3 per cent of all accidents occurring in the whole group.

The explanation of this kind of result seems to be that the liability to become involved in accidents is due more to chance factors and the behaviour of others than to an inherent quality in the worker. On the other hand, accident statistics have sometimes shown that even in different periods the same workers have an above-average proneness to accidents, but only when their jobs have not changed. The generally accepted view at present is that accident proneness in the sense of a disadvantage that certain workers always take with them wherever they go is very rare; we must think instead of accident proneness as a result of the interaction between the worker and his job situation.

Thus insofar as accident proneness exists at all, it is due to:

(a) unsuitability for the job, or lack of training in it;
(b) temporary factors, e.g. frustration, worry or ill-health;
(c) a very small number of inherently unsafe workers.

XXIII will deal with practical measures for reducing accidents and will outline the legal position. A great contribution to industrial safety may also be made by ergonomics, described in the next section.

ERGONOMICS

7. Definition. Ergonomics is the study of equipment, methods, layout and environment at work in terms of human abilities and limitations. It regards the worker not as an adjunct to the machine but as part of a man/machine production unit, behaving according to the following sequence.

(*a*) Stimulus, e.g. instruments, warning lights and buzzers, appearance, sound or smell of work in progress.

(*b*) Perception (through the appropriate senses) and decision-making.

(*c*) Response, e.g. operating controls, using tools or hands, communicating with others.

(*d*) Result, i.e. a change in the work, which produces new stimuli, thus repeating the sequence.

(NOTE: In the USA the terms human factors engineering or human engineering are used instead of ergonomics.)

8. Ergonomic design of equipment. Although designers of working equipment have always considered the human operator to some extent, there are many machines which are unnecessarily difficult for him, i.e. stimuli are hard to recognise and responses cannot be made easily or quickly. These problems were very important in the 1939–45 war when ergonomics was rapidly developed and applied to the design of tanks, guns and aircraft.

The ergonomicist tries to fit the process to the man, rather than expect the man to do the best he can with equipment which has been designed with engineering, rather than human, considerations in mind. He adopts the following approach.

(*a*) *Displays*—are the things the operator looks at and listens to providing information quickly, easily and unambiguously? Should dials, gauges, warning lights, etc., be redesigned? Is perception difficult?

(*b*) *Controls*—can the operator change the state of the machine and materials, quickly, easily and naturally? Are levers, wheels, switches, etc., in the most convenient position?

(*c*) *Working environment*—is the operator's place of work well lit, heated to an appropriate temperature and free from excessive noise or humidity?

THE WORKING ENVIRONMENT

9. Illumination. Research has established minimum standards of illumination necessary for many industrial tasks. Examples of these standards, expressed in lux, are:

(a) Very fine assembly work	1,500
(b) Medium assembly work	300
(c) Weaving of light cloth	300
(d) Weaving of dark cloth	700
(e) Sheet metal work	200

A lux is the light given by a standard candle at a distance of one metre from the work; very approximately 10 lux are equivalent to the light given by one-fifth of a watt passing through a filament lamp, or by one-fifteenth of a watt passing through a fluorescent tube.

The minimum lighting for the areas surrounding the actual task—environmental or amenity lighting—should not be less than 150 lux. The degree of illumination can easily be measured with light-meters, and the installation of suitable lighting is not usually difficult or expensive. Expert advice is available from illumination engineers, but some of the most important rules are as follows:

(a) Task lighting should be focused on the task itself; focusing on an area adjacent to the task will cause fatigue and loss of attention.

(b) Too much contrast between the lighting of the task and the lighting of the environment causes eye fatigue, and may lead to accidents because the worker may find difficulty in adjusting his vision when he moves from a bright to a relatively dark area.

(c) Glare can produce discomfort or poor vision. It can be minimised by ensuring that lights do not shine in workers' eyes and that working surfaces do not reflect light.

(d) Some variety in the visual environment should be provided by walls of different colours or the sight of some distant object, e.g. a view through a window.

(e) Even when workshops and offices appear to be well-lit by daylight from windows and glass roofs, the illumination may have to be supplemented by artificial light because some areas may be in shadow. The colour of the supplementary lighting should then be a good match to daylight.

(f) Dirty windows, walls or light sources reduce the illumination available. They should be cleaned and maintained regularly.

10. Noise. Like illumination, noise can be measured by meters and its intensity expressed in numerical terms, the unit of measurement being the *decibel*.

Confusion can sometimes occur because the scale of decibels is logarithmic, i.e. an increase of x units in the scale means that sound intensity has increased by *x times* the previous amount, not *plus x*. Therefore an increase from 70 to 80 decibels means that the sound is ten times louder. The noise made by a hydraulic press (approximately 130 decibels at one metre) is 10,000,000,000,000 times the intensity of the faintest sound the average person can hear (one decibel).

There are four unfortunate effects of noise in industry.

(*a*) *Deafness*—exposure to loud and prolonged noise will in most people produce deafness, beginning with inability to hear high notes. Deafness may occur so slowly that the worker may not notice it; an enlightened employer will test the hearing of his employees to see if their hearing is deteriorating in noisy conditions (very roughly an intensity of eighty decibels or more).

(*b*) *Efficiency*—research shows that repetitive work which is not mentally demanding does not suffer when carried out in noisy conditions. On the other hand, work which requires accuracy, concentration and alertness will deteriorate. For example, inspection and calculation become less efficient under noise, and scrap or spoiled work becomes more frequent. It is also probable, though not definitely proved, that noise increases the number of accidents.

(*c*) *Annoyance*—employees seem to be able to become accustomed to practically any level of noise in time, but they will complain about it when the noise is:

    (*i*) occasional (particularly when high-pitched);
    (*ii*) apparently unnecessary;
    (*iii*) unexpected;
    (*iv*) unexplained.

Therefore the annoyance caused by noise can often be reduced by explanations or warnings.

(*d*) *Interference with communication*—oral messages may be unheard or misunderstood in noisy conditions.

Noise may be reduced by silencing the machine or enclosing it in insulating material, and by facing interior walls, floors and ceilings with sound-absorbent surfaces. If it is still above an acceptable level, employees should be given ear-defenders to wear, though quite often complaints are made that they are cumbersome. It may be necessary for supervisors to enforce their use.

11. Heating and ventilation. In this field three factors are important: temperature, humidity and air movement. All three can affect performance and comfort at work.

(a) *Temperature*—in factories the optimum air temperature for light work is 10°C (65°F) and the range in which most people feel comfortable is 15° to 20°C (60° to 70°F). Heavy work in factories is best carried out within a range of 12° to 15°C (55° to 60°F). In offices the comfort zone is 19° to 23°C (67° to 73°F).

(b) *Humidity*—this is only important when conditions are extremely damp or extremely dry. In the first case employees complain of stuffiness and in the second they feel uncomfortable because of dryness of the nose and throat.

(c) *Air movement*—it is generally agreed that an air movement of about 10 metres per minute should be aimed at; at this level movement is just perceptible. If temperatures are above or below the ideal, then air movement should be greater or less, respectively, than 10 metres per minute. Air movement may be improved by the use of fans or by an air conditioning system.

Unlike illumination and noise, which can be fairly easily modified at any time, the heating and ventilation characteristics of the working environment are much less flexible and often depend on the way in which the building was designed. It can be very expensive to install air conditioning or improve the central heating after a building is complete; they should be fully considered at the time when the building is being planned.

PROGRESS TEST 6

1. What are the two most important laws of physical fatigue? (2)

2. State the ways in which psychological fatigue can be reduced. (3)

3. Is there such a thing as accident proneness? (6)

4. Describe how ergonomic principles can be applied to the design of machines and equipment. (8)

5. How should a large workshop containing several machines used for high precision work be illuminated? (9)

6. In what ways does deafness detract from a worker's efficiency? (10)

7. Explain why heating and ventilation can be a more difficult problem than illumination or noise. (11)

CHAPTER VII

Social Psychology at Work

THE BEHAVIOUR OF WORKING GROUPS

1. The formation of a working group. So far in this book the employee has been studied mainly as an individual, responding in various ways to the psychological and physical conditions in which he works, without reference to his fellow-employees. This assumption is very often quite unrealistic. Work is rarely an activity carried out in solitude; most of us have colleagues whose wishes and personalities we have to learn to understand because we work closely with them. When we work with others, merely understanding them is not enough; it is necessary for us to modify our behaviour to some extent, acting in ways which are acceptable to them rather than completely satisfying to ourselves.

After people have worked closely and continuously with each other for some time, the mutual adjustment of behaviour settles down into a fixed pattern, a set of mental attitudes becomes established which all share, and very often certain customs become so strongly entrenched that they are almost compulsory. A collection of individuals has now been transformed into a *working group*, which is a special type of *social group*.

2. The work of Elton Mayo. The importance of the working group was first shown clearly by Elton Mayo and his colleagues in a detailed study of worker behaviour at the Western Electric Company factory at Hawthorne, near Chicago, between 1924 and 1932.

Mayo had been called in by the management because production at the factory was thought to be too low. At first Mayo experimented with the illumination, following the current belief that if physical conditions were suitable and the pay adequate there was no reason why employees should not work hard. A puzzling result of the experiment was that output increased even when lighting was made worse. Because definite conclusions were difficult to draw from the behaviour of a large department when its working conditions were varied, he eventually segregated five female operators into a separate room so that their behaviour could more easily be controlled and observed.

3. The relay assembly test room. During the period 1927 to 1929 variations in rest pauses and working hours were made and compared with the output of the five girls. Throughout the period, even during the times when working conditions had been made worse, output steadily increased. When the girls were interviewed to find an explanation for this unexpected result they said:

(a) they enjoyed working in the test room, and worked harder there than in the factory because they felt special;

(b) they did not regard the observer who was present in the room with them as a normal supervisor because he explained things to them and reassured them;

(c) the experiment seemed to show that management was interested in them;

(d) they helped each other at work and had developed close friendships with each other away from work;

(e) they felt united and had a common purpose.

4. The bank wiring room. Between November 1931 and May 1932 a group of men were put into a special room but in other respects continued working under their usual conditions. The group, which was engaged in the assembly of banks for use in telephone exchanges, consisted of nine wiremen, three soldermen and two inspectors. An observer also sat in the room but did not participate in any way, the men sometimes being interviewed outside the room by another member of Mayo's staff. A supervisor was formally in charge of the men, but was present in the room only part of the time. Payment was made according to a rather complicated piece-work scheme. The following observations were made.

(a) The men worked to an unofficial level of output; if anyone worked harder than this he was abused by the others.

(b) Reported figures for output and delay time (when stoppages occurred for reasons beyond a worker's control) were false; they showed a constant, instead of a variable, output week by week.

(c) The men often exchanged jobs, contrary to management instructions. They often helped each other.

(d) The supervisor knew about these practices, but did not try to stop them. He was not regarded by the group as their leader.

(e) One wireman, though conforming with the unofficial norms of production, used to tell the foreman about the irregular practices. He was the outcast of the group, and was called "squealer".

(f) Unofficial leaders in the group were more influential than the official leader, the foreman.

5. Conclusions from the Hawthorne studies. The steadily increasing level of output in the relay assembly room was ascribed by Mayo to the beneficial effects of a united working group outweighing the deteriorating physical working conditions. The bank wiring room study had shown, however, that a united working group could oppose management interests by restricting its output. Thus the working group was shown to be powerful enough to override working conditions on the one hand and a payment-by-results scheme on the other.

When the Hawthorne results were published the relay assembly room received most attention, and the human relations movement which appeared soon afterwards emphasised the encouragement of united working groups because it was thought that good performance would follow. This advice did not always bring the hoped-for result, firstly because it is not always possible to manipulate employees into cohesive groups, and secondly because it is never certain that the groups, if formed, would agree that their own objectives coincided with those of management, i.e. they might resemble the bank wiring room rather than the relay assembly room.

6. Working groups—benefits to the employee. An individual at work can derive certain benefits from becoming a member of a group:

(a) satisfaction of social needs;

(b) the benefits of shared experience, e.g. an experienced worker showing the ropes to a newcomer;

(c) mutual support, e.g. colleagues backing up someone who is having a dispute with management;

(d) a basis for self-expression, because the security afforded by the group often encourages creativity.

7. Formation of working groups. A collection of individual employees does not automatically become a working group.

The conditions which will cause a group to form and make it cohesive are as follows.

(*a*) The employees must be near enough to each other for easy face-to-face communication.

(*b*) The work they are doing must be related; e.g. they form parts of a chain (like a progressive assembly line), are doing similar jobs (as in the relay assembly room), or have the same purpose (like a committee organising a works outing).

(*c*) The individuals must be compatible, without great differences in status, skill or education.

(*d*) The total number should not exceed about twelve, though this depends on physical arrangements in the workplace.

(*e*) An external threat will often cause a collection of individuals to form themselves into a group.

8. Behaviour of working groups. When a working group has come into existence it will behave in certain characteristic ways, very much as if it had a life of its own independent of the lives of the individuals included in it.

(*a*) The group will produce a settled system of personal relationships and customs.

(*b*) These customs sometimes include restrictions on output (*see* XXII, **5**).

(*c*) An individual will often behave more in the way the group expects than as he would if left to himself.

(*d*) The group exerts great pressure on all its members to conform to its own standards of behaviour.

(*e*) Newcomers to the group are often made to feel unwelcome. Groups vary in this respect just as individuals vary in their ability to become easily accepted by a group.

(*f*) The group tends to resist change imposed on it, and will react to it slowly because of the threat to its existence, its security, its customs and its pattern of relationships.

(*g*) Unofficial leaders emerge in the group, changing according to the needs of the situation at the time. When the group is in open conflict with management, for example, it may choose as its leader a person whom normally its members would describe as an agitator. When conditions settle down, a new leader might emerge who would be a more diplomatic person.

(*h*) A group often seems to follow the same motivation process as an individual—searching for and eventually perceiving satisfying goals. It can be frustrated and show the negative reactions of aggression, regression, resignation and fixation.

(*i*) The character of a group will not change because one person leaves it or joins it, unless that person is extremely influential.

(*j*) An external threat or the competition of another group will increase the cohesiveness of a group.

9. Group cohesiveness. The extent to which individuals feel that they are members of a group, and the strength of their attachment to the group is called cohesiveness or morale. It is shown by the frequent use of the word "we" instead of "I", the help group members give each other and the perseverance and enthusiasm they show. Cohesive working groups usually have low rates of labour turnover (*see* XVII) and absence.

A high degree of cohesiveness is not always linked with high productivity. Restriction of output by working groups is widespread, and is usually found in groups cohesive enough to be able to rely on the observance of limits of output by its members. On the other hand when organisation structure or work methods are rearranged to facilitate the formation of working groups, productivity is sometimes increased.

It is possible to find any combination of cohesiveness and productivity; no doubt many people have encountered happy united groups who do very little work, or sections composed of workers who dislike each other but nevertheless show above-average rates of output. The relationship between cohesiveness and productivity is similar to that between individual job satisfaction and productivity (*see* II, **23**), that is it depends on the group's perception of its own interests. However, although the effect of group cohesiveness on output is uncertain, an employer's costs will nearly always be reduced by the presence of cohesive working groups because labour turnover and absence will be comparatively low.

10. Working groups: implications for management. Research shows that working groups can be powerful forces within an organisation. Sometimes their presence is beneficial to management, e.g. the relay assembly room, and sometimes the reverse, e.g. the bank wiring room, because there is no reliable connection between the cohesiveness of a group and its rate of production.

The working group must also be considered in relation to the formal structure of the organisation; does the group coincide with an official section or department, or does it draw its membership from several of them? Frequently a company is organised by function, i.e. production workers belong to one department, maintenance workers to another and clerks to a third. An informal working group, consisting of people working near each other on the same task, could possibly include members of each of these three departments. A somewhat similar situation occurs when the unofficial leader of the group and the officially appointed foreman or manager are rivals for the allegiance of the group, creating confusion and lack of control.

If management wishes to make constructive use of informal working groups, and minimise the difficulties they can sometimes bring, the following measures are often recommended.

(a) By ensuring that working conditions are good, that employment policies are fair and by taking a personal interest in the employees, encourage groups to perceive the company's interests as coinciding with their own, thus increasing productivity.

(b) In any case, making it easier for cohesive groups to form because labour turnover and absenteeism will be reduced.

(c) When making changes, remember the instinctive opposition of the working group.

(d) Arrange for competition between groups, so that cohesiveness will increase. Greater output may also occur.

(e) Examine incentive schemes to see if they can be based on the output of the group instead of the individual (see XXII, 6).

(f) If practicable, make the working group coincide with the official section or department. In some cases the functional division of authority may have to be abandoned.

(g) If it is not possible to give the unofficial leader an official post, give some sort of recognition perhaps by including him in joint consultation procedures. Train foremen and managers in human relations skills so that the group will be more satisfied with its official leadership.

11. Contemporary views about working groups. In recent years the human relations movement (see 5) has become less influential; although the working group is still regarded as a very important factor in industrial behaviour it is no longer thought to be supreme. The reasons for this change of view are as follows.

(a) An increasing recognition of the importance of ego and self-actualisation needs (see II, 2), placing more emphasis on the content and meaning of the job. It is often thought more useful to make the work intrinsically interesting than to try to manipulate social groupings.

(b) Many human relations writers seem to adopt a paternalistic attitude, accepting the jobs as they are and merely advocating more attention to the social climate.

(c) It is difficult to predict the behaviour of working groups, except as regards labour turnover and absenteeism. Sometimes a cohesive group has high productivity, sometimes the reverse (*see* **9**).

(d) Evidence that many workers expect to satisfy only their physiological and security needs at work (*see* X, **7**), forming few friendships there and accepting uninteresting jobs providing a good wage is paid.

(e) Changes in technology which sometimes break up working groups, separating individuals from each other and making communication difficult because of noise or pressure to work at a certain pace.

The human relations movement has, however, been very valuable in opening up the study of non-economic incentives at work, though the emphasis has now changed from the rewards of social satisfaction to the rewards of job extension (*see* II, **15–16**). It also stimulated research into leadership in commerce and industry, described in the next chapter.

ATTITUDES

12. Definition of attitude. An attitude is an individual's characteristic way of responding to an object or situation. It is based on his experience and leads to certain behaviour or the expression of certain opinions.

In contrast to a need, which is short-lived and transitory, an attitude is long-lasting and exists even when all needs are for the moment satisfied. For example, a professional social worker will have taken up that occupation because he has a certain attitude towards the care of others, but within that occupation he will be motivated from time to time by the considerations discussed in II. Attitudes provide a predetermined set of responses, so that a person's behaviour or opinions can often be forecast in certain situations. Knowing a person's attitude towards politics, for example, one can be fairly accurate in predicting what he will say when asked to comment on a topical issue.

Attitudes may be held on any subject, though frequently it appears that attitudes held by a person may be grouped together under a general heading such as authoritarian or permissive. Someone having a certain attitude will hold corresponding beliefs, but a person having an opposite attitude will hold equally sincerely beliefs of a quite different kind. Perception is also strongly influenced by attitudes; thus some people will perceive a situation as favourable to them while others will perceive the same situation as unfavourable. In extreme cases attitudes can prevent people from believing facts which a very large majority consider true and abundantly proved.

At work, attitudes towards management will strongly influence the reactions of employees towards any management communication; in extreme cases practically any announcement will be greeted with complete scepticism.

13. How attitudes are formed and changed. Research shows that experience within a social group is the most important factor in determining attitudes, starting with experience in the family group and continuing in groups at school, among friends and at work. The process of attitude formation is somewhat mysterious but need not be examined in detail here.

Attitude change is more important at work, since it may explain why an employee's behaviour has altered and it may be necessary sometimes to attempt to bring about a change in a desired direction for training purposes (*see* XX, 1–3) or to improve industrial relations. There are three main ways in which attitudes are changed.

(*a*) The pressure exerted by a social group on an individual member to conform with group standards, which include the accepted attitudes of the group. This may occur naturally when a newcomer joins a group, or may be contrived as a part of training. In the latter case the group is made to undergo an experience like discussing or acting out a real or imaginary situation which it is hoped will cause the attitudes of all the participants to change to some extent.

(*b*) Through the influence of a highly-respected individual.

(*c*) As a result of a severe shock or intense pressure, e.g. a wartime experience.

Process (*a*) is the one most likely to occur in commerce and industry and it will be dealt with in XX, **2**.

14. The measurement of attitudes. It is useful for management to know the nature and strength of the attitudes of its employees as a guide to future policy and to show possible causes of poor industrial relations. For example, if a large number of employees were leaving the company an enquiry into attitudes might reveal the reasons and indicate what could be done to retain more employees. The chief ways in which attitudes may be detected or measured are as follows.

(a) A *searching interview* in which the employee is encouraged to express his attitudes. Because this method is so lengthy and costly it is usual to apply it to a random sample of employees rather than to all. To encourage frank speaking the interviewing is done by people independent of management, e.g. a firm of consultants.

(b) An *exit interview* given when an employee is leaving the company. He is asked to explain fully why he is leaving, his reply often revealing the attitudes of himself and his colleagues. Although it seems reasonable to expect that someone who is leaving a company will speak more freely than someone who is not, experience shows that often the leaver is guarded in his remarks, partly to protect his colleagues and partly to be able to leave in a friendly and placid atmosphere.

(c) *Attitude surveys*, which ask employees to comment on a list of statements or questions, indicating those with which they agree. The two principal types are those devised by Thurstone and Likert; both enable an attitude to be given a numerical score which can be correlated by statistical methods with other measurable behaviour (see *Statistics* by W. M. Harper, M. & E. HANDBOOK series).

The attitudes of employees are shown, of course, in their everyday conversation and behaviour at work. A supervisor or manager whose communications with his subordinates are good will from this evidence know many of their attitudes and how strongly they are held, though the difference in status will probably prevent his knowledge from being complete.

PROGRESS TEST 7

1. Summarise the results of the experiment in the relay assembly test room at Hawthorne.   (3)
2. What were the main observations made in the bank wiring room at Hawthorne?   (4)
3. What benefits does an employee obtain from membership of a working group?   (6)
4. Under what conditions is a working group likely to form?   (7)

5. Describe some of the main characteristics of a working group. (8)

6. What is the relationship between group cohesiveness and productivity? (9)

7. How can the existence of working groups affect management policy? (10)

8. Define attitude. How can an attitude be changed? (12, 13)

9. In what ways may attitudes be measured? (14)

CHAPTER VIII

Leadership and Participation

UNOFFICIAL AND OFFICIAL LEADERS

1. The unofficial leader. In psychological studies, a leader is usually defined in terms of the group he leads; he is the person who directs and controls the group so that the purposes of the group are achieved. When a group forms spontaneously by a process of social interaction, it quite frequently has more than one leader at any one time. The leaders in such a situation may be rivals, but more frequently share between themselves the various leadership functions of planning, directing, reviewing, etc. Different circumstances may bring about a change in leadership, different leaders emerging who seem more capable of dealing with the new situation.

In commerce and industry the unofficial leader can be a very important person, particularly when the working group is strongly united. He is sometimes given the semi-official status of shop steward (*see* XXV, **8**), which recognises his importance and his place in relations between management and employees. Even when they do not have this status, unofficial leaders are often given special and privileged treatment by management. However, the importance of the unofficial leader tends to be intermittent, becoming active at times of crisis and quiescent in more placid circumstances. On the other hand, the official leader, the person given formal authority over others, is always important because of his function of seeing that a certain area of the firm's business is effectively dealt with.

2. The official leader. Extending the definition in the preceding section, an official leader is a person who motivates and controls his subordinates to work towards goals which are regarded by the organisation as desirable and possible. The subordinates must therefore be led in such a way that they value the rewards they are able to obtain from their work; these may be money, friendship, status, approval, a sense of achievement or a mixture of these.

The official leader, who may be called, for example, supervisor, section leader or manager, possesses *authority* partly because he has been appointed by the owners of the company (or their representatives) and partly because of his competence to hold the post. Subject to employment law, he has *power over his sub-ordinates*, i.e. he can get them to do things they would otherwise not do, through his right to punish or reward, his control of resources, his knowledge of the job, his skills in handling people and the respect for authority they may have. The way he combines these factors is called his *management style*, and a great deal of research has been carried out to try to identify the style which a manager should adopt to bring the best results from his subordinates.

LEADERSHIP STUDIES

3. Research in leadership. Early writers on leadership took the view that the *personality* of the leader was all-important; they said that leaders were born, not made, perhaps coming from a certain class of society. They compiled lists of the personal qualities (intelligence, integrity, steadfastness, etc.) that were needed in a successful leader. These lists reflected of course the writers' own prejudices and were not based on careful observation and research. It was not an approach which could lead to any ways of improving leadership behaviour.

Later work on leadership has been conducted from a *behavioural* point of view; leaders and their subordinates are studied in actual work situations in order to discover whether certain kinds of leadership behaviour are more effective than others. Research of this kind has obvious difficulties, e.g. the presence of observers may distort normal behaviour, effectiveness is often difficult to measure, leaders' behaviour may be influenced by the quality of their subordinates, and descriptions of different management styles easily become very subjective. However, quite consistent results have been obtained from many hundreds of studies, two of the most important being summarised below.

4. The Prudential Life Insurance Company study. This important American study, carried out in the late 1940s, endeavoured to study managers and supervisors in their normal circumstances, rather than create an artificial experimental environment.

A large office organisation was divided into relatively high-

producing and relatively low-producing departments, using the
available records of the clerical time taken to deal with a certain
amount of work. The supervisors of all the departments were
then interviewed to find out how they approached their jobs and
their attitudes towards the company, their subordinates and their
colleagues. As a result of these interviews it was possible to divide
the supervisors into two classes.

(a) *Employee-centred*, in which emphasis was given to relationships within the department, and to the preferences, needs
and capacities of individual subordinates. The supervisor believed
in helping his subordinates to get promotion and in giving them
general rather than close supervision.

(b) *Production-centred*, in which the subordinates were closely
supervised and controlled, both as to the pace and the method of
work. The need to get the work done on time was continually
emphasised.

When the productivity of the departments and the management
styles of the supervisors were compared, it was found that there
was a very strong tendency for the high-producing departments
to be run by employee-centred supervisors and for the low-producing departments to be under production-centred supervisors,
the efforts of the latter to push the work through being apparently
self-defeating.

The lesson drawn from this study was that supervisors should
be encouraged or trained to move away from a production-
centred approach and adopt an employee-centred style of management to obtain the best results from their subordinates.

5. The Ohio State University study. In this investigation a large
amount of miscellaneous information about management style
was collected by means of interviews, observation and questionnaires. A preliminary examination of this material suggested that
nine dimensions of management behaviour might exist. Statistical
analysis was applied to the data, and two major factors emerged
by which managerial style could be described.

(a) *Consideration*—including emphasis on mutual trust and
respect between manager and subordinate, consideration for subordinates' feelings, and two-way communication.

(b) *Initiating structure*—the close definitions of the jobs of
subordinates, great activity by the manager in planning, controlling, initiating new ideas and criticising his subordinates.

It will be seen that these definitions of two independent dimensions of management behaviour are very similar to the definitions of employee-centredness and production-centredness which were assumed to be at the opposite ends of one dimension. For convenience and clarity, the two dimensions will be called emphasis on task and emphasis on people.

In the first the manager regards his subordinates as factors of production at his disposal for performing a certain task. He will direct and control them in precise terms, their reward for accepting this being monetary payment. It is improbable that they would obtain satisfaction of ego or self-actualisation needs in these circumstances.

When the manager puts the emphasis on people he regards his subordinates almost as his equals and does not exercise strict authority over them. He assumes that they have ideas to contribute and that it is part of his function to draw out these ideas. Another assumption he makes is that they will produce good work without close or detailed supervision, i.e. that the job itself provides part of the motivation, perhaps by the satisfaction of the higher needs.

Another part of the Ohio State University study was concerned with the relationship between management style and employee satisfaction, as expressed in the rate of labour turnover and the number of grievances. It was found that both turnover and grievances were highest when the management style showed low consideration, irrespective of the degree of initiating structure that was shown. The lowest rates of turnover and grievances were found when the management style showed medium to high consideration together with low initiating structure. Thus the degree of consideration seems to be the dominant factor in determining this area of employee behaviour. The research did not, however, show a similar clear relationship between a particular management style and productivity.

6. Subsequent research. Subsequent research has confirmed the Ohio findings, though the dimensions are often given other names.

(*a*) The analysis of leadership behaviour worked out by Blake and Mouton and known as the managerial grid uses the terms concern for people and concern for production.

(*b*) Another approach, by W. J. Reddin, calls the dimensions relationships orientation and task orientation, but adds a third dimension, effectiveness.

(c) F. E. Fiedler, in his research into leadership, uses the terms permissive, non-directive and task-controlling, directive.

(d) Douglas McGregor's theory X and theory Y which are described in **12** are similar in that theory X has a resemblance to initiating structure and theory Y to consideration.

(e) R. Likert uses the terms co-operative-motivation system and job-organisation system.

EFFECTIVE LEADERSHIP

7. Management style and effectiveness. Although reductions in labour turnover and grievances are very valuable, the principal aim of the research into management style is to establish its relation to effectiveness, that is the degree to which it facilitates adequate or high productivity.

The studies at the Prudential Life Insurance Company showed a clear relationship, i.e. that the effective manager emphasised people. Later studies, however, did not produce such clear-cut results, some in fact showing the reverse relationship. Various other factors were then examined, among them the size of the firm, the personalities of the subordinates, the nature of the production process, the liking the subordinates had for the manager and the power the manager held in the organisation. It appears from all this research that no managerial style can be identified which will be effective in every situation; different work situations require different styles if they are to be managed effectively.

It is sometimes said that a manager's main skill is *diagnostic*; he assesses all the relevant factors in the work situation and diagnoses what management style will be the most effective. Unfortunately diagnosis cannot always be followed by appropriate behaviour, since many managers find it difficult to change their style (*see* **10**).

8. The importance of the process. An important factor determining which particular management style is effective is the task structure—the extent to which the work is defined or programmed. Task structure in most cases depends on the technology, and is best illustrated by describing its two extremes.

(a) Structured or highly-programmed work, e.g. assembly line work in a mass-production factory, is strictly defined as to method and time. Each individual job is specialised and must be carried out as defined in order that it may fit into a complex production system. There are few work decisions the subordinate can make.

(b) Unstructured or loosely-programmed work, e.g. as found in a research laboratory, is defined in very broad terms and gives the subordinate a large number of decisions regarding methods and sequence. Sometimes the task itself is rather vague, and there may be many possible ways of accomplishing it. The subordinate is often given the freedom to choose the way he prefers.

In highly-programmed work the manager will almost inevitably emphasise the *task*, for it is his responsibility to ensure that jobs are done according to their precise specification. There is little purpose in asking employees for their suggestions about the way the work should be done, and it is impracticable to allow them to work at their own pace; such deviations would certainly upset the efficiency of the process, and might indeed be dangerous.

In contrast, the manager of unstructured work will as a rule obtain the best results by emphasising *people*, because most employees prefer to control and arrange their own work rather than be closely supervised, and they often welcome the opportunity to contribute suggestions and ideas. When the work is loosely-programmed close supervision is unnecessary and tends to be resented. The manager's job should be to see that his subordinates are self-motivating and self-directing. The success of the employee centred managers at the Prudential Insurance Co., where the work was comparatively unstructured, is an example.

In this analysis, individual differences among subordinates should not be overlooked; some do not expect or wish to contribute suggestions or take responsibility, while others (probably an increasing proportion) expect management to emphasise the people dimension and arrange jobs so that they will be less structured. The manager must therefore use his judgment to decide whether the attitudes of his subordinates must override the requirements of the process.

9. Fiedler's theory of leadership effectiveness. The American psychologist F. E. Fiedler has put forward a theory, based on several studies, which modifies the simple relationship which has just been described. Fiedler suggests that although in general the task-centred approach is best for structured work, it may also be effective when the work is unstructured, relations between the manager and his subordinates are poor and the manager's formal powers, e.g. of dismissal or promotion, are weak. In other words, when conditions are unfavourable for the manager his best plan is to take firm control of his subordinates.

The theory goes on to confirm that in general the people-centred approach is best for unstructured work, but adds that this approach may also be effective when the work is structured and the manager powerful but not well-liked. Fiedler's analysis thus uses four variables:

(a) emphasis on task or people;
(b) task structure;
(c) manager–subordinate relationships;
(d) powers of the manager.

It shows that management style, to be effective, should take account of technology, social relationships and the place of the manager in the organisation.

10. Changing managers. It may sometimes be quite obvious that a manager's style is quite unsuitable for the work he is responsible for, and that he would be more effective if he could change his style.

The most usual example is the authoritarian, task-centred manager, in charge of relatively unstructured work. Because attitudes of this kind are deeply rooted in the manager's personality, they are very difficult to change, except superficially and temporarily. The techniques most often attempted are role-play and group discussions of various kinds (*see* XX, **2**), but there is no guarantee of their success. It is much easier to improve a manager's knowledge, both of his immediate job and of new management techniques which he might find useful. Possibly the added self-confidence this knowledge brings may modify his management style.

When a manager's style is reasonably appropriate, but not quite suitable, knowledge of leadership theory and discussions with other managers may well bring about an improvement. This change will not be maintained, however, unless the company where he works is sympathetic to the change and has a work pattern which is compatible with the changed management style. For example, in a company which from top to bottom is run on very authoritarian lines, with rigid rules and procedures, it is impossible for one manager to maintain a people-centred style; he must conform to the prevailing code of managerial conduct in the company.

Since the style of many managers cannot be changed, it may be necessary in order to make the best use of their abilities to transfer them to work more appropriate to their style. Another possibility might be to change the degree to which the work is structured, but this would have great difficulties in practice.

PARTICIPATION

11. Definition. Worker participation is the inclusion of the employees in the decision-making process of the organisation. It implies also that the employees have access to sufficient information on which to base their share in decisions. Sometimes the power of the employee in making decisions is complete because he is also regarded as a co-owner, as in the kibbutzim in Israel and factories in Yugoslavia. On the other hand, in many companies in Great Britain participation may merely consist of the management informing employee representatives of decisions that have already been made, and asking for their comments.

The extent to which worker participation is possible and desirable is a very controversial subject, with political overtones. In this field Douglas McGregor and N. R. F. Maier have made useful contributions, though they are concerned mainly with decisions at departmental level rather than policy decisions for the organisation as a whole.

12. Theory X and Y. The American writer Douglas McGregor described two contrasting assumptions about the behaviour of employees, called theory X and theory Y.

(*a*) Theory X takes the view that the average employee dislikes work, will try to avoid responsibility, and will only be made to work by a mixture of close control and threats.

(*b*) Theory Y assumes that work is a natural and welcome activity which need not be externally controlled if the employee is adequately motivated, that employees will seek responsibility and that they can give valuable help in solving work problems.

McGregor took the view that theory Y was the correct assumption to make, and that firms should be organised on that basis. He said that theory X gave employees the opportunity to satisfy only basic and security needs at work, but a theory Y management attitude would enable them to satisfy Maslow's higher needs, in particular ego and self-actualisation needs. A man's job should be so constructed that it gave him the opportunity for full self-development.

There are similarities between theory X and task-centred management on the one hand, and theory Y and people-centred management on the other, and the comments made in the previous section about styles of management apply to a large extent to theories X and Y. Most employees would no doubt welcome the opportunity to have more control over their work and to put into practice their own ideas. There is undoubtedly a large fund of valuable expertise, experience and orginality among employees that is often untapped by management.

Unfortunately some jobs are so closely limited, defined and integrated into a complex production process that opportunities to satisfy the higher needs at work are completely absent. Workers in jobs like these must quite often be treated in a theory X manner, i.e. coerced and controlled, if adequate effort is to be obtained. Moreover, there are many employees who do not expect to take responsibility at work and avoid it if they can. Therefore, management is sometimes justified in making theory X assumptions about employees.

13. Quality and acceptance in decisions. The previous discussion of management style was concerned with the general tone of the manager's behaviour and his typical way of dealing with work situations, but of course the manager will have decisions of many kinds to make and should deal with them in different ways.

The psychologist N. R. F. Maier has suggested a way of analysing the various decisions which have to be made by a manager which should help him to decide how they should be handled. According to Maier, decisions may be described according to their *quality* and their *acceptance*.

(*a*) *The quality of a decision* is the extent to which it uses objective facts, particularly as regards technical knowledge or financial resources. A high-quality decision would involve the consideration of complex technical data or the expenditure (or saving) of large sums of money.

(*b*) *The acceptance of a decision* is the extent to which it affects the personal feelings of subordinates, how much their emotions and need-satisfactions are involved.

14. The four types of decision. This analysis is illustrated in Fig. 4, in which four types of decision are shown, involving various proportions of quality and acceptance.

(*a*) *High acceptance, low quality decisions* do not need expert technical knowledge or incur large financial outlay, but they matter a great deal to the subordinates. Canteen questions are an obvious example, others being holiday rotas and arrangement of desks in an office.

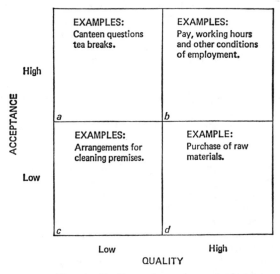

FIG. 4   *Quality and acceptance in decisions.*

(*b*) *High acceptance and high quality decisions* not only affect subordinates' personal lives to a great extent but also have important technical and financial implications for management. Wages and salaries are the obvious example, others being changes in hours or working methods.

(*c*) *Low acceptance and low quality decisions* are trivial and unimportant; they arouse little interest among subordinates and do not require very much money or technical knowledge.

(*d*) *Low acceptance and high quality decisions* do not affect subordinates very much personally, but have a high technical or financial content. The purchase of raw materials, the design of products, and the prices charged for products are examples of this type of decision.

15. How to deal with decisions. This analysis is useful because it can guide a manager in the way he should deal with the different decisions which come his way. He can assume that if a decision matters a great deal to his subordinates they will want some part in making the decision, but that if it does not affect their interests the decision can be made without involving them.

A decision which has to be based on complex technical and financial considerations, perhaps affecting the long-term interests of the company, needs the expertise of qualified managers, who must keep in mind the requirements to maximise profits or comply with the law. In many cases the subordinates do not have the knowledge necessary to make decisions of this type, nor are they interested in them. Obviously the most difficult decisions to make are those which are not only of high quality but also affect the subordinates personally.

A manager may therefore deal with the four main types of decision.

(a) *High acceptance, low quality*—by consultation with subordinates, sometimes allow them to play the major part in making the decisions. In many companies canteen committees have been formed, consisting almost entirely of rank-and-file employees, to supervise the running of the canteen.

(b) *High acceptance, high quality*—by negotiation with the subordinates. Management and employees both have interests they wish to protect, which in many ways are incompatible. The usual way of resolving the conflict is by bargaining and compromise, neither side being completely satisfied with the decision but both accepting it as fairly reasonable.

(c) *Low acceptance, low quality decisions*—either by the manager without reference to his subordinates, or by delegation to a lower level of supervision. Maier suggests that in many cases they may be decided by tossing a coin.

(d) *Low acceptance, high quality decisions*—by the manager alone, or with the advice of experts. The employees would not expect to be consulted, nor would they have the knowledge to make a useful contribution.

Maier's method of describing decisions is therefore very useful in identifying the extent to which employees should participate in decisions affecting themselves or their work. It guides a manager in his day-to-day work, but does not claim to deal with participation on the larger scale, i.e. at the level of the organisation as a whole.

16. Participation in company-level decisions. McGregor and Maier were concerned above all with the employee's participation in decisions affecting him directly and in the short term. There is plenty of evidence that most, though not all, employees are more than willing to take part in decisions of this type, but not very much evidence about their willingness to be involved in decisions at the highest level, e.g. manufacturing or investment policy.

In the great majority of organisations there is very little participation by employees in policy decisions; sometimes there are varying degrees of *consultation*.

(*a*) Employees are consulted before a decision is made, but the management is not bound by their views, though it usually tries to take them into account.

(*b*) Employees are informed of decisions and are consulted about their effects. The decisions may be modified in detail.

(*c*) Employees are informed of decisions, and negotiations take place between them and the management about implementation. The detailed application of a redundancy decision is an example.

(*d*) There is a company suggestion scheme.

In many companies there is neither participation nor consultation, but merely information to employees about the decisions that have been made.

17. Participation—a summing up. In such a controversial subject, influenced so much by individual attitudes, it is impossible to come to a clear conclusion. The reader might like to make his own judgment, based on the following arguments, firstly in favour of participation and secondly against it.

(*a*) *In favour*.

(*i*) It makes use of the knowledge and experience of employees, which are usually at least as valuable as a manager's.

(*ii*) Employees are more motivated in their work if they can take part in decisions affecting their work. If they think that decisions are unfair to them, they will be less motivated.

(*iii*) The greater the number of people involved in a decision, the less the possibility of important factors being overlooked.

(*iv*) Unworkable impracticable decisions are avoided.

(*v*) Many decisions impinge directly on employees' lives; it is only right that they should help to make them.

(*vi*) Employees by their efforts contribute to the prosperity of the company; it is right that their voice should be heard.

(*vii*) Modern educational methods and policies encourage independent, informed thinking. Employees should be encouraged to apply this to their work.

(*b*) *Against.*

(*i*) Involving the employees in decisions is time-consuming; many decisions have to be made urgently.

(*ii*) Most employees do not have the technical knowledge on which to base the majority of decisions.

(*iii*) Employees have no responsibility for making the best use of the company's assets and maximising profits; the managers of the company have this responsibility and their decisions must recognise it.

(*iv*) Employees tend to take the short-term view, and may oppose decisions which may benefit the company in the long run but do not offer many rewards to employees in the immediate future. Innovation and enterprise may be discouraged.

(*v*) Employee participation at company policy level needs such cumbersome machinery that it is only possible and genuine in small companies.

(*vi*) Many employees take the view that they are not paid to make decisions, and will only become involved in decisions which affect them directly.

(*vii*) There is a fundamental conflict of interests between employers and the employees; negotiation is more realistic than participation.

The arguments against participation are much weaker, some would say non-existent, when the employees are also the owners of the company. There are a few companies, usually rather small, of this type in Great Britain; they seem to be both commercially successful and stable. Most have been created and built up by a single owner who has then given them away to his employees. Possibly the number of such companies is too small for reliable conclusions to be drawn.

18. The Bullock Committee. In recent years all the political parties have said that they want to encourage more worker participation, though they do not agree about its extent or its methods. It is common in Europe, where most countries have laws compelling companies to include employee representatives on their boards. Trade unions in this country have varying views, some enthusiastically supporting participation, others opposing it completely, saying that negotiation is more realistic and serves the interests of their members better.

The report of the Bullock Committee on Industrial Democracy was published in 1977. It proposed that in companies of over 2,000 employees the board of directors should consist of equal numbers of shareholder and employee representatives (the latter elected through trade union machinery), plus a smaller group of co-opted independent members—the "$2x + y$" formula.

This proposal was generally not well received, although since 1977 there has been a gradual voluntary growth in participation within individual companies, the extent and procedures being agreed between management and employees.

Participation will no doubt be accelerated by the amendment in 1982 to the Companies Act 1967, which requires companies with 250 employees or more to make an annual statement of the action they have taken to:

(*a*) provide employees with relevant information;

(*b*) consult employees or their representatives on a regular basis;

(*c*) encourage the involvement of the employees in the company's performance, e.g. through an employees' share scheme;

(*d*) make the employees aware of the financial and economic factors affecting the performance of the company.

PROGRESS TEST 8

1. What is the difference between an unofficial and an official leader? **(1, 2)**

2. Define employee-centred and production-centred leadership. **(4)**

3. What is the relationship between management style and labour turnover? **(5)**

4. Define unstructured work and describe the most appropriate management for it. **(8, 9)**

5. What is worker participation? **(11)**

6. Summarise theories X and Y. Is theory Y always preferable to theory X? **(12)**

7. Describe the different types of decision which confront a manager. **(13–15)**

8. Summarise the arguments for and against worker participation. **(17)**

CHAPTER IX

Communications and Change

COMMUNICATIONS

1. Definition. Communications consist of all the processes by which information is transmitted and received. The subject matter may include facts, intentions, attitudes, etc., and the chief purpose of communications is to make the receiver of a communication understand what is in the mind of the sender. Therefore a communication is incomplete unless it is received and understood. As the usual result of the understanding is a change in behaviour, effective communications can be regarded as part of a learning process (*see* III).

2. The importance of communications. An organisation may consist of management, employees, premises, equipment, materials, etc., but it will not come to life unless communications effectively link all these parts together and co-ordinate their activities. The decisions of management must be made known to employees, and some kind of control system arranged to ensure that these decisions are acted on; the decisions themselves should be based on a flow of information reaching management from all parts of the organisation. Communications in a large, complex organisation with many departments and locations are obviously more difficult than those in a small single organisation; in a large company errors and inefficiency can easily occur because an individual or a department has not informed another of its actions, or has not been informed.

From the psychological point of view, communications have an importance which goes beyond the transmission and reception of information. The form which a communication takes (or, of course, whether communication takes place at all) can profoundly affect the attitudes of the employees and the degree to which they understand and support management policies. Many industrial disputes originate in a failure of communications—a misunderstanding by the employees of the intentions of management (or vice versa) or a misinterpretation of company policy.

3. Types of communications. It is useful to divide communications within an organisation into two kinds: *formal*, meaning arranged or approved by the management; and *informal*, meaning unofficial and unplanned methods of communication.

Another distinction that can be made is between *one-way* communication, in which the sender makes no provision for a reaction from the receiver, and *two-way* communication, which is framed in such a way that a response from the receiver is provided for and encouraged. One-way communication is quick and preserves management authority; two-way communication is much slower and indicates a more participative approach to decision-making.

The written or spoken word dominates formal communications, but informal communications also include for example gestures, facial expressions, what is *not* said, or who is present or not present at a meeting. Many rumours begin because someone has drawn conclusions from several non-verbal indications. A glimpse of a senior manager studying a plan of the offices, accompanied by a stranger who holds a large tape-measure, would no doubt start a rumour that the office accommodation is to be changed.

Communications may be analysed yet again according to their *direction*. They may be:

(*a*) *downwards*—from a higher level in the organisation to a lower;

(*b*) *upwards*—from a lower level to a higher;

(*c*) *lateral* or *sideways*—from one level to another of approximately the same level.

Most formal communications are downwards, while informal communications are mostly upwards or lateral. It seems that many organisations have communications problems because they do not make formal arrangements for communications to flow upwards or laterally, thus cutting management off from employees' ideas and opinions and making co-ordination between departments unnecessarily difficult.

4. Formal methods of communication. The various formal methods of communication may be summarised as follows.

(*a*) Written instructions and announcements by notices on boards, internal memoranda, notices in pay-packets, company magazines, letters to each employee. One-way, downwards and permanent.

(*b*) Broadcast messages over a public address system. One-way, downwards and not permanent, i.e. misunderstandings cannot be checked.

(*c*) Large meetings of employees addressed by a senior manager. One-way (because response is inhibited in a large meeting), downwards, and not permanent unless the information given is confirmed later in writing.

(*d*) Small meetings of no more than about twenty employees. Two-way (because comments and questions are easy). Mainly downwards, but with some provision for upwards communication. Not permanent.

(*e*) Inter-departmental committees. Two-way and lateral. Not permanent in themselves, but usually followed by a written summary of the discussion and decisions reached.

(*f*) Interviews to give instructions or information or to review a subordinate's performance, i.e. appraisal (*see* XVIII). One-way or two-way according to the manner in which the interview is conducted. Downwards and not permanent. If this method is used to transmit instructions through several layers of the organisation by a series of interviews, distortion is possible because the original instructions may be reworded or misunderstood on their way down.

(*g*) Joint committees of management and employee representatives. Two-way, downwards, upwards and lateral, usually followed by published minutes of proceedings and therefore permanent. These committees may meet regularly, or meet only when required, e.g. to hear appeals against dismissal.

(*h*) Suggestion schemes. Mainly one-way and upwards, but to some extent two-way and downwards (*see* XXIII, **23–25**). Permanent, because suggestions are submitted in writing.

(*i*) Attitude and other questionnaires (*see* VII, **14**). One-way, upwards and permanent.

5. Informal methods of communication.

(*a*) The normal casual conversations which occur between employees at all levels. Two-way, multi-directional, not permanent.

(*b*) A private network of telephone or personal contacts in other parts of the organisation, to help in getting the work done more quickly than by using the official methods of communication. This network, often based on mutual favours or personal friendships, is extremely active in most organisations. It is two-way, multi-directional and not permanent.

(c) Surreptitious written material circulating within the organisation, e.g. caricatures, satirical poems. One-way, multi-directional, permanent.

(d) Secret signs and gestures, e.g. warning others of the approach of a manager. One-way, lateral, not permanent.

(e) Rumour, or the grapevine, spread by a combination of the four methods above, and based on miscellaneous sources of information and guesswork. It is rarely entirely false but concentrates on the more sensational aspects of a situation.

It is probably true to say that when the formal communication systems of an organisation are comparatively inefficient, the informal systems become more active.

6. The psychology of communications. It is possible to improve the effectiveness of communications by applying the psychology of attention, perception and motivation. The subjective and objective factors of attention (*see* I, **7**) are important in the following ways.

(a) The wording of a message should show that it is directed towards the receiver personally, e.g. "You will be pleased to hear that ...", not "It has been decided that ...".

(b) Rumours spread rapidly because they emphasise the subjective factors of attention.

(c) A crowded untidy notice board carrying many out-of-date notices will not be looked at; it should carry only relevant material, arranged in such a way that it is easily read, and that new notices are immediately obvious.

(d) An urgent or important notice should be very large, printed on coloured paper, have a title printed in unusual type or appear more than once on the same notice board.

7. The importance of perception. Communication is also affected by perception (*see* I, **9–10**).

(a) A communication, written or spoken, which uses words which appear long and unfamiliar to the receiver may be perceived as condescending and may therefore arouse resentment. The meaning of the words may be misinterpreted. Short words in clearly constructed sentences should be used where possible.

(b) The intention of the communication may not be understood, sometimes because the sender of the message is not clear in his own mind as to what he wants to say and why but more often because the perceptions of the sender and the receiver regarding the subject of the communication are different. The attitudes of management and employees regarding a change in working arrangements may well be diametrically opposed; a well-meant communication about them from management will probably then be perceived by the employees as a threat of some kind. A statement by a manager to a subordinate that he wishes to discuss the previous year's work may be made in a helpful, problem-solving spirit but perceived by the subordinate as some kind of accusation against which he must put up a defence.

8. One-way and two-way communication. The sender of a communication should always try to motivate the receiver to understand the message and put it into practice. People can become frustrated quite easily when they try to understand a difficult communication, especially when it is unexpected (*see* II, **7**). When they hear an announcement about important matters concerning their personal welfare, or about topics on which they could express useful opinions, frustration is again likely to occur because it is obvious that decisions have been made without consultation. The conclusions that may be drawn are as follows.

(*a*) *One-way communication*, which is easy and quick, is quite adequate for subjects which are straightforward, expected or urgent. Methods which can be used are notices, letters, public address announcements, and talks to large meetings.

(*b*) *Two-way communication*, which can be quite time-consuming and demands some patience and personal skill, should be used for subjects which are complicated, unexpected, of personal concern to the receivers or about which they could make a worthwhile contribution. A better decision may be reached, and it will be accepted more readily. Methods which can be used are small meetings, interviews and committees.

9. Communication and participation. The subject of communication has much in common with leadership and participation, discussed in the previous chapter. Whatever style a manager uses, he must communicate effectively. Even if he adopts an extremely task-centred approach he will obtain a better response if he communicates his instructions clearly, if possible explaining the reasons for them. A manager whose style is to work through his subordinates must obviously foster effective and frequent two-way communication with them.

Participation, which by definition involves a sharing of decision-making by the employees, can only be successful if communications are two-way and efficient. The decisions must be based on adequate information reaching the employees or their representatives, and management and employees must both be assured of the other's good faith. This again implies efficient and frequent two-way communication.

DEALING WITH CHANGE

10. The effects of change. Since the end of the 1939–45 war radical changes have been occurring in all parts of commerce, industry and the public services. A very rapid rate of technical innovation has produced new materials, new methods and new products. Some companies have ceased to exist, some have been taken over by larger and more successful competitors, while others have grown very quickly and changed their character completely.

Eventually, these changes will affect the individual employee.

(*a*) He may be expected to learn a new skill, or modify his present skill.

(*b*) He may find that he is expected to become an adjunct to a computer instead of a traditional clerk.

(*c*) His job may become part of a complicated production system.

(*d*) He may be asked to move to another part of the country.

(*e*) He may be promoted, demoted, or made redundant.

The results of change so far as the employee is concerned can be beneficial or they can be disastrous. At one time the disadvantages of change, e.g. demotion or redundancy, were suffered above all by the shop-floor worker, other employees being shielded from them to a large extent. Nowadays the adverse effects of change can be felt by all levels, including management.

11. Resistance to change. Research and experience show that there is a widespread tendency among employees to resist change, even though it might appear to outside observers that working conditions would be improved. The resistance may, of course, disappear eventually, the employees then saying that they prefer the new arrangements to the old, but before this happens opposition from employees, accompanied sometimes by industrial action, can make the introduction of change very difficult.

The main reasons for resistance to change are as follows.

(*a*) Important and permanent decisions about an employee's working life are made by people who are often unknown and remote.

(*b*) The employee may lose his job or be transferred to a lower-paid job.

(*c*) The skill and experience he has acquired over the years may suddenly become valueless.

(*d*) His status in the firm may be lower.

(*e*) Cohesive social groups may be broken up, together with established relationships, roles, and customs.

(*f*) New relationships must be established, new customs learned.

(*g*) Familiar things represent security: unfamiliar things insecurity.

(*h*) Personal life may be upset by new working times or a move to a new district.

There are individual differences in employees' attitude to change. Some people welcome change, enjoying the excitement and the disturbance of familiar routine. Others dislike change of any kind, even in their private lives. The great majority lie between these two extremes, their reaction to change at work being influenced partly by the nature of the change and partly by the way it is handled. Again, some companies have a tradition of frequent change and tend to attract employees who like uncertainty and variety. In these companies changes are not likely to be resisted by the employees unless they are obviously unreasonable.

12. Reducing resistance to change. Investments in technological or organisational innovations will not bring the benefits that management expect if the employees show resistance to change. The costs of dealing with disputes and the low level of productivity that is often found can be so great that some managers, particularly in companies where industrial relations are poor, prefer to retain an out-of-date technology rather than face the turmoil that the introduction of new methods would bring. A manager should therefore realise that resistance to change is likely to occur, is not based on stupidity or obstinacy, and can be reduced, if not overcome, by some forethought.

The essential first step is to ensure that when changes in working methods or in the organisation of the company are being planned, full consideration is given to the changes that will occur in the human resources of the company. Therefore some kind of manpower plan is required (*see* XII), which will include for example recruitment, transfer, promotion, re-training, and redundancies. When this has been done, careful thought should be given to the method of communicating the effects of the change to the employees.

(*a*) Where it is practicable, there should be some participation by the employees in decisions which affect their daily work. If the decision cannot be changed in principle then there should be participation about the way it is put into effect.

(*b*) The threat to security which many employees feel may be reduced by telling employees individually, and at the earliest possible moment, what their new jobs will be and their position in the new organisation structure.

(*c*) The loss of valuable skill and experience can be counterbalanced by a programme of re-training, emphasising that no one will be expected to do work he is unfitted for, and that an opportunity to learn a new skill is being offered.

(*d*) It is occasionally possible to preserve existing social groups, transferring them to new work as a unit instead of dispersing them.

(*e*) The employees who will suffer financially should be at least partially compensated, e.g. by removal and settling-in expenses if they are required to move house, by guaranteeing their previous income for a period if they are transferred to a lower-paid job, and by giving generous *ex gratia* payments if they are made redundant.

(*f*) Even when the change is comparatively small, perhaps affecting only a few people, resistance will be reduced if the top management of the company show that they know about the change and understand its effects on the employees.

(*g*) The change should be made known by a two-way communication process (*see* **8**), and two-way communication should be encouraged while the change is proceeding.

In some companies it must be admitted that the procedures described above would not be practicable. Employees in a company which has very bad industrial relations may not respond favourably to participation and may not believe statements made to them by management. In such cases, the advice often given is to plan the change in all its aspects very carefully, but secretly, and then implement it very suddenly and without warning. Drastic action of this kind is rarely justified, however, and managers usually have to make their own diagnosis of the situation and decide what position to take up between participation and two-way communication on the one hand and complete authoritarianism on the other.

PROGRESS TEST 9

1. Why are communications important in an organisation? **(2)**

2. What is the difference between these types of communication:

(*a*) formal and informal;

(*b*) one-way and two-way;

(*c*) downwards, upwards and lateral? **(3)**

3. Describe three methods of formal communication. **(4)**

4. Describe three methods of informal communication. **(5)**

5. What is the connection between perception and communication? **(7)**

6. When should two-way communication be used in preference to one-way? **(8)**

7. Why do most employees resist change? **(11)**

8. How can resistance to change be reduced? **(12)**

CHAPTER X

Other Influences on Employee Behaviour

INTRODUCTION

1. The importance of the work situation. In the preceding chapters various influences on the behaviour of people at work have been discussed. These can be summarised under the following headings.

(*a*) *Physique*, making the individual more suitable for some jobs than for others.

(*b*) *Intelligence*, which also affects suitability for jobs and the capacity for learning.

(*c*) *Personality*, which includes the important factors of perception, motivation, and social adjustment.

(*d*) *Physical working conditions*, which should make the immediate job environment suitable to the employee and minimise fatigue and accidents.

(*e*) *The working group*, imposing its own standards of conduct and output on the individual but offering some advantage in return.

(*f*) *Style of leadership*, which to be effective should take account of the nature of the process and the type of employee.

(*g*) *Participation*, the degree to which employees can share in decision making.

(*h*) *Communications*, the spread of knowledge about policies, intentions and attitudes within the company. Particular reference was made to the connection between communication and the handling of change.

It has been shown, for example in the discussion on job satisfaction and leadership, that the type of production process is an important factor in behaviour at work. It is logical to assume, therefore, that the actions of an employee depend not only on his individual qualities and the influence of the working group but also on the type of job he is doing and the type of company he is in. The same individual in a different job, or in a different company, could behave in quite a different way.

A great deal of research has been done in recent years to see if certain work situations produce characteristic behaviour among employees; the most important results of this research will be described later in this chapter (*see* **2–7**). An accepted name for this area of study has not yet appeared; the most popular term is possibly structural determinants of behaviour.

STRUCTURAL DETERMINANTS

2. The docks. For many years dock workers had been regarded as particularly strike prone. In 1965 a report appeared of a Committee of Enquiry, under the chairmanship of Lord Devlin, which had been set up to investigate conditions of work in the docks. It showed that most dockers were casual workers, never sure of continued employment and moving frequently from one employer to another. The work itself was arduous, often unpleasant, and remunerated by means of a very complex payment-by-results system. Many dockers lived in communities near the docks and mixed socially as well as at work.

The Report argued that these conditions affected behaviour at work in the following ways.

(*a*) Because the employee had no loyalty to a particular employer, and vice versa, behaviour was irresponsible and erratic on both sides. The dockers were ready to strike on trivial matters, and the employers sometimes attempted to evade agreements.

(*b*) Loyalty to other dockers took the place of loyalty to an employer, increased by the fact that so many dockers lived in communities. Therefore a strike would quickly spread through the docks because of the solidarity among dockers.

(*c*) The complex payment system gave rise to many disputes.

The report made recommendations which were subsequently put into effect. Dock workers were gradually transferred into permanent employment and their pay system made more simple. Industrial relations in the docks have now greatly improved, but other factors, e.g. the rapid growth of container traffic and the increased use of small ports, may be partly responsible. The Devlin Report is, however, an interesting demonstration of the importance of the effect of organisation and working conditions on employee behaviour.

3. Two contrasting factories. Tom Lupton studied conditions in two factories in north-west England; the first made heavy electrical equipment and the second made garments.

In the electrical factory the employees had formed cohesive working groups imposing output norms and manipulating the payment-by-results system so that weekly pay did not fluctuate very much. The management knew this was happening but made no attempt to stop it.

In the garment factory no working groups had formed and each worker did his best to earn as much as he could. The management kept a very tight control on piece-rates, altering them if it became too easy to earn a bonus.

The differences between behaviour in the two factories were explained as follows. The electrical factory enjoyed stable and prosperous market conditions, with orders in hand for a long period. Labour costs were low in proportion to total costs. The employees decided that it was desirable to aim for constant earnings and restriction of output in case management decided that bonus earnings were too easy to get and that the scheme should be made tighter. Management connived at this because labour costs were low, because they wished to avoid disputes which might hold up production, and because they knew that most of their employees, having transferable skills, could easily obtain jobs elsewhere.

On the other hand, the garment industry is seasonal and uncertain. Labour costs are high and competition intense. This particular factory, like most in the industry, was small, its management having close contact with the shop floor. The employees, whose skills were not easily transferable, had decided to work hard while work was available rather than manipulate the payment system. The management kept close control of wages because of their importance in total costs.

4. Coal mining. The Tavistock Institute of Human Relations investigated the effects on worker behaviour of changes in the method of coal-mining in Durham.

The old system was almost entirely manual; a small group of miners hacked at the coal, loaded it, and propped up the roof, each man being skilled at any of these tasks. The group were self-selected, a vacancy being filled by the choice of the remainder, and its members spent much of their free time together. They were paid as a group and had little supervision. As would be expected, the group was extremely cohesive.

After the 1939–45 war the Longwall system of mining was

introduced. This system used a complex and noisy machine which cut the coal and automatically loaded it into trucks. Between forty and fifty men worked on a shift, each being trained in a special skill. Payment varied according to the job. Each shift was also specialised; one was engaged in preparation, another in getting, the other in advancing. Although the Longwall method was technologically much more advanced than the traditional method, its results were disappointing. Not only was output lower than expected but there were many disputes and much absence.

The Tavistock investigators suggested that the change in technology had produced a new social system which compared unfavourably with the old. There was friction between the shifts, which themselves were too large and dispersed to form a cohesive working group.

A different method of organising the work was then proposed which was shown to have beneficial effects on production and job-satisfaction. The specialisation of task which was the logical outcome of the new technology was partly abandoned; the shifts did not specialise, but continued where the previous shift had left off, and within each shift each man was able to do several jobs rather than specialise in one. The men to each shift were again self-selected and were allowed to allocate jobs themselves. The group output bonus was restored.

This new method of work, although by engineering standards less efficient than the previous method, gave higher production with less absence and fewer accidents.

5. Technology, organisational structure, and employee behaviour. A most important study was carried out between 1953 and 1957 in Essex. Its purpose was to enquire whether the application of the principles of organisation laid down by management theorists had any relation to success in business. The research was led by Miss Joan Woodward, who described it in a booklet *Management and Technology* (HMSO, 1958).

The investigations covered the whole structure of management and supervision and showed considerable variations in the pattern of organisation, which could not at first be related to the size of firm, type of industry or business success. However, when the firms were grouped according to production system, some clear relationships appeared concerning both organisational structure and employee behaviour. The three main classes of technology used in the study were:

(*a*) unit production and small batch—articles made to customers' orders either singly (one-off) or in small quantities;

(*b*) large batch and mass production—articles made on assembly lines, in large or very large quantities;

(*c*) process production—articles made by a highly controlled process, the materials being handled almost entirely by non-human means and rarely visible, e.g. an oil refinery.

6. Results of the Essex research. The research showed that within each class of technology the most successful firms had approximately the same type of organisation in terms of the number of levels of management, the span of control, the ratio of managers and supervisory staff to total personnel and the degree to which jobs were precisely defined.

More relevant for this book are the relationships which were found to exist between the type of technology and the behaviour of employees; in firms which used the same production arrangements it was extremely probable that the employees in all of them would tend to behave in much the same way and be satisfied in their jobs to approximately the same degree. This area of the research can be summarised as follows.

(*a*) *Span of control*—in unit and process production the span of control was smaller than it was in mass production. The closer relationship between the supervisor and his subordinates in unit and process production tended to contribute to better industrial relations.

(*b*) *Management specialisation*—in unit production the managers responsible for production were expected to have a wide range of technical skills, but in mass production there were large numbers of specialists, e.g. in production planning, methods engineering and work study, whose existence limited the authority each line manager could exercise. In process production there were few staff specialists, the managers of the process usually possessing the necessary scientific and technical competence. The employees in unit and process production were able to get immediate decisions from their managers but in mass production might often have to wait while their managers referred to the specialists for guidance.

(*c*) *Pressure on the employees*—in unit production it was recognised that to get the best results, i.e. to produce an article precisely to a customer's specification, the employees should not be pushed or controlled very much. In mass production, in contrast, supervision put considerable pressure on employees to use the expensive plant to its full capacity to reach higher levels of production and to maintain good time-keeping. At first sight the pressure on employees in process production was at a minimum, but although supervisors and managers exerted little pressure on their subordinates there was in fact considerable pressure of another kind; the employees were aware that the plant could not be left unattended and required monitoring and control to be carried out according to a specified routine if breakdowns and even explosions were to be avoided. The employees seemed to resent the pressure that was put on them by the process far less than the pressure they might have received from a human supervisor.

These results lead to the conclusion that industrial relations in mass production will almost inevitably be poorer than they are in unit or process production because of the consequences of that particular type of technology. Moreover, there are in mass production a large number of employees doing boring repetitive jobs, compared with unit production in which the typical employee is a skilled craftsman and process production in which he is a highly trained operator with considerable responsibility. Job satisfaction, therefore, would seem to be less in mass production than in the other types of technology.

7. The affluent worker. This is the title of a book (Cambridge University Press, 1968) in which J. Goldthorpe and his collaborators described an investigation carried out in Luton among a sample of 229 manual workers, all earning at least £17 a week, high earnings for that period. They enquired into the attitude and behaviour of employees in three firms, engaged in small batch, mass and process production respectively.

The most striking result of the research was the instrumental approach shown by the majority of semi-skilled workers, i.e. the machinists in small batch, the assemblers in mass and the process workers in process production. They regarded their jobs simply as a means to an end; a way of obtaining a high income which they could use to satisfy their needs in their leisure time. In many cases they had left interesting and responsible jobs to take up their present employment, only because the pay was higher. They did not expect to obtain satisfaction from their work, they took no interest in the social activities offered by the company and made few friends at work. They preferred the type of supervisor who left them alone. In contrast with the findings of Joan Woodward in Essex, there were few differences in attitudes between the employees of the small batch, mass and process production firms.

The conclusion drawn by Goldthorpe was that the employees in his study were influenced to some extent by the job satisfaction and social conditions they found in the particular technology in which they worked, but much more by the instrumental attitude to work which they all shared. This attitude was based on the great importance the employees placed on leisure pursuits and the family and on an acceptance that few jobs offer satisfaction of ego and achievement needs. The job is regarded as the means of satisfying basic and security needs and providing enough money to satisfy the higher needs outside work. Attitudes to work cannot therefore be properly understood without knowing employees' attitudes to leisure.

8. The influence of occupations on behaviour. The behaviour of an employee is influenced not only by the type of company in which he works but by the traditions, physical effort and mental demands of his occupation. Examples of occupations which are often associated with typical behaviour are as follows.

(a) *Professional workers*, e.g. lawyers, architects and doctors, who have undergone a long course of training carefully controlled by a professional body which usually has statutory recognition. There is a strict code of ethics, and often some restriction on the numbers entering the profession. Most professional workers seem to have high job satisfaction, their working life often extending into their leisure time. When they are employed by a company their loyalties appear to be divided between their profession and their employer.

(b) *Craftsmen*, e.g. skilled manual workers in engineering, building, printing, etc., who have served an apprenticeship which is controlled jointly by the employer and the trade union, the latter frequently restricting the numbers entering the craft. They enjoy high status among other manual workers, have an independent outlook because they can use their skills fairly easily with another employer, and become more valuable as they get older because of their increased experience and skill. There are many similarities between the craftsman and the professional.

(c) *Machine minders and assembly workers*, who apply a moderate level of skill to a very restricted range of operations. Training is short, the work has little interest or variety and generally is part of a tightly controlled process. These workers often become less valuable as they get older because their stamina and speed of reaction decrease. When they change employers they frequently change their occupation also. They tend to have a detached attitude to the job and company, often showing an instrumental approach.

(d) *Process workers*, who monitor processes which are almost entirely automatic, e.g. chemical manufacture and oil refining. They have to be intelligent enough to understand the science and technology on which the process is based so that they may deal with emergencies and breakdowns. A fairly long training period is necessary, emphasising theory and procedures rather than manual skills. Their job satisfaction is often high because of the responsibility they feel for the safety of the process, the lack of human pressures to increase production and the special training they have received. On the other hand, the need to do shift work to keep the process continuously operating may cause some job dissatisfaction.

(e) *White collar workers*, who traditionally are expected by employers to share management attitudes rather than associate themselves with manual workers. They enjoy greater fringe benefits, shorter hours and less discipline than manual workers, and are on progressive salaries. They are usually treated by managers as individuals rather than as categories; differences in salaries usually reflect this. Their job satisfaction can be quite high when they are able to control their own work and see its results, but low when they do routine and apparently meaningless clerical operations. Their experience is often valuable to one employer only, and is difficult to transfer.

9. Total influences on employee behaviour. It has been shown that an employee's attitudes and behaviour are influenced not only by his own personal qualities but by the technology in which he works and the constraints and opportunities of his occupation. In addition the working group, the style of leadership and the extent of participation can be important.

These influences are not, of course, in one direction; the employee chooses a certain occupation because he thinks it suits his circumstances and personal qualities, he may enter a certain industry because he likes the conditions he knows he will find there, and he may not welcome any form of participative management, avoiding any companies where it is practised. Furthermore, the nature of his work will also affect his leisure, and the way he wishes to spend his leisure may well govern his choice of occupation. Social class, which sometimes opens occupational doors and sometimes closes them, is another important factor, though class in its turn is partly dependent on occupation.

Many interdependent factors, forming a very complex system, influence the behaviour of people at work. It is the task of personnel management to formulate and administer policies, methods and institutions which take account of these factors.

PROGRESS TEST 10

1. Describe an investigation into the effects of the work environment on employee behaviour. (2–4)

2. Summarise the results of Joan Woodward's research in Essex. (5, 6)

3. What is meant by the "instrumental approach" to work? (7)

4. Give two examples of the way in which a person's occupation can affect his leisure time. (8)

PART TWO

PERSONNEL MANAGEMENT

CHAPTER XI

What is Personnel Management?

1. Definition. The Institute of Personnel Management has published the following definition.

Personnel management is that part of management concerned with people at work and with their relationships within an enterprise. Its aim is to bring together and develop into an effective organisation the men and women who make up an enterprise and, having regard for the well-being of the individual and of working groups, to enable them to make their best contribution to its success.

In particular, personnel management is concerned with the development and application of policies governing:

Manpower planning, recruitment, selection, placement and termination;

Education and training; career development;

Terms of employment, methods and standards of remuneration;

Working conditions and employee services;

Formal and informal communication and consultation both through the representatives of employers and employees and at all levels throughout the enterprise;

Negotiation and application of agreements on wages and working conditions; procedures for the avoidance and settlement of disputes.

Personnel management is also concerned with the human and social implications of change in internal organisation and methods of working, and of economic and social changes in the community.

2. The application of industrial psychology. Another way of defining personnel management is to regard it as a range of policies, institutions and procedures which enable the principles of industrial psychology to be put into practice. Its purpose is not only to make effective use of people at work and develop satisfactory relationships among them but to motivate them both by providing them with jobs which are satisfying in themselves (if this is practically possible) and by offering them financial and other rewards.

To emphasise the psychological basis of personnel management, it may be re-defined as that part of management which deals with people at work as regards:

(a) *utilisation*—recruitment, selection, transfer, promotion, separation, appraisal, training and development;

(b) *motivation*—job design, remuneration, fringe benefits, consultation, participation, negotiation and justice;

(c) *protection*—working conditions, welfare services, safety, implementing appropriate legislation.

These three divisions are not separate and self-contained. For example, an employee who has been well selected and trained for his job will be more motivated in it than someone who has been carelessly selected and untrained. The use of consultation and participation, besides motivating employees, will often show how they can be better utilised. A well-designed and safe working environment will enable better use to be made of people's abilities and will in most cases help to provide satisfaction of human needs.

3. Employees as a resource. In recent years the term management of human resources has begun to be used instead of personnel management, emphasising the fact that the people employed in a company are resources which are at least as important as financial or material resources and must be given careful and expert attention.

Employees will not submit passively to manipulation or dictatorial control by management but more and more expect and demand some influence in the way they are employed. Research in the behavioural sciences shows that an appropriate response by management will benefit the company (*see* II, VIII, **8**, VIII, **17–18** and IX, **12**). Personnel management techniques in, for example, appraisal, training and job evaluation can only be successfully applied with the consent and support of the employees.

4. Differences in personnel management. In the same way as behaviour at work is influenced by technology and organisation (*see* X), the practice of personnel management varies in different types of company.

In a large progressive company the full range of personnel procedures is found, the personnel department is active and influential, and quite often there are well-established arrangements by which employees can participate in decisions, or at least be consulted about them.

In a smaller company a specialist personnel department may not exist, and personnel management functions may be carried out by the various managers as part of their normal duties. The emphasis here may be on recruitment, selection, wage structures, compliance with employment law and perhaps industrial relations; other matters such as training, appraisal, job evaluation and participation are probably dealt with in an unplanned, informal and almost intuitive way. Organised and thoroughly documented personnel procedures are instinctively felt to be inappropriate in a small company.

Publicly-owned organisations are usually large and accountable to electors or a government department on behalf of the electors. They develop detailed procedures in all aspects of their work, and particularly so in matters concerning their employees. The personnel department is traditionally almost entirely administrative, seeing that agreed procedures are observed, controlling numbers and grades of staff and emphasising welfare, since employees are expected to make a life-long career with the organisation. However, some bodies which have a commercial role, for example electricity and gas boards, show a more creative approach to personnel management, particularly in training and management development, and their example is gradually being followed elsewhere in the public sector.

This book will describe "middle of the road" personnel management; it must be realised, however, that there are wide variations among employers in the way it is practised.

5. Outline of the following chapters. In order that personnel management may be seen as a whole, an outline will now be given of the following chapters, under the three main headings of utilisation, motivation and protection.

(*a*) *Utilisation* begins with a description of manpower planning, followed by the analysis and description of jobs. The next group of topics together form what is sometimes called the employment process, which in many large personnel departments is the responsibility of a specialist officer. It comprises recruitment, selection, transfer, promotion, demotion and separation, together with the relevant legislation. Appraisal, training and development, which together are sometimes called the development process, complete the subject of utilisation.

(b) *Motivation* is implicit in many of the topics dealt with under utilisation, because to make the best use of an employee a manager must try to motivate him. Job satisfaction is also increased by being employed in suitable work. The areas of personnel management which are particularly concerned with motivation are job evaluation, methods of payment, fringe benefits, participation and justice.

(c) *Protection* includes the study of working conditions, e.g. hours of work, overtime and shift working, and safety, together with the relevant statutory and common law provisions.

PROGRESS TEST 11

1. Define personnel management. (**1, 2**)
2. What is the meaning of the term human resources management? (**3**)
3. Is personnel management carried out in the same way among all types of employer? (**4**)

CHAPTER XII

Manpower Planning

1. Definition. Manpower planning, which has received considerable attention in recent years, may be defined as an attempt to forecast how many and what kind of employees will be required in the future, and to what extent this demand is likely to be met.

2. Purpose. Manpower planning can help management in making decisions in the following areas:

(a) recruitment;
(b) avoidance of redundancies;
(c) training—numbers and categories;
(d) management development;
(e) estimates of labour costs;
(f) productivity bargaining;
(g) accommodation requirements.

Company manpower planning needs continuous readjustment because the goals of an organisation are unstable and its environment uncertain. It is also complex because it involves so many independent variables—invention, population changes, resistance to change, consumer demand, government intervention, foreign competition and above all domestic competition. It must include feedback because if the plan cannot be fulfilled the objectives of the company may have to be modified so that they are feasible in manpower terms.

3. The importance of company objectives. Figure 5 shows that the essential first step in company manpower planning is a statement of company objectives which covers products, methods, markets, etc. From this is derived the demand for labour, which is then related to the supply of labour to produce the manpower plan.

The implications of the manpower plan must then be considered by the top management of the company in case company objectives need amendment—for example, it may not be possible to increase production by the planned amount because labour of the kind required is either impossible to train in the time available, or does not exist in the quantity needed.

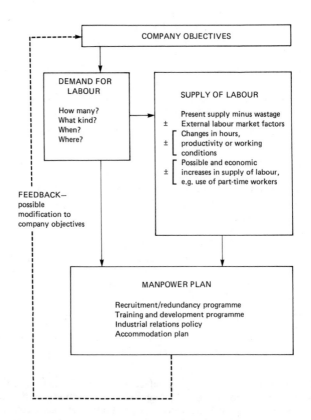

FIG. 5   *The manpower planning process.*

4. Steps in long-term company manpower planning. A long-term company manpower plan is usually regarded as one which attempts to forecast for about five years ahead.

As shown in Fig. 5 the company must consider the demand for labour, its potential supply (with corrections for its present misuse, over-use or under-use) and the external environment. By studying the interaction of all these factors it can then produce a plan showing how many and what kind of employees are expected to be required in the future. The main points to be considered are as follows.

(*a*) *The creation of a company manpower planning group*, including the managers in charge of the main functions within the company.

(*b*) *The statement of manpower objectives* in the light of company objectives by considering:

    (*i*) capital equipment plans;

    (*ii*) reorganisation, e.g. centralisation or de-centralisation;

    (*iii*) changes in products or in output;

    (*iv*) marketing plans;

    (*v*) financial limitations.

(*c*) *The present utilisation of manpower*, in particular:

    (*i*) numbers of employees in various categories;

    (*ii*) statistics of labour turnover and absence;

    (*iii*) amount of overtime worked;

    (*iv*) amount of short time;

    (*v*) appraisal of performance and potential of present employees;

    (*vi*) general level of payment compared with that in other firms.

Note that for all the above, accurate and complete personnel records are essential.

(*d*) *The external environment of the company:*

    (*i*) recruitment position;

    (*ii*) population trends;

    (*iii*) local housing and transport plans;

    (*iv*) national agreements dealing with conditions of work;

    (*v*) government policies in education, retirement, regional subsidies, etc.

(*e*) *The potential supply of labour*, in particular:

    (*i*) effects of local emigration and immigration;

    (*ii*) effects of recruitment or redundancy by local firms;

    (*iii*) possibility of employing categories not now employed, e.g. part-time workers;

    (*iv*) changes in productivity or working practices.

5. The final company manpower plan. After considering and co-ordinating these factors a manpower plan may then be made, showing in detail, by function, occupation and location, how many employees it is *practicable* to employ at various stages in the future. The following should appear in it:

    (*a*) jobs which will appear, disappear, or change;

    (*b*) to what extent re-deployment or re-training is possible;

    (*c*) necessary changes at supervisory and management levels;

    (*d*) training needs;

    (*e*) recruitment, redundancy or retirement programme;

    (*f*) industrial relations implications;

    (*g*) arrangements for feedback in case modifications in manpower plan or company objectives are necessary.

When agreed, the plan must be communicated to all levels of employees, but particularly to managers and unions or employee representatives; it is often necessary and advisable to negotiate with the trade unions on the detailed implementation of the plan.

6. Short-term company manpower planning. This type of plan, which usually covers a period up to one year ahead, is much more common than a long-term plan. Many firms do not have the quality of management to forecast long-term objectives, or they feel that the nature of their business makes it impossible to look ahead for more than one year.

A short-term manpower plan is comparatively easy because a firm will usually make a production or marketing plan for a year ahead involving budgets, orders for new materials and components, and sales quotas. From this can be derived the amount of *direct labour* in terms of man-hours required in future, and then, by dividing into this figure the number of available working hours, the number of men can be obtained. Overtime and the average level of sickness absence and machine breakdowns must be taken into account when available working hours are calculated.

The amount of *indirect labour* may be estimated partly by fixed commitments and partly as a rule of thumb percentage of indirect to direct labour. From the total labour requirements a recruitment or redundancy plan can be derived, but the period is usually too short for any worthwhile training plan to be made.

An advantage of the short-term plan is the ease with which the forecast can be compared with the manpower that was actually required, and any discrepancies analysed.

7. Limiting factors. In practice, manpower planning can be diffi-cult and often inaccurate. The chief reasons are as follows.

(*a*) The type of industry: some depend on new product develop-ment in an extremely competitive environment; others may depend on political decisions which are impossible to forecast; while others work on a tendering basis, so that plans can only be short-term because it is never known whether a tender will be accepted.

(*b*) Opposition or scepticism among members of management; all must be convinced of the value of manpower planning if it is to be a success.

(*c*) Resistance to the changes expressed in the plan. The fore-casts of labour structure, with their effects on skills and status, may be regarded as a threat.

(*d*) The difficulty of making accurate forecasts of social and economic changes.

(*e*) The need to have very complete and accurate employee records, maintained for at least the last five years.

(*f*) The plan may indicate recruitment and training pro-grammes which although desirable may be impossible to put into practice because the money to pay for them may not be available now. Because of its financial position the company may find long-term plans useless.

In general, the longer the period over which the plan is made, the greater the effect of these limiting factors. Nevertheless long-term manpower planning is a growing practice, particularly in large companies which have to plan their expenditure on capital equip-ment several years ahead in any case. The difficulties of recruiting, selecting and training human resources on the one hand, or of making them redundant on the other, are so great that manpower planning is amply justified, even though its results may be some-what inaccurate.

PROGRESS TEST 12

1. Define manpower planning. What is its purpose? (**1, 2**)

2. What are the main points to be considered in formulating a long-term manpower plan? (**4**)

3. What is a short-term manpower plan, and what are its ad-vantages? (**6**)

4. What factors reduce the accuracy or the benefits of man-power planning? (**7**)

CHAPTER XIII

Job Analysis and Job Specifications

JOB ANALYSIS

1. Purpose of job analysis. In personnel management it is very often necessary to obtain and record a description of a job (*see* **5**). The description must then be kept up to date to take account of changes in organisation or technology. Job analysis is the process by which a description of a job is compiled.

2. Methods and difficulties. There are many difficulties in job analysis, some practical, some concerned with the attitudes of employees. The following are the most important methods which may be used.

(*a*) *Direct observation*—this is always necessary but has several drawbacks.

(*i*) A skilled worker can make his job look easy.

(*ii*) An experienced worker can make his job look difficult.

(*iii*) Mental processes are not revealed.

(*iv*) Some manual work is too fast or intricate to be observed accurately, unless film or video is used.

(*b*) *Interview with the job-holder*—this is nearly always necessary but difficulties often occur, largely because the worker may be suspicious of the job analysis. He may decide to exaggerate the importance of the job or occasionally try to make it seem unimportant. The main problems with these interviews are as follows.

(*i*) The worker's attitude may influence his account of the job.

(*ii*) He may, even if co-operative, forget some details of the job, and emphasise the most recent events.

(*iii*) He may not be able to express himself clearly.

(*c*) *Interview with the supervisor*—this again is an inevitable occurrence, though its value varies for the following reasons.

(*i*) Supervisors are surprisingly often out of touch with the details of the job.

(*ii*) They frequently have never done the job themselves.

(*iii*) They sometimes allow their description of the job to be influenced by their opinion of the job-holder.

(*iv*) They may exaggerate the duties and responsibilities of the job in order to increase their own importance.

(*d*) *Materials of work*—a study of the tools, working materials, machines, documents, communication media, etc., frequently provides a useful check on information obtained in other ways, and may suggest questions to be asked.

(*e*) *Previous studies*, e.g. work study records, training manuals and accident reports, are sometimes available and can be brought up to date or added to other information.

(*f*) *Do-it-yourself*—in some jobs it is feasible for the analyst to spend some time actually performing the work himself. He should then be careful not to form too subjective an impression, e.g. if he himself is not good at figures he may tend to over-estimate the difficulty of an accounting job.

(*g*) *Questionnaires* are sometimes used, but are highly unreliable. The job-holder is asked to fill in answers to written questions about his job, but he may be suspicious of the questionnaire (*see* (*b*) above), may not understand the questions, and feel unduly restricted by them.

(*h*) *Work diaries* are sometimes used, chiefly for managers and clerical workers. The job-holder records his activities in detail throughout the day over a period of about a month. The diary is then analysed to obtain a list of duties and their frequency. If kept conscientiously and accurately, a work diary can be very helpful, but often the job-holder forgets to complete it until the end of the afternoon when his recollection of the day's work is not reliable.

In order to analyse a job with some degree of accuracy it is obviously necessary to use a combination of several of the above methods, each checking the other.

JOB SPECIFICATIONS

3. Definitions. The Department of Employment has published a glossary of training terms from which the following definitions have been taken.

(*a*) Job description—a broad statement of the purpose, scope, duties and responsibilities of a particular job.

(*b*) Job specification—a detailed statement of the physical and mental activities involved in the job and, when relevant, of social and physical environmental matters. The specification is usually expressed in terms of behaviour—i.e. what the worker does, what knowledge he uses in doing it, the judgments he makes and the factors he takes into account when making them.

4. Use of job descriptions. For general discussions of jobs, a broad description is all that is necessary. For example, when examining the staffing of a department for manpower planning purposes a detailed statement of activities is not required.

A job description can be written under these headings:

(*a*) title of job;
(*b*) scope of job (in broad terms);
(*c*) reporting to . . .;
(*d*) responsible for . . ..

5. Use of job specifications. For several personnel functions a detailed account of the job is necessary. The most important of these are:

(*a*) selection;
(*b*) promotion;
(*c*) appraisal;
(*d*) setting performance standards;
(*e*) job evaluation;
(*f*) training.

The job specification is therefore of fundamental importance in personnel management, though it should be used with discretion. When relations are poor between manager and subordinates, the latter may use their job specifications (if they have been issued) as self-defensive weapons, refusing tasks or responsibilities because they do not appear in the specifications.

There are few companies where job specifications can genuinely remain unchanged for any length of time, since they are partly the result of organisational needs (which frequently change) and partly the result of the way in which successive employees have carried out the job. Many companies therefore prefer to keep job specifications confidential, giving employees copies of their job descriptions only.

6. Drawing up a job specification. There is no standard layout or set of headings for a job specification; it is found that variations are necessary according to the type of work, e.g. manual or non-manual, and to the organisation.

The statement in the definition (*see* **3**) that a job specification should emphasise activities and behaviour is most important. A specification written in terms of responsibilities, for example, can be very misleading. To say that someone is responsible for obtaining and collating information from the company's branches may sound very important but in fact that person may simply receive straightforward sales statistics on standard forms and copy them on to an analysis sheet.

Whenever possible the job specification should show *what* the person does, and by *what means*. It is also desirable to indicate approximately what proportion of working time is spent on each activity, or group of activities, and how frequently any occasional duties occur.

The job specification should begin with the job description (*see* **4**) and then continue with a more detailed account of the job, perhaps using these headings:

    (*a*) major responsibilities and results expected;
    (*b*) routine duties under the headings in (*a*);
    (*c*) non-routine or infrequent duties under the same headings;
    (*d*) working conditions;
    (*e*) equipment and materials used;
    (*f*) personal contacts.

For appraisal and training purposes, performance standards should also be included; these are dealt with below. An example of a job specification for a manual job appears in Appendix I.

PERFORMANCE STANDARDS

7. Purpose. It is sometimes necessary to specify the quantity or quality of work which should be attained by the holder of a certain job. As stated above, the most frequent use of performance standards is found in appraisal and training; to assess an employee either in his normal work or after training it is essential to have a criterion against which to compare his actual performance. Performance standards are also used in some wage systems (*see* XXII, 3).

8. Setting standards. Performance standards are most easy to set when some kind of physical activity takes place. They can state how many articles should be produced, how many documents completed or how many selling calls made in a day. When the task becomes varied, e.g. when articles of several different types are made during a working day or the calls are scattered over a large area, standards expressed in such simple terms become misleading. A performance standard should also contain some reference to the quality of work.

In many cases, therefore, they are less easy to set than may appear at first sight; the standard of output may have to refer to a period considerably longer than one day in order to include a typical range of tasks, or subjective judgments introduced, e.g. "performs work satisfactorily". To reduce these difficulties it may sometimes be possible to select from the range of tasks the employee performs a very small number which must be done satisfactorily if the complete job is to be accomplished well. Careful analysis of the job may reveal these key points or critical incidents for which it may be possible to set performance standards expressed in measurable behaviour.

9. Standards for managers and supervisors. It is a very difficult problem to set performance standards for managers and supervisors because their work is extremely varied and emphasises mental rather than physical activity.

In some cases there may be obvious targets, e.g. a sales manager may be expected to maintain sales at a certain minimum level, or a foreman to keep waiting time in his section below a certain level. Criteria such as these which are similar to the key points or critical incidents mentioned in **8**, are particularly valuable when they can be measured objectively and are within the control of the person concerned. A target for a foreman to "maintain satisfactory industrial relations within the section" would be valueless, first because of the subjective interpretation of the word satisfactory and secondly because the quality of industrial relations would depend on many factors outside the foreman's control.

It is often claimed that careful analysis aided by ingenuity will show that any job contains elements for which performance standards can be expressed in terms of measurable behaviour, and some approaches to appraisal (*see* XVIII, **10**) and training (*see* XIX, **3**) are based on this assumption.

PERSONNEL SPECIFICATIONS

10. Definition. According to the Department of Employment's glossary of training terms a personnel specification (sometimes called a man specification) is an interpretation of the job specification in terms of the kind of person suitable for the job.

11. Purpose. A personnel specification is used above all in recruitment, selection and promotion as part of the process of utilisation, i.e. finding the most suitable person to fill a job. It contains a series of desired attributes against which candidates for a job are judged; in some cases it may be possible to set an achievement or aptitude test (*see* IV, **16–17**) to obtain a more exact measure of their suitability.

12. Method. For convenience, and to ensure that no important points are overlooked, it is common practice to use a standard set of headings in a personnel specification. These headings often correspond with those used in recording the interview (*see* V, **7**), e.g. the seven-point plan or the five-fold grading, so that the candidate can be matched more easily against the requirements of the job.

The personnel specification must always be based on the job specification; every statement in it must be justified by evidence obtained from the analysis of the job. Phrases like "possessing outstanding initiative", which are sometimes found in personnel specifications, are not only vague but often have no relation to the actual demands of the job. The specification is intended to describe the person who is capable of doing the job adequately, not an impossible ideal.

13. Adapting the job to the employee. It is unrealistic and somewhat inhuman to suppose that a candidate will be found who fits the personnel specification exactly or can be precisely moulded into it by training. Quite often the job is changed after it has been analysed, sometimes deliberately, sometimes gradually and unconsciously by the job-holder to suit his abilities, personality and experience. In any case job analysis can never produce a completely reliable result (*see* **2**) and job and personnel specifications based on it must always be interpreted flexibly.

PROGRESS TEST 13

1. Describe, with comments, the chief methods of analysing a job. (**2**)
2. What is the difference between a job description, a job specification and a personnel specification? (**4, 5, 10**)
3. For what purposes is a job specification used? (**5**)
4. Define performance standards. (**8**)
5. For what purposes is a personnel specification used? (**11**)

CHAPTER XIV

Recruitment and Selection

RECRUITMENT

1. Definitions. It is useful to make a distinction between recruitment and selection.

(*a*) *Recruitment* is the first part of the process of filling a vacancy; it includes the examination of the vacancy, the consideration of sources of suitable candidates, making contact with those candidates and attracting applications from them.

(*b*) *Selection* is the next stage, i.e. assessing the candidates by various means, and making a choice followed by an offer of employment.

2. Examining the vacancy. If the vacancy is additional to the present workforce, i.e. it has occurred because of some new or increased activity, then in all probability the need for the new employee has been established and a job specification compiled. The majority of vacancies, however, occur as replacements for people who have left the company or as the final event in a chain of transfers and promotions following on a reorganisation. In these cases consideration may be given to the following points.

(*a*) It may be possible to fill the vacancy from within the company.

(*b*) It may be filled by a different kind of employee, e.g. a school-leaver or a part-timer.

(*c*) The job and personnel specifications may need to be revised.

3. Internal sources. The advantages of filling the vacancy internally rather than externally are:

(*a*) better motivation of employees because their capabilities are considered and opportunities offered for promotion;

(*b*) better utilisation of employees, because the company can often make better use of their abilities in a different job;

(*c*) it is more reliable than external recruitment because a present employee is known more thoroughly than an external candidate;

(*d*) a present employee is more likely to stay with the company than an external candidate;

(*e*) internal recruitment is quicker and cheaper than external.

4. External sources. Very many vacancies are filled from external sources; even when an internal candidate is transferred or promoted the final result is usually a vacancy elsewhere in the company which has to be filled from outside. External recruitment can be time-consuming, expensive and uncertain, though it is possible to reduce these disadvantages to some extent by forethought and planning.

External sources may be divided into two classes; those which are comparatively inexpensive but offer a limited choice, i.e. (*a*) to (*f*) below, and those which are comparatively expensive but give the employer access to a wider range of candidates, i.e. (*g*) and (*h*) below.

(*a*) Recommendations by present employees.
(*b*) Unsolicited.
(*c*) Direct links with universities, colleges and schools.
(*d*) Trade unions.
(*e*) Jobcentre or Careers Office.
(*f*) Professional bodies' appointments service.
(*g*) Private agencies.
(*h*) Advertising.

5. Recommendations by present employees. This is sometimes encouraged by rewards to employees who introduce successful candidates. It gives a limited field of choice, but it costs very little and, as a rule, the candidates are of good quality.

6. Unsolicited. Applications are sometimes received from candidates who either call personally at the place of work or write letters of enquiry. This is another inexpensive source which provides a limited choice, but the candidates are of variable quality.

7. Direct links with educational establishments. Many employers maintain connections with universities, colleges and schools. Candidates are usually available from these sources only at one time of the year, but this difficulty can often be overcome if companies begin their internal training courses in the autumn, or fill junior vacancies with temporary staff until school-leavers are available.

8. Trade unions. Some companies recruit certain kinds of employees through the appropriate trade unions. The choice is limited, but there is some certainty that the candidate has the skill or knowledge the job requires.

9. Government agencies. The Careers Service and the various services of the Department of Employment provide a means of recruitment which is either free of charge or costs very little. The choice offered by these services is limited, however, because many types of employee prefer to seek jobs by other methods and do not register with the appropriate government agency.

10. Professional bodies. Many professional bodies have an employment service with which their members can register, supplying details of their experience and the kind of job they are looking for. An employer who uses this service can be sure that all the candidates submitted to him are professionally qualified, and if the vacancy he wishes to fill requires a certain qualification the limited choice offered is not a disadvantage.

Instead of running an employment service, which needs careful administration, some bodies prefer to encourage employers to advertise in their journal.

11. Private agencies. Organisations which are run as commercial enterprises for supplying employers with candidates for jobs are of two main types.

(*a*) *Office staff employment agencies*, which mainly deal with clerical, typing and office machine operator vacancies. The employer informs the agency of the vacancy he wishes to fill, and the agency submits any suitable candidates on its register. When a candidate is engaged the employer pays a fee to the agency, part of which is usually refunded if the employee leaves within a specified time. There is no charge to the candidate, who of course is at liberty to register with several agencies if he or she likes. Unless the agency takes care to submit only reasonable candidates for the vacancy its services can be expensive because of the time taken up in interviewing, testing and processing applications.

(*b*) *Senior selection agencies*, which usually undertake the complete recruitment process and the first stages of selection for managerial and professional vacancies. The agency analyses the job, prepares job and personnel specifications, advertises, sends out application forms and interviews selected candidates, sometimes testing them also. The employer is then presented with a short list of candidates, the career and qualifications of each being described, so that he may make the final choice. This method of recruitment is expensive because it is usual for the employer to pay a substantial fee whether or not a suitable candidate is found. It has two disadvantages.

(*i*) In many cases it is impossible for an outside body to understand in a short time what kind of a person will fit in with the present management of the company.

(*ii*) It is very difficult for the agency to follow up and validate its recommendation (*see* **22**).

12. Advertising. The most popular method of recruitment is to advertise the vacancy and invite candidates to apply to the company. It has been estimated that about 10 per cent of all advertising expenditure is devoted to situations vacant advertising; there is no doubt that much of this huge sum is wasted, chiefly because so little research has been carried out compared with research in the field of product advertising.

Many employers have been able to reduce their job advertising costs with no adverse effect on the quality or quantity of candidate response by experimenting with styles of advertisements, media and wording, and keeping careful records of the number of replies received to each advertisement and the candidate who was eventually selected. The only reliable guidance about advertising comes from the person who receives and analyses the replies, i.e. the employer himself; newspapers and advertising agencies, which often claim to advise on the style and size of advertisements, are not usually in a position to know and evaluate the response.

Job advertisements should aim at procuring a small number of well-qualified candidates quickly and cheaply. An advertisement which produces hundreds of replies is bad; the employer will then be faced with the lengthy and expensive task of sorting out a few candidates for interview. The advertisement can become the first stage in selection by describing the job and the qualifications required so comprehensively that borderline candidates will be deterred from applying and good candidates encouraged.

The small amount of research that has been done in this field shows that information about the job contributes much more to the effectiveness of an advertisement than its style or size. There is also general agreement that including the word training in an advertisement increases the response.

Advertising may be made more effective and less expensive if the following principles are observed.

(a) The advertisement should contain a job specification and a personnel specification in miniature, including the following:

(i) job title;

(ii) description of job and employer (including location);

(iii) experience, skills and qualifications required;

(iv) age range;

(v) working conditions, e.g. wage or salary, fringe benefits;

(vi) training given (if relevant);

(vii) what action the candidate should take, e.g. write a letter, telephone for an application form, etc.

(b) It should appear in the appropriate publication, e.g. local press for manual and routine clerical jobs, national press for senior jobs, professional journals for specialists.

(c) Experiments should be made to test the response for different sizes, headings, wording, page position, day of the week, etc.

(d) Careful records should be kept showing:

(i) which publication was used;

(ii) which date and day of the week;

(iii) which position on the page;

(iv) which style and size, e.g. display, semi-display, run-on;

(v) names of the candidates replying to each advertisement;

(vi) names of the candidates who are selected for interview;

(vii) name of the candidate who is successful.

(e) The response should be analysed so that advertising expenditure can be directed towards the publication and the style of advertisement which give the best result for a particular type of vacancy.

(f) Rejected candidates should be sent a prompt and courteous letter; inconsiderate treatment will eventually detract from a company's reputation and adversely affect the response to future advertisements.

Sometimes other considerations besides cost and response must be kept in mind. For example, suppose that evidence has been collected which shows that small advertisements are just as effective as large, providing the information given is the same (a not uncommon finding). The company may decide that small advertisements are not consistent with its prestige and that large advertisements must be used even though they can be shown to be wasteful. In this case part of the cost of the advertisement should logically be paid out of the company's general advertising account as it is concerned as much with public relations as with recruitment.

On the other hand, the prestige of the company can sometimes be made use of; a recruitment campaign is very often more successful if it follows a national advertising campaign for a new product which has brought the company into the public eye.

13. Box numbers. Occasionally a company decides to use a box number in a job advertisement instead of its own name and address. The reasons for this decision are usually:

(*a*) the company is beginning a new venture which at present it wishes to keep secret; *or*

(*b*) the present holder of the job is to be transferred or dismissed and has not yet been told; *or*

(*c*) the company wishes to state a salary in the advertisement but its salary policy is secret (*see* XXII, **12–13**).

Only the first of these three reasons is entirely creditable. The response to box number advertisements is usually poor in quality and quantity partly because of the mystery incorporated in them and partly because they inevitably contain less information than a normal advertisement which specifies the company's name, address and business.

Some large companies who wish to preserve their anonymity ask a senior selection agency to advertise on their behalf; the prestige of the agency may to some extent counterbalance the disadvantages of the use of a box number.

SELECTION

14. The application form. Whatever method of recruitment is used, the candidate should be asked to fill in an application form, firstly to ensure that no important details are omitted and secondly to provide information about the candidate in a logical and uniform order.

The layout of application forms varies, but most of them contain the following headings, usually in this order:

(*a*) job applied for;

(*b*) name, address, telephone number;

(*c*) date and place of birth, marital status, nationality;

(*d*) education;

(*e*) training and qualifications;

(*f*) medical history, e.g. any serious illnesses, whether disabled;

(*g*) employment history (names of previous employers, description of jobs held, dates of employment, reasons for leaving);

(*h*) any other information the candidate wishes to provide;

(*i*) a signature under the words "This information is correct to the best of my knowledge";

(*j*) date.

The application form is not only the basis of selection, but is the fundamental document in an employee's personnel record (*see* XXIV, **2**) and has legal importance in the contract of employment (*see* XVI, **1**).

15. Selection method. The manager's next step is to compare the application form with the personnel specification, looking for attributes which show the candidate to be apparently suitable for the job and shortcomings which may either rule out the candidate from consideration or necessitate special training if he were engaged. From this comparison he can make a list of candidates for interview and a list of those to be rejected. The latter should be written to at once regretting their lack of success (*see* **12**, (*f*)).

He will have decided what type of interview should be given—individual, successive, or panel (*see* V, **10–12**), and what tests should be used, e.g. an intelligence test (*see* IV, **8**), an aptitude test (*see* IV, **16**) or an achievement test (*see* IV, **17**). He may also decide to use leaderless group discussion if the vacancy is appropriate (*see* IV, **14**). The interview, which is the main and indispensable part of the selection process, is described in V, **3–9**. Notes are made, and filed for a reasonable period, of each candidate's performance in the interview and tests in case an unsuccessful candidate questions the decision, e.g. under the Race Relations Act (*see* Appendix V).

16. Offer of the job. Assuming that a suitable candidate has emerged from the selection process, he must now receive an offer. It is usual for him to be made an oral offer, and if he accepts it (perhaps after an interval for consideration) he is given a written offer. The initial offer of a job needs special care, particularly as regards the following points.

(*a*) The wage or salary offered must not only be appropriate to the job and attractive to the candidate but consistent with the earnings of present employees.

(*b*) The job must be named and any special conditions stated, e.g. "for the first six months you would be under training at our Birmingham branch".

(*c*) The candidate must know the essential conditions of employment, e.g. hours, holidays, bonuses and fringe benefits.

(*d*) Any provisos must be clearly stated, e.g. "subject to satisfactory references and medical examination".

(*e*) The next stage must be clearly defined; if the candidate asks for time for consideration, it must be agreed when he will get in touch. If the candidate accepts the oral offer, the manager must say what will happen next, and when.

17. References. A clear, unbiased and comprehensive description of a candidate's abilities and behaviour by his previous employer would be of enormous value in selection, particularly if the employer also supplied a job specification. Unfortunately this ideal is never realised, for several reasons.

(*a*) Most candidates are employed at the time of their application, and do not wish their employers to know they are looking elsewhere.

(*b*) Because of (*a*) a prospective employer would be breaking a confidence if he asked for a reference before an offer of a job had been made and accepted.

(*c*) By the time an offer has been accepted, selection is over and the reference is too late to affect it.

(*d*) An offer may be made "subject to satisfactory references", but as most references are received after the candidate has started work they can only be used to warn managers of possible faults in the candidate which in serious cases may eventually lead to warnings followed by dismissal.

(*e*) Employers giving references are usually extremely cautious; many references merely state the job title, the dates of employment, and the reason for leaving.

(*f*) References are occasionally biased, giving a good reference to hasten an employee's departure or a poor one because of a grudge.

Most references do not give rise to second thoughts about the selection of a candidate, but in a few cases information is given (usually by a telephone call) which shows the request for a reference to have been worth while.

18. Medical examinations. Preferably, every candidate should have a medical examination before the offer of a job is confirmed (*see* IV, **3**). It will show whether he is physically suitable for the job and what risk there is likely to be of sickness absence or injury—though some doctors maintain that a very thorough medical examination indeed is necessary to fulfil these requirements.

Many employers, perhaps the majority, dispense completely with medical examinations because of their cost, the delay they cause in allowing the candidate to start work, and the very large number of jobs in which physique is not important (*see* IV, **3**). Others require candidates to be interviewed by a nurse who will refer them to a doctor if she suspects that any serious disability is present.

Medical examinations should always be given:

(*a*) when the candidate is applying for a particularly arduous job, or when he will work alone, e.g. a security officer;

(*b*) when the job demands high standards of hygiene, e.g. catering and food manufacture;

(*c*) when the interview or other source reveals a doubtful medical history;

(*d*) to any employee whose health may be in danger because of his work—this decision is made by the Employment Medical Adviser, who has the statutory power (if the employee consents) to carry out the examination;

(*e*) to candidates who are known to be disabled, e.g. registered disabled persons (*see* **19**).

It is wise to include in the application form, above the space for the signature, a statement to the effect that the candidate agrees, if engaged, to be medically examined at any time.

19. Employment of disabled persons. Many employers believe they have a social duty to employ disabled people where possible, adapting production lines or telephone exchanges, for example, to allow this. There is also statutory backing for the employment of the disabled in the Disabled Persons (Employment) Acts 1944 and 1958, which provide for the following.

(*a*) A register of disabled persons, open to all who are substantially handicapped in getting or keeping suitable employment.

(*b*) A requirement that every employer with twenty or more workers should employ a number or quota of registered disabled persons equal to at least 3 per cent of the total numbers of workers.

(*c*) An employer may not dismiss a registered disabled person without reasonable cause if he is below his quota or if the dismissal would bring his numbers below it.

(*d*) The designation of two jobs, passenger lift attendant and car park attendant, which may only be filled by registered disabled persons.

The Acts have helped many disabled persons to find work, but in some areas employers find the quota difficult to fulfil, although they employ a reasonable number of disabled people. The reason for the difficulty is that although there is a legal requirement for employers to maintain a 3 per cent quota there is no legal requirement for disabled persons to register. Indeed, many disabled people maintain that being registered may be a drawback in their careers and that they prefer not to indicate that they regard themselves as in a separate category from other people. Employers who are not able to meet the quota of registered disabled persons must approach their local Jobcentre to explain their difficulties.

The "designated employments" in the Acts are another problem, because both the occupations (*see* (*d*)) can be quite arduous and require regular attendance. It is often difficult to find candidates who are registered as disabled but yet are fit enough to meet the physical requirements of these jobs.

20. The written offer of employment. Assuming that the oral offer has been accepted (*see* **16**) the employer must now confirm in writing. He will repeat in his letter the conditions he has already stated, taking great care that they are accurate because they will be on permanent record as the basis of the contract of employment. In many companies it is the rule that written offers may only be sent by the personnel manager or company secretary to ensure their accuracy.

The Employment Protection (Consolidation) Act 1978 requires that employees must be given a statement of their conditions of service within the first thirteen weeks of employment. Some employers combine the written offer of employment with the statutory statement which must contain:

(*a*) names of employer and employee;

(*b*) date when employment began;

(*c*) pay, or method of calculating pay;

(*d*) intervals at which payment is made, i.e. weekly, monthly, etc.;

(*e*) terms and conditions relating to:

(*i*) hours of work;

(*ii*) holiday pay, including the pay due on termination of employment;

(*iii*) sick pay;

(*iv*) pension scheme;

(*f*) the length of notice of termination the employee is obliged to give and entitled to receive;

(*g*) a note indicating the employee's right to join, or not to join a trade union, or the effect on him of a union membership agreement (*see* XXV, **21**);

(*h*) a description of the manner in which an employee can seek redress of any grievance relating to his employment;

(*i*) the title of the job;

(*j*) a note showing whether any period of employment with another employer counts as part of the period of employment for notice purposes (*see* XVI, **2**);

(*k*) reference to a document stating the disciplinary rules, and naming a person to whom the employee can apply (and by what method) if he is dissatisfied with a disciplinary decision.

It is not necessary for the written statement to cover all these points in detail; the employee may be directed to documents which are easily accessible to him for the full particulars. These documents could include, for example, pension scheme handbooks or copies of the works rules.

Employees must be informed in writing of any changes in conditions not more than one month after the change has been made.

21. Induction. The process of receiving the employee when he begins work, introducing him to the company and to his colleagues, and informing him of the activities, customs and traditions of the company is called induction. It may be regarded as the beginning of training or the final stage of the selection process. It has also been shown to have a close relationship with labour turnover (*see* XVII).

Induction may be divided into two stages.

(*a*) Introduction to the working group (*see* VII, **8**, (*e*)) is important psychologically and is best done by the employee's immediate supervisor, who should introduce him to his colleagues and show him round the department.

(*b*) Company background (in a large company), which may be described by lectures, films or visits. Probably this should not be done in the first day or week of employment because the employee is at that time more concerned with his immediate surroundings and his own job. He will become interested in the wider scene two or three months after he has joined the company and can then take part in a second-stage induction course at some central point in the firm, if the company is a large one, or his supervisor may talk to him informally if the company is small.

22. Follow up. All selection should be validated by follow-up. The employee himself is asked how he feels about his own progress and his immediate superior is asked for his comments, which are compared with the notes taken at the selection interview. If a follow-up is unfavourable it is probable that selection has been at fault; the whole process from job specification to interview is then reviewed to see if a better choice can be made next time.

An employee can be followed-up about three months after he has started if the job is fairly straightforward, and after a longer period if the job is more complex and responsible.

EFFICIENCY IN RECRUITMENT AND SELECTION

23. Costs. As in other management processes, careful control should be exercised over recruitment and selection to ensure that money is not being spent unnecessarily. The recording of advertisements and response (*see* 12) is one control that may be used. Others include the following.

(*a*) Can new sources of candidates be found which are less expensive?

(*b*) Could a less expensive selection procedure be used?

(*c*) Is the application form too complicated, containing unnecessary information, or is it too simple, omitting important information?

(*d*) Are internal candidates being considered sufficiently?

(*e*) Are selection standards too high or too low?

24. Efficiency ratios. A manager who recruits and selects on a large scale can check his efficiency by calculating some of the following ratios, which give a numerical measurement of the efficiency of his procedures.

(*a*) Average time during which a vacancy remains unfilled.

(*b*) $\dfrac{\text{Number of candidates replying to an advertisement}}{\text{Number of candidates called for interview}}$

(*c*) $\dfrac{\text{Number of interviews}}{\text{Number of offers made}}$

(d) $\dfrac{\text{Number of offers made}}{\text{Number accepted}}$

(e) $\dfrac{\text{Number starting work}}{\text{Number judged satisfactory in follow-up}}$

(f) $\dfrac{\text{Number starting work}}{\text{Number still employed after one year}}$

(g) $\dfrac{\text{Cost of recruitment and selection}}{\text{Number starting work}}$

(h) $\dfrac{\text{Number of vacancies}}{\text{Number filled internally}}$

(i) $\dfrac{\text{Total value of wages and salaries offered}}{\text{Cost of recruitment and selection for those vacancies}}$

A downward trend in any of these ratios, except (i), will show that an improvement is taking place in the efficiency of recruitment and selection.

PROGRESS TEST 14

1. What is the difference between recruitment and selection? (1)

2. What are the advantages of filling a vacancy internally? (3)

3. Describe, with comments, three inexpensive external sources of recruitment. (4–10)

4. How can the cost of recruitment advertising be reduced? (12)

5. Are there any circumstances in which an employer is justified in advertising over a box number? (13)

6. Outline the steps in selection which occur before the candidate is called for interview. (14, 15)

7. What should the initial offer of a job contain? (16)

8. To what extent are references useful in selection? (17)

9. State the circumstances in which candidates should be medically examined. (18)

10. Outline the law regarding the employment of disabled persons. (19)

11. What information must be given to an employee under the Employment Protection (Consolidation) Act 1978? (20)

12. What is induction? (21)

13. What is the purpose of follow-up in selection? (22)

CHAPTER XV

Promotion, Transfer, Demotion and Retirement

PROMOTION

1. Definition. A promotion is a move of an employee to a job within the company which has greater importance and, usually, higher pay. Frequently the job has higher status and carries improved fringe benefits and more privileges. Its purpose is to improve both the utilisation and motivation of employees.

2. Methods. There are two main ways in which a company may promote its employees.

(*a*) *By management decision*, in which an employee is selected for promotion on the basis of information already known to the management. This method is quick and inexpensive and obviously suitable for a small company or for jobs for which the field of possible candidates is small and well known. In large companies it may cause discontent because the decision is arrived at in secret, possible candidates not having the opportunity to state their qualifications for the post. In all cases, this method depends for its success on complete and up-to-date employee records which can be used to identify all possible candidates for any job.

(*b*) *By internal advertisement*; employees are told by notices or circulars that a post is vacant and they are then invited to apply. Some or all of the candidates are interviewed and one finally selected. It is a comparatively expensive and time-consuming method, but is particularly suitable to a large organisation in which management cannot be expected to have personal knowledge of possible candidates. It does not rely on accurate employee records, and, being open rather than secret, appears fairer to the candidates than the management decision method. In the public sector promotions are made almost entirely through internal advertisements.

3. Promotion and motivation. Normally, employees derive

satisfaction from a company policy of promotion from within, but badly handled promotions can cause dissatisfaction. The important points to note are:

(*a*) the criteria for promotion must be fair—usually a combination of ability, relevant experience and length of service;

(*b*) the method must be fair;

(*c*) selection for promotion must be based on appraisals by present and past managers (*see* XVIII);

(*d*) the wage or salary offered to the promoted employee must be what the job deserves rather than what the management thinks he will accept;

(*e*) unsuccessful candidates must be sympathetically treated;

(*f*) there must be no discrimination (*see* Appendix V).

TRANSFER

4. Definition. A transfer is a move to a job within the company which has approximately equal importance, status and pay.

5. Selection for transfer. To manage human resources in a constructive way it is sometimes necessary to transfer employees to other jobs, sometimes because of changed work requirements and sometimes because an employee is unhappy or dissatisfied in his present job.

In some companies it is the custom for the least satisfactory employees to be transferred from one department to another with the result that a transfer is regarded as discreditable, particularly if it occurs at short notice and without explanation. An unhappy employee may therefore prefer to leave the company rather than seek a transfer.

In other companies transfers are used as a means of developing promising employees by giving them experience in several departments. A few companies advertise all vacancies internally and consider applicants for whom the new job would be a transfer rather than a promotion.

6. Transfer policy. Transfers can increase job satisfaction and improve utilisation under the following circumstances.

(*a*) A transfer is regarded as a re-selection.

(*b*) The need for a transfer is explained.

(*c*) Unsatisfactory employees are not dealt with by transferring them to other departments.

(*d*) Requests by employees for transfers are fully investigated.

(*e*) No employee is transferred to another district against his will.

(*f*) An employee transferred to another district is given financial assistance from the company to cover removal costs, legal fees, re-furnishing, etc.

DEMOTION

7. Definition. A demotion is a move to a job within the company which is lower in importance. It is usually, though not always, accompanied by a reduction in pay.

8. Reasons for demotion. An employee may be demoted for these reasons.

(*a*) His job may disappear or become less important through a company reorganisation.

(*b*) He may no longer be thought capable of carrying out his present responsibilities efficiently.

9. Effects of demotion. Unless the employee has himself asked for it, demotion will probably have adverse effects.

(*a*) There will be less satisfaction of esteem and self-actualisation needs. The employee may show negative reactions to frustration (*see* II, **7–8**).

(*b*) He may become a centre of discontent in the company.

(*c*) Other employees may lose confidence in the company.

An employee who resigns because he has been demoted without his agreement may complain of unfair dismissal under a special category known as "constructive dismissal".

RETIREMENT

10. Age of retirement. State retirement pensions are at present paid at sixty-five for men and age sixty for women, providing retirement from work takes place. The retirement policies of employers are usually based on these ages, though in some kinds of public employment men may retire at age sixty. An employer's pension scheme (if one exists) is designed to conform with retirement policy, giving an entitlement to pension at the age when the employee is expected to retire.

There are two schools of thought about the age of retirement;

one maintains that the age is a minimum only and suitable and fit employees should be allowed to work on after this age. The other believes in a fixed retirement age.

11. Flexible retirement.

(a) *Advantages.*

(i) Many employees are fit and active well beyond the official retirement age. By working on, they benefit financially and the employer profits from their knowledge and experience.

(ii) The financial burden on the pension scheme may be relieved.

(b) *Disadvantages.*

(i) Eventually the employer must decide that an employee is no longer fit to work; the decision may not be accepted by the employee, who may make accusations of favouritism if others older than himself are still working.

(ii) Promotion may be held up if a senior employee does not retire, causing promising employees to leave the company.

(iii) The employee, not knowing when he will be asked to leave, cannot easily plan for retirement.

(iv) The company cannot plan its manpower when retirement ages are uncertain.

12. Fixed retirement. A company which adopts a fixed retirement age policy insists on all its employees retiring from their present jobs at a certain age, although sometimes they are offered re-employment in a junior capacity for a limited period.

(a) *Advantages.*

(i) Employees can plan for retirement more easily.

(ii) No invidious judgments about efficiency have to be made.

(iii) The company can plan its manpower more precisely.

(iv) Promotion is not held up.

(b) *Disadvantages.*

(i) The services of experienced and fit employees may be lost, though sometimes retired employees are used as consultants.

(ii) It is unfair to employees with a small company pension, e.g. those with short service.

PROGRESS TEST 15

1. Describe two methods which a company may use to promote its employees. **(2)**

2. What is the connection between promotion and motivation?   **(3)**

3. In what ways can transfers increase job satisfaction?   **(6)**

4. Summarise the relative merits of a flexible or fixed age of retirement policy.   **(11, 12)**

CHAPTER XVI

Resignation and Dismissal

THE CONTRACT OF EMPLOYMENT

1. Legal aspects. A contract of employment exists when, in return for a wage or salary, an employee undertakes to put himself at the disposal of an employer during the agreed hours of work. The employer has the legal right to supervise the employee's actions and decide the manner in which the work should be done, and the employee has the duty to put the employer's interests before his own. He also guarantees, by statements, written or spoken at the time he was engaged, that he is competent to do the work in question.

Under the Employment Protection (Consolidation) Act 1978, the employer must state certain of the terms of employment in writing (*see* **XIV, 20**); other terms may be either written, spoken or implied by customary practice in that particular occupation or industry.

2. Termination of the contract. The contract of employment may be terminated by either side, i.e. employer or employee, giving notice making clear the date on which the contract will end. If the contract does not expressly state what period of notice must be given, the period can be deduced by reference either to accepted custom in the occupation or to previous case law. In many instances it has been held that the interval at which wage or salary is paid should be the notice period, e.g. an employee who is paid monthly is entitled to one month's notice.

The many difficulties which occur when the period of notice has not been clearly stated are removed to a large extent by the Employment Protection (Consolidation) Act 1978. This Act lays down minimum periods of notice which apply after an employee has completed four weeks' continuous service with the employer. Until that time has elapsed the period of notice, if not expressly stated, depends on custom or case law. The Act states that after four weeks' continuous employment an employee must give his employer at least one week's notice. The employer must give the employee minimum notice which increases with length of service as follows:

After four weeks' service	one week
After two years' service	two weeks
After three years' service	three weeks

and so on, up to a maximum of:

After twelve years' service	twelve weeks

These are only minimum periods of notice, and if the contract clearly or by custom provides for longer periods then the latter will prevail. The Act does not affect the right of the employer to dismiss an employee without notice under certain circumstances (*see* 6) or for the employer and employee to terminate the contract without notice if they both agree to do so.

RESIGNATION

3. Definition. A resignation occurs when an employee gives his employer notice to terminate the contract of employment. The minimum period of notice may be whatever is customary, the period laid down in the Employment Protection (Consolidation) Act 1978, i.e. one week, or the period expressly stated in the contract. There is no legal requirement that a resigning employee should tell the employer why he is leaving. During the period of notice the employee remains, as before, under the control of the employer.

4. Treatment of resignations. Some resignations are disguised dismissals, the employee being allowed to resign as a face-saving measure. There is no objection to this if the employee has another job to go to, but if he has not he may find difficulty in obtaining unemployment benefit. He should be warned of this possibility before he agrees to resign.

When an employee resigns it is not only courteous but necessary for a manager to interview him to find out his reasons for leaving—the exit interview (*see* VII, **14**). Although many employees are not entirely frank about their reasons for leaving they may give information which throws light on employee attitudes and may thus lead to a reduction in labour turnover (*see* XVII).

DISMISSAL

5. Definition. An employee is dismissed when his employer terminates the contract of employment between them, whether or not the employee agrees.

6. Dismissal without notice. In most circumstances the employer must give the employee the notice due under the contract (*see* **2**), but in rare cases the conduct of the employee is such that the employer is legally entitled to dismiss the employee without notice. Examples of misconduct which justify instant dismissal are as follows.

(*a*) Refusal to obey a reasonable instruction, providing the refusal is serious enough to indicate that the employee is repudiating the contract; a refusal in a fit of temper would not justify instant dismissal unless it was maintained afterwards.

(*b*) Serious neglect of duties.

(*c*) Absence from work without permission or good cause.

(*d*) Activities in private life which might adversely affect the employer's business, e.g. running a business in competition with the employer or discreditable behaviour which might drive customers or clients away from the company.

(*e*) Dishonesty towards the employer.

(*f*) Violence towards the employer or other employees.

It will be seen from these examples that there is considerable room for argument about the degree of misconduct in any particular case and whether it is sufficient to justify dismissal without notice. Unless the employer is sure that the necessary degree of misconduct has occurred he often prefers to dismiss with notice, or with money in lieu of notice.

7. Dismissal with notice. An employer is not automatically required by law to give a reason for dismissal, although of course he normally would do so. He may, however, at the initiative of the employee be asked to state a reason in accordance with the provisions of the following statutes:

(*a*) Employment Protection (Consolidation) Act 1978;

(*b*) Sex Discrimination Act 1975 (*see* Appendix V);

(*c*) Race Relations Act 1976 (*see* Appendix V).

Because dismissal is such a serious matter, the employer must be careful to ensure not only that it is done for good reason but that the manner in which the employee is dismissed is fair. Capricious dismissals carried out in an unjust way adversely affect the motivation of employees, lower the reputation of the company, create an industrial relations problem and expose the employer to legal action (*see* **9**).

8. Model disciplinary procedure. The code of practice prepared by the Advisory, Conciliation and Arbitration Service contains a model disciplinary procedure which may be summarised as follows.

(*a*) A disciplinary procedure which is fair, full and quick should be agreed between management and employee representatives.

(*b*) Each employee should know what the procedure consists of, its rules and the offences which can lead to dismissal.

(*c*) The procedure should state who has power to dismiss, provide that senior management should be consulted, give the employee an opportunity to state his case and be accompanied by an employee representative, and provide for a right of appeal.

(*d*) Before dismissal takes place a previous warning should be given. In serious cases this warning should be in writing, and in cases of gross misconduct an employee may be dismissed without warning.

The code of practice is not legally binding but it may be taken into account in any proceedings before an industrial tribunal or the Employment Appeals Tribunal. The procedure it suggests is in any case good personnel management practice.

9. Unfair dismissal. Wrongful dismissal occurs when insufficient notice is given; unfair dismissal is defined under the Employment Protection (Consolidation) Act 1978 as dismissal which has occurred for reasons other than:

(*a*) the employee's capability, qualifications or conduct;

(*b*) redundancy (*see* **11**);

(*c*) a statutory requirement.

It is also unfair to dismiss an employee because he has joined an independent trade union or is active in its affairs, but it is sometimes fair to dismiss him if he refuses to join a union in a closed shop (*see* **XXV**, **21** and **23**). An employee who is not dismissed but resigns because he is forced to by his employer's conduct may complain of unfair dismissal.

Certain categories of employees are excluded from the unfair dismissal provisions, the most important being those with less than 52 weeks' service, those who work for less than 16 hours a week, those over normal retirement age and those (under the Employment Act 1980) who have had less than two years' service if they work for a firm whose employees do not exceed twenty.

An employee who considers he has been unfairly dismissed may, not later than three months afterwards, present a complaint to an industrial tribunal. The employer will then be required to state the reason for dismissal and justify it as being fair in accordance with the Act. An attempt is then made to settle the dispute by conciliation, but if this is unsuccessful the tribunal will hear the case, when the employer will try to show not only that the dismissal was fair but that it was reasonable in all the circumstances, for example that warnings had been given and that the employee had been given the opportunity to defend himself.

If the tribunal finds that the dismissal was unfair it will first, if the employee agrees, make an order for him to be reinstated, i.e. restore him in the job as though the dismissal had never happened, or re-engaged, i.e. return to his previous employer but in a different job. If the employee does not wish to return to his former employer, if reinstatement or re-engagement is judged by the tribunal to be impracticable or if the employer refuses to comply with an order for reinstatement or re-engagement, then monetary compensation must be paid by the employer. It consists of:

(a) a basic award calculated in the same way as redundancy pay (see 11); and

(b) a compensatory award assessed by the tribunal as being just in the circumstances, taking into account what the employee has suffered in hardship or in company benefits lost;

(c) a special additional award, usually of between 13 and 26 weeks' pay, which is given when the employer refuses to comply with an order for reinstatement or re-engagement.

Under the Employment Act 1980, if an employer claims that he was induced to dismiss an employee who was not a union member because of pressure from a union or person, an industrial tribunal, if it agrees, may require the union or person to pay part of the compensation.

The Employment Protection (Consolidation) Act 1978 gives dismissed employees the right to be given by their employers, on request, a written statement of the reasons for dismissal, provided they have had 26 weeks' service. The employee can ask for the statement whether or not he intends to complain of unfair dismissal, or he may ask for it in order to decide if he wishes to make a complaint.

10. Management action. In addition to complying with the code of practice summarised in **8**, a company should take the following steps to ensure that no one is dismissed unfairly and that there is a defence if a dismissed employee complains to a tribunal.

(*a*) Managers and supervisors must know whether or not they have the power to dismiss.

(*b*) Records of performance, attendance, timekeeping, etc., must be maintained and preserved.

(*c*) Job specifications must wherever possible include performance standards.

REDUNDANCY

11. Legal definition. Under the Employment Protection (Consolidation) Act 1978 a dismissed employee is redundant when the whole or main reason for his dismissal is that the employer's needs for employees to do work of a particular kind in the place where he was employed have diminished or ceased. If an employee is no longer required in one section but instead of being made redundant is transferred to another section of the firm and displaces another employee who is dismissed, that employee is then redundant.

Acceptance by an employee of another job in the firm will prevent the employee from claiming he is redundant, even if that job has inferior conditions, prospects and pay to his previous job. If he refuses the offer of another job in the firm he will only be regarded as redundant if the alternative job is inferior to the previous job, unsuitable to his skill and training, or an unreasonable distance from his home.

An industrial tribunal hears disputed cases of redundancy; it requires the employer to prove that the employee was not redundant or that the alternative job that may have been offered was reasonable. The working of the Act is described in diagrammatic form in Fig. 6.

A redundant employee, providing he has had at least two years' service and has worked for at least 21 hours a week is entitled to redundancy pay at the following rates:

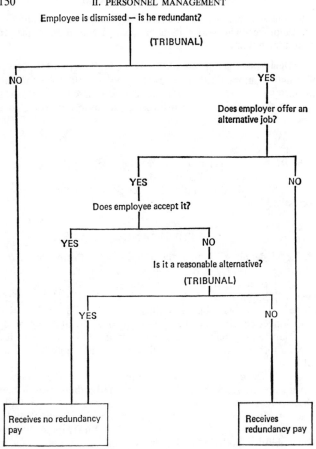

FIG. 6 *Eligibility for redundancy pay.*

(*a*) for each year of employment between ages 18 and 21, half a week's pay;

(*b*) for each year of employment between ages 22 and 40, one week's pay;

(*c*) for each year of employment between ages 41 and 65 (60 for women) one-and-a-half weeks' pay.

These payments are tax free and are in the first instance made by the employer, who may then claim part of the amount from the redundancy fund to which all employers contribute.

12. Dealing with redundancy. The legal provisions for redundancy payments are reasonably clear and simple and are often supplemented by *ex-gratia* payments from the employer. The human problems of redundancy are much more difficult and if badly handled can have most unfortunate effects. A perfect manpower plan (*see* XII) would avoid redundancy completely because all changes in a company's activities would have been foreseen and their effects on employees provided for. Even a rudimentary plan can reduce redundancy or give some warning of it.

A company may try to avoid redundancy by encouraging early retirements and by ceasing to recruit until the number of its employees has fallen to the desired level. This method is often slow, but it avoids the personal disasters that redundancy can bring. The recruitment "freeze", if continued for too long, creates a gap in the age structure of the work-force which can be very serious in later years. To some extent the employer loses control over the situation because he is never sure which of his employees will leave and at what rate. Doubts about their future may cause many of the most valuable employees to resign, lowering the general quality of the staff.

If redundancy is going to occur the company should, where possible, deal with it according to the method described in IX, **12**. It must also observe the relevant provisions of the Employment Protection Act 1975.

(*a*) The employer must consult the appropriate independent trade union so that discussions may be held with a view to reducing the number of redundancies or mitigating their effect. The consultation must take place at the earliest opportunity, but not later than the following times:

(*i*) if 10–99 employees are to be dismissed over a period of 30 days or less at one establishment, at least 30 days before the first dismissal;

(*ii*) if 100 or more employees are to be dismissed over a period of 90 days or less, at least 90 days before the first dismissal.

The trade unions must be told in writing the reasons for the redundancy, the numbers and descriptions of the employees affected, the present number of employees of those descriptions, the proposed method of selection for redundancy and the proposed method of carrying out the dismissals. The employer must reply to any representations made by the unions, giving his reasons if he rejects any of them.

(b) If a union believes any of these requirements have not been met it may complain to an industrial tribunal. A conciliation officer of the Advisory, Conciliation and Arbitration Service will then be given the opportunity to try to bring about a settlement, but if this is not possible the tribunal will hear the complaint. The employer may offer the defence that consultation as required by the Act did in fact take place or that in the circumstances it was not reasonably practicable. If the tribunal finds the union's complaint justified it may either require the employer to postpone dismissal to enable consultation to take place or it may make a "protective award", i.e. an award of pay to employees for a period regarded by the tribunal as "just and equitable". The length of the protected period will be determined by the tribunal but will not be more than:

(i) 90 days where 100 or more employees are to be made redundant over a period of 90 days or less;

(ii) 30 days where 10 or more employees are to be made redundant over a period of 30 days or less;

(iii) 28 days in any other case, e.g. for fewer than 10 employees.

(c) The employer must inform the Secretary of State, not later than the times shown in (a), in order that the Department of Employment may assist in redeployment or retraining, or possibly avoid or minimise the effects of the redundancy. If the Secretary of State is not informed the employer's rebate from the redundancy fund (see 11) may be reduced, or the employer may be prosecuted and fined.

(d) An employee who accepts an offer of a different job in his company may have a trial period of four weeks (or longer by agreement) in the new job, without loss of the right to redundancy pay (see 11).

Finally, under the Employment Protection (Consolidation) Act 1978, an employee may complain of unfair dismissal if he believes he has been unfairly selected for redundancy, for example if the employer has not followed the agreed procedure or has not considered the possibility of offering him alternative employment.

PROGRESS TEST 16

1. What period of notice should be given to a dismissed employee? **(2, 6)**

2. What are the main reasons why a dismissal may be unfair? **(7–9)**

3. Define redundancy. **(11)**

4. How can a company try to avoid making its employees redundant? **(12)**

CHAPTER XVII

Labour Turnover

1. Definition. Labour turnover is the movement of people into and out of the firm. It is usually convenient to measure it by recording movements out of the firm on the assumption that a leaver is eventually replaced by a new employee. The term separation is used to denote an employee who leaves for any reason.

2. Measurement. Two formulae are in common use for measuring labour turnover.

(*a*) The separation or wastage rate, which expresses the number of separations during the period (usually one year) as a percentage of the average number employed during that period. It is therefore:

$$\frac{\text{Number of separations during period}}{\text{Average number employed during period}} \times 100$$

(*b*) The labour stability index, which shows the percentage of the employees who have had at least one year's service. It is usually expressed as follows:

$$\frac{\text{Employees with at least one year's service}}{\text{Number of employees employed one year ago}} \times 100$$

Quarterly periods of service			*Number of leavers*	*% leaving*	*% remaining*
First	(1–13	weeks)	200	40	60
Second	(14–26	weeks)	100	20	40
Third	(27–39	weeks)	50	10	30
Fourth	(40–52	weeks)	25	5	25
Fifth	(53–65	weeks)	15	3	22
Sixth	(66–78	weeks)	10	2	20
Seventh	(79–91	weeks)	5	1	19
Eighth	(92–104	weeks)	5	1	18

Another method of measuring labour turnover is to study a group of employees recruited during a certain period (usually three months) and record the rate at which they leave the company. An example is shown on p. 154 based on the assumption that the company engaged 500 new employees during the period.

These figures are sometimes presented graphically by plotting the percentage leaving against quarterly periods of service. The result is called a survival curve.

3. Use of turnover measurements. The separation rate is easy to calculate and is widely used. It also has the great advantage of indicating costs because separations and replacements can involve the company in considerable expense (*see* **4**). It can be somewhat misleading, however, for two reasons.

(*a*) Recently engaged employees are more likely to leave than long service employees (*see* table in **2**), and therefore an increase in the separation rate may simply be due to some increased recruitment a few weeks previously rather than to a sudden deterioration in worker satisfaction.

(*b*) Some jobs in the company may be vacated and filled several times during the year. Suppose, for example, that in a company employing 1,000 workers 250 leave during the year, giving a separation rate of 25 per cent. The true position might be as follows:

```
        150 jobs vacated and filled once        = 150 leavers
         25 jobs vacated and filled twice        =  50 leavers
         10 jobs vacated and filled three times  =  30 leavers
          5 jobs vacated and filled four times   =  20 leavers
Total: 190 jobs vacated during year.     Total: 250 leavers
```

In such a case the separation index can give a false impression because 100 of the 250 leavers are short-service employees (though the cost of replacing them can still be considerable).

The stability index is best used in conjunction with the separation rate, showing the extent to which the company is retaining its experienced employees. On the figures shown above, the stability index would be

$$\frac{1,000 - 190}{1,000} \times 100 = 81\%$$

Survival rates always show that the tendency for employees to leave is greatest during their early weeks with the company; they are useful in showing if the company is losing a particularly large number of employees early in their service compared with a previous period. It is often instructive to compare survival rates in different departments or for different employee categories, e.g. by age groups or occupations.

4. Cost of labour turnover. Separations and their consequent replacements can be surprisingly expensive. The cost of labour turnover increases when employees are more specialised, more difficult to find and require more training. It is made up of some or all of the following components:

(*a*) lower production during learning period;

(*b*) lost production while the employee is being replaced;

(*c*) payment to other employees at overtime rates while waiting for a replacement;

(*d*) possible diversion of efforts of more highly skilled employees while waiting for a replacement;

(*e*) possible sub-contracting of work;

(*f*) cost of scrap and spoiled work while job is being learned;

(*g*) cost of recruitment, selection and medical examination;

(*h*) training cost;

(*i*) administrative cost of removing from and adding to payroll.

Therefore, when the separation rate is high the employer can incur considerable costs which are not always immediately obvious.

5. Reducing labour turnover. All employers expect to have a certain degree of labour turnover; without it the company would stagnate. No doubt many companies would be content if their separation rates lay between 10 and 15 per cent, though few rates in the private sector of industry and commerce are as low as this. If an employer wishes to reduce his labour turnover because he feels it is excessive for his district and his industry, he may take the following action.

(*a*) *Recalculate* the separation rate for various categories of his employees, e.g. departments, age groups, occupations, to see if turnover in any of these categories is particularly high; if so it can be specially investigated.

(*b*) *Ensure* that his selection procedures are adequate; suitable employees are more likely to stay than unsuitable.

(*c*) *Ensure* that the immediate supervisor, by being involved in selection, feels some responsibility towards a new employee.

(*d*) *Check* that employees are being fully utilised—some may be leaving because of boredom or job dissatisfaction.

(*e*) *Overhaul* pay structure, perhaps using job evaluation (*see* XXI).

(*f*) *Introduce or improve* an induction course (*see* XIV, **21**).

(*g*) Give new employees appropriate *training*.

(*h*) *Show that prospects* in the company are good by promoting from within wherever possible.

(*i*) *Ensure that physical working conditions are adequate.*

In general, an increase in job satisfaction (*see* II, **22**) and in the cohesiveness of working groups (*see* VII, **9**) will decrease the rate of labour turnover.

PROGRESS TEST 17

1. State two formulae by which labour turnover may be measured. (**2**)

2. Which labour turnover formula indicates costs? (**3**)

3. What items make up the cost of labour turnover? (**4**)

4. State some ways in which labour turnover may be reduced. (**5**)

CHAPTER XVIII

Appraisal

TRADITIONAL APPRAISAL METHODS

1. Definition. Appraisal is the judgment of an employee's performance in his job, based on considerations other than productivity alone. It is sometimes called merit rating, more frequently when its sole object is to discriminate between employees in granting increases in wages or salaries.

All managers are constantly forming judgments of their subordinates and are in that sense continuously making appraisals; the term is, however, applied in personnel management to a formal and systematic assessment made in a prescribed and uniform manner at a certain time.

2. Purpose of appraisal. The principal uses of appraisal are:

(*a*) to help a manager decide what increases of pay shall be given on grounds of merit;

(*b*) to determine the future use of an employee, e.g. whether he shall remain in his present job or be transferred, promoted, demoted or dismissed;

(*c*) to indicate training needs, i.e. areas of performance where improvements would occur if appropriate training could be given;

(*d*) to motivate the employee to do better in his present job by giving him knowledge of results, recognition of his merits and the opportunity to discuss his work with his manager.

Appraisal therefore is concerned both with utilisation (future use and training) and with motivation (pay and feedback).

3. Appraisal methods. There are many kinds of appraisal schemes, though usually they are elaborations or variations on one of the following.

(*a*) *Ranking*, which requires the manager to rank his subordinates in order of merit, usually on their total ability in the job but sometimes according to a few separate characteristics.

It is quite easy for a manager to use this method for a small number of subordinates, and usually quite close agreement about the rank order is found among various judges who know the subordinates well. It can be used to decide pay, and to some extent to determine future use, but not to identify training needs or provide motivation. However, although it puts subordinates in order of merit it does not show how much better the first is than the last.

(*b*) *Grading*, which allots employees into a pre-determined series of merit categories—usually five—on the basis of their total performance.

It works reasonably well for a homogeneous group of subordinates, and fair agreement among raters is usually obtained. There is, however, a strong tendency for extremes to be avoided (the central tendency), i.e. very few subordinates are rated poor or exceptional. To overcome this, a forced distribution is sometimes used; managers are instructed to ensure that subordinates are put into the five categories in the following proportions, ensuring that the assessment of merit is distributed normally:

Poor	Below Average	Average	Above Average	Exceptional
10%	20%	40%	20%	10%

The forced distribution is, however, an unsound method to use if the number of subordinates is below about forty. Grading has the same uses and limitations as ranking.

(*c*) *The rating scale* is by far the most common method of appraisal. It consists of a list of personal characteristics or factors against each of which is a scale, usually of five points, for the manager to mark his assessment of the subordinate. An example is shown in Appendix II. Instead of entitling the points of the scale "Poor", "Below average", etc., they are frequently defined (as shown in Appendix II) to encourage consistency of judgment among the raters. The factors are also defined, and there are sections at the end of the form for general remarks and suggestions for future action.

This method can be used for deciding pay, determining future use and indicating training needs. It is rather difficult to use for motivating an employee, as he may well be inclined to argue about the details of the ratings rather than discuss his job constructively.

The rating scale method is in some ways rather dangerous because it gives a false impression of analysis and exactitude. If it is to be successful the managers who use it must be trained, and the factors included in it carefully considered. Some of the faults often found, and ways by which they can be reduced, are described in **4**.

(*d*) *The open-ended* method is a comparatively recent innovation, introduced because of dissatisfaction with rating scales. Instead of requiring a manager to assess a number of personal characteristics, not all equally relevant, the method emphasises the way the job is performed and expects the manager to write a few sentences about the subordinate rather than put ticks in columns. The method has many varieties, a common one being to ask the manager four questions about the subordinate.

(*i*) What are his strong points in relation to his job?

(*ii*) What are his weak points in relation to his job?

(*iii*) What is his promotion potential?

(*iv*) What are his training needs?

Another approach is simply to ask the manager to write a general account of the subordinate's work over the past year and suggest any action that might be taken to improve his performance. In some companies the subordinate simultaneously writes his own version of his year's work and suggests transfers or training that might help his career. The two documents are exchanged before the appraisal interview (*see* **6**) takes place.

The open-ended method cannot be used directly to decide pay but it fulfils the other purposes of appraisal very well. It is more intellectually demanding than the other methods and is perhaps at its best when the subordinates' jobs are relatively unstructured, allowing differences in performance to be clearly shown. In contrast, the rating scale can be completed with much less thought and seems to be suitable for subordinates who have similar and rather routine jobs.

All methods of appraisal require employees to be matched against the demands of their jobs; therefore it is necessary to have job specifications which include performance standards expressed as precisely as possible.

4. Rating scale problems. Unreliable judgments may be made when using the rating scale method.

(*a*) Managers are often unwilling to use the extreme ratings (known as the central tendency).

(*b*) They have different standards of judgment, sometimes influenced by strong prejudices.

(*c*) They do not all attach the same meaning to the names of the factors, e.g. co-operation and initiative, unless these are carefully defined.

(*d*) They are strongly influenced by a subordinate's recent behaviour rather than by his work throughout the appraisal period.

(*e*) Their judgment is influenced by any particularly strong or weak characteristic of the subordinate, causing them to take a generally favourable or unfavourable view of his other qualities (the halo effect).

(*f*) It is difficult to design a rating scale which is suitable for all types of employee. The scale shown in Appendix II would not, for example, be appropriate for managers.

These problems may be reduced by defining the factors and ratings and by training managers in the use of the rating scale.

5. Need for appraisals. There has been in recent years a reaction against formal appraisals, largely because of their tendency to decay into routine form-filling, managers sometimes copying what they wrote the previous year.

It has been said that a manager should, as a normal part of his job, continually assess the merits of his subordinates and consider what training they need to improve their performance or meet new demands. He should take action, e.g. initiate a transfer, if his assessment indicates it and be ready to give a written appraisal whenever it is specifically required, e.g. if a subordinate has applied for promotion. There is general agreement, however, that an annual meeting between the manager and subordinate to review the latter's work during the year is useful because it gives formal recognition of the subordinate's efforts.

6. The appraisal interview. In many companies appraisal is one-way and secret; it can therefore only fulfil the first three purposes of appraisal in **2** and cannot be used to motivate the employee by reviewing his performance in his job.

A two-way and open appraisal requires that an interview takes place between manager and subordinate based on the techniques described in V, **14–15**. A problem-solving approach is usually recommended, encouraging the subordinate to talk freely about his successes and failures over the period. The self-criticism that may occur in this process is much more likely to lead to action by the subordinate to remedy his faults than criticism by the manager.

On the other hand, it is said that in many companies relations between manager and subordinate are not good enough to permit a problem-solving interview to take place. The subordinate will try to hide his shortcomings rather than discuss them. Managers who have the time, patience and social skills to conduct problem-solving interviews are also rather rare. Moreover one of the functions of a manager is to assess his subordinates and tell them if their work is unsatisfactory; his subordinates expect him to do this and will not respect him if he appears to avoid the task.

The first approach to the appraisal interview emphasises motivation and participation while the second emphasises utilisation and authority. In practice many managers successfully combine both, beginning the appraisal interview with criticism and concluding with a discussion on ways of improving performance.

MANAGEMENT BY OBJECTIVES

7. Definition. Management by objectives is a system which attempts to improve the performance of the company and motivate, assess and train its employees by integrating their personal goals with the objectives of the company. It is frequently abbreviated to MBO.

8. Psychological background. In order to understand and benefit from management by objectives all employees who are included in it must understand the psychological principles on which it is based. When management by objectives is introduced into a company a training course is therefore given which explains Maslow's hierarchy of needs (*see* II, **2**), Herzberg's theory of motivational hygiene (*see* II, **13**) and MacGregor's theory X and theory Y (*see* VIII, **12**). The merits of the problem-solving appraisal interview are also discussed (*see* **6** and V, **14–15**). Together these emphasise the virtues of employee participation and the increase in job satisfaction which occurs when the employee feels a sense of achievement and involvement with his work. Unless management by objectives is carried out in this spirit it becomes merely another method by which subordinates can be controlled.

9. Steps in the process. Management by objectives consists essentially of a joint setting of objectives and a joint review of their achievement or non-achievement by a manager and his subordinate (referred for convenience in the rest of the chapter as M and S). The details of the process are as follows.

(*a*) Clarification and review of the company's objectives by the senior management of the company.

(*b*) A repetition of this for departmental objectives so that they are consistent with company objectives.

(*c*) M (who is himself included in management by objectives as a subordinate) interviews S to discuss the purpose of S's job, the key results he must achieve, and what performance standards he should attempt to achieve (*see* XIII, **9**).

(*d*) M and S jointly agree on an action plan for S, i.e. the programme he should try to follow to ensure that he meets the objectives agreed in (*c*).

(*e*) M arranges for control information to be available so that S's performance can be compared with his objectives.

(*f*) At the end of the review period, e.g. three, six or twelve months, M and S meet again to discuss to what extent S has achieved his objectives, as far as possible in a problem-solving manner.

(*g*) M advises S how to build on the strengths revealed in (*f*) and how to overcome his weaknesses.

(*h*) Key results, performance standards (*see* **10**) and an action plan are agreed for the forthcoming period.

10. Key results and performance standards. From the items in his job specification S is encouraged to pick out the tasks which are essential to the job—those which if done well will cause the whole job to be done well. For these tasks M and S agree on objectives or performance standards which are challenging but not impossible and can for preference be expressed in quantitative terms, e.g. improvement in sales by x per cent, reduction in costs by £y, delays to be reduced by z weeks. M must encourage S to suggest his own objectives as far as possible but he must not sanction those which are too easy to achieve or are inconsistent with company policy.

11. Advantages of MBO. The advocates of management by objectives claim that a wide range of advantages may be gained by its introduction into a company.

(*a*) An increase in general efficiency because employees are clear about their objectives.

(*b*) Improved motivation because employees will try harder to achieve objectives they have shared in setting than objectives which have been imposed on them.

(c) An improvement in the quality of work as a result of problem-solving review of performance.

(d) Better identification of training needs as a result of the performance review.

(e) The results of training are easier to assess because its object is to bring performance up to known standards.

(f) The examination of S's job in order to identify key results areas and agree on objectives is useful training both for S and M.

(g) The discussions between M and S may reveal shortcomings in the organisation of the company.

(h) Control systems are improved.

(i) Communications between M and S are improved.

(j) Subordinates are no longer appraised on the basis of subjectively-judged personal characteristics but on their performance against clearly stated objectives.

(k) Motivation, appraisal and training become very much the concern of line management instead of the company's personnel and training specialists.

12. Disadvantages of MBO. Although management by objectives has been very successful in some companies, often being credited with a great increase in their profitability, experience has shown that the system has disadvantages which in many cases seem insuperable.

(a) Even after a training course, the joint setting of objectives and performance review is sometimes not successful, either because the staff of the company do not have the ability to take part in these difficult interviews or because the traditions or management style of the company are inconsistent with the MBO approach. For example, the construction industry tends to inculcate an authoritarian style of management which makes it difficult for construction firms to adopt MBO successfully. The difficulties found in problem-solving interviews are relevant here (*see* **6**).

(b) Although MBO is supposed to improve the organisation of the company, sometimes a reverse influence occurs; MBO is unsuccessful because the company is badly organised and directed.

(c) The system is complicated, difficult and lengthy. It therefore easily degenerates into a routine, particularly when the psychological basis is not understood or top management enthusiasm wanes. In one company known to the writer the setting of objectives is done by an exchange of memoranda.

(*d*) It is often difficult to set new objectives each year. The objective then becomes to maintain present standards.

(*e*) MBO is not appropriate when jobs are structured because S has little control over his objectives or performance.

(*f*) MBO is not possible when the company cannot plan very far ahead, because it is, for example, at the mercy of unforeseeable market conditions.

(*g*) If M is less technically qualified than S, e.g. in some parts of the Civil Service, he may accept objectives which are too easily attainable.

(*h*) S may place undue emphasis on the measurable parts of his job and neglect others, e.g. the creative or innovative parts.

(*i*) MBO may lead to rivalry between subordinates rather than co-operation. Sometimes group objectives are set to avoid this, but they make individual appraisal much more difficult.

(*j*) S's failure to achieve his objectives may be due to factors outside his control which could not be foreseen.

(*k*) S may achieve his objectives but use dubious methods.

(*l*) MBO often encourages concentration on the short-term at the expense of the long-term.

(*m*) MBO in some companies is regarded by subordinates as another weapon of control used by managers. Objectives, although supposed to be set jointly, are in fact imposed by M and the performance review, if objectives are not reached, becomes inquisitorial and accusatory in nature.

PROGRESS TEST 18

1. What are the purposes of appraisal?   (**2**)
2. Describe the rating scale method of appraisal.   (**3**)
3. What are the difficulties in conducting appraisal interviews?   (**6**)
4. What is the psychological basis of management by objectives?   (**8**)
5. Describe the procedure in management by objectives.   (**9**)
6. What are the main advantages and disadvantages of management by objectives?   (**11, 12**)

CHAPTER XIX

Training Principles and Administration

THE SYSTEMATIC APPROACH

1. Purpose of training. Under favourable circumstances, training has the important dual function of utilisation and motivation. By improving employees' ability to perform the tasks required by the company, training allows better use to be made of human resources; by giving employees a feeling of mastery over their work and of recognition by management their job satisfaction is increased. When circumstances are unfavourable, these results may not be obtained, for example when the trainee sees no purpose in his training (*see* III, **6**), when it is regarded as a punishment or sign of displeasure or when the training seems irrelevant to the trainee's needs.

In detail, the gains which it is hoped training will bring are:

(*a*) greater productivity and quality;

(*b*) less scrap or spoiled work;

(*c*) greater versatility and adaptability to new methods;

(*d*) less need for close supervision;

(*e*) fewer accidents;

(*f*) greater job satisfaction showing itself in lower labour turnover and less absence.

It is always desirable to attempt to validate a training course to see if any of these results have been achieved (*see* **10**).

2. Reasons for training. Sometimes training is a routine, e.g. all new employees in certain jobs automatically go through a training course. More often training is given as a response to some event, for example:

(*a*) the installation of new equipment or techniques which require new or improved skills;

(*b*) a change in working methods;

(*c*) a change in product, which may necessitate training not only in production methods but also in the marketing functions of the company;

(*d*) a realisation that performance is inadequate;

(*e*) labour shortage, necessitating the upgrading of some employees;

(*f*) a desire to reduce the amount of scrap and to improve quality;

(*g*) an increase in the number of accidents;

(*h*) promotion or transfer of individual employees.

Training which is routine and traditional sometimes becomes out of date, irrelevant or inadequate. A review may show that the purposes, methods and standards of the training should be changed.

3. The systematic approach to training. Like any other business process, training can be very wasteful if it is not carefully planned and supervised. Without a logical systematic approach some training may be given which is not necessary, and vice versa, or the extent of the training may be too small or too great. When the training is complete, *validation* will show whether it has been successful in achieving its aims and *evaluation* will attempt to measure its cost-benefit.

The systematic approach to training follows this programme.

(*a*) The job is analysed and defined (*see* XIII, **1–6**).

(*b*) Reasonable standards of performance are established, perhaps by reference to experienced employees.

(*c*) The employees being considered for training are studied to see if the required performance standards are being attained.

(*d*) The difference (if any) between (*b*) and (*c*) is considered. It is often called the "training gap", though it may be partly due to faults in the organisation, poor materials or defective equipment.

(*e*) Training programmes are devised to meet the training needs revealed in (*d*) (*see* XX).

(*f*) Training is given and appropriate records kept.

(*g*) The performance achieved after training is measured; if the training programme has been successful the performance standards set in (*b*) should now be achieved (validation).

(*h*) An attempt is made to calculate the cost of the training and compare it with the financial benefit gained by the improved performance of the employees. The training programme may be revised if a method can be seen of achieving the same result at lower cost (evaluation).

The following mnemonic may be useful:

Analyse job
Performance standards
Performance attained
Requirements of training
Originate training programme
Administer training
Check results
How can training be improved next time?

4. The assessment of individual training needs. The systematic approach to training will show the training needs of an individual employee or a group of employees engaged on the same work.

Careful analysis of the job including the setting of performance standards is the first step; management by objectives is a special example of this (*see* XVIII, **9–10**). The performance now being attained by employees can sometimes be measured, but more often it is assessed through an appraisal scheme (*see* XVIII, **1–5**). Management by objectives again shows a different technique by reviewing measurable performance in previously agreed key areas of the job. Any disparities between standards and performance levels show possible training needs.

Often, of course, the assessment is done almost by intuition, particularly when an individual employee's performance could obviously be improved by clearcut training action, e.g. giving him more knowledge of the product or showing him how to use an office machine. Validation of the training may be equally straightforward in such cases.

5. The assessment of long-term training needs. Many training programmes, e.g. apprenticeships, are lengthy, and can therefore be wasteful unless plans are made well in advance. A sudden need for skilled engineering craftsmen will not be met by increasing the number of apprentices entering a four-year scheme; on the other hand it is possible for a company to have jobs for only a small proportion of its apprentices when they complete their training because it is reducing or giving up some of its manufacturing activities.

The assessment of long-term training needs, usually carried out for a whole company, is therefore part of manpower planning (*see* XII). By estimating the expansion or contraction of the labour force, what categories will be affected, the probable number leaving the company and the present utilisation of employees, it is possible to plan what kind of training will be required in the future, when it should begin and how many present or new employees need to be trained. If financial or material resources are limited the analysis may also help to decide which training activities should be given priority.

TRAINING DESIGN

6. Training principles. The psychological principles of training have been dealt with in III, **6–9**; motivation of the trainee is particularly important and is influenced a great deal by the design of the training programme and the methods which are used.

The first step in designing a training course is to consider the training requirements under three headings:

Attitudes
Skills
Knowledge

For example a shop assistant in a men's outfitters would require a certain *attitude* towards customers, *skill* in selling, measuring, wrapping and displaying, and *knowledge* of his stock, sales procedures, current fashions and his company's general policy. Methods of training in these three aspects of a job will be described in the next chapter.

7. On- or off-job training. The methods of training will to a large extent dictate whether the training shall take place on or off the job.

(*a*) *On-job* training is given in the normal work situation, the trainee using the actual tools, equipment, documents or materials that he will use when fully trained. He is regarded as a partly productive worker from the time his training begins.

(*b*) *Off-job* training takes place away from the normal work situation, usually employing specially simplified tools and equipment. The trainee is not regarded as a productive worker from the beginning, his initial work often consisting of exercises. Off-job training may take place on the employer's premises, at a training centre attended by trainees from several employers, or at a college.

8. Advantages and disadvantages of on-job training.

(*a*) Advantages.

(*i*) It is less costly than off-job training because it uses normal equipment in normal surroundings.

(*ii*) Learning will take place on the equipment which will be actually used when the trainee is proficient; there are no transfer of learning problems (*see* III, **8–9**).

(*iii*) The trainee is in the production environment from the beginning; he does not have to adjust to it after the rather sheltered conditions of off-job training.

(*b*) Disadvantages.

(*i*) The instructor (usually a supervisor or a nearby worker) may be a poor teacher and may not have enough time to give proper training.

(*ii*) If there is a payment-by-results scheme it may discourage the instructor from training and the trainee from learning properly.

(*iii*) The trainee may be exposed to bad methods and learn these instead of more efficient methods.

(*iv*) A large amount of spoiled work and scrap material may be produced.

(*v*) Valuable equipment may be damaged.

(*vi*) Training takes place under production conditions which are stressful, i.e. noisy, busy, confusing and exposing the trainee to comments by other workers. Stress usually inhibits learning.

(*c*) Some forms of training can only take place on-job, e.g. job rotation, coaching, and those skills which are so uncommon that it is not worthwhile to set up off-job training facilities for these.

(*d*) Conversely, theoretical training can hardly ever take place on-job; the trainee must attend a college, which is off-job training.

9. Advantages and disadvantages of off-job training.

(*a*) Advantages.

(*i*) As the training is given by a specialist instructor, it should be of higher quality.

(*ii*) Special equipment, simplified if necessary, can be used.

(*iii*) The trainee can learn the job in planned stages, using special exercises to enable him to master particularly difficult aspects.

(*iv*) In the long-term off-job training may be less costly because it enables workers to reach higher standards of speed and quality.

(*v*) It is free from the pressures of payment-by-results schemes, noise, danger or publicity.

(*vi*) The trainee will learn correct methods from the outset.

(*vii*) He does not damage valuable equipment or produce spoiled work or scrap.

(*viii*) It is easier to calculate the cost of off-job training because it is more self-contained than on-job.

(*b*) Disadvantages.

(*i*) The higher costs of separate premises, equipment and instructors can only be justified if there is a regular, fairly large intake of trainees (though this may be overcome by participation in group training schemes in which several employers co-operate).

(*ii*) Sometimes there are transfer of learning difficulties when a trainee changes from training equipment to production equipment and from a training school environment to a production environment.

(*c*) No training can be entirely off-job; some aspects of the task can only be learned by doing them in the normal production setting, with its own customs and network of personal relationships. To illustrate this point, training in driving might be given to a very high standard on a private track, but the driver will not be truly expert until he has experienced driving on public roads; only then can he learn to react to the behaviour of other drivers.

(*d*) Some methods of training which have become important in recent years can only be off-job, for example programmed learning, skills analysis and discovery learning (*see* XX); even here the final stages of training must be on-job.

VALIDATION AND EVALUATION

10. Validation of training. The systematic approach to training (*see* 3) provides a means of validating a training programme. The trainee may be given a test to see if he is now able to reach the performance standards that have been set, or the quantity and quality of his production may be measured for the same purpose.

Unfortunately, training programmes are often extremely difficult to validate. Many jobs are not measurable in any significant way and therefore validation of training for them can only be subjective. For example, the performance of a manager who has attended a management training course may be assessed by his superiors before and after the course. They may well agree that an improvement has occurred, but could this not be due to the fact that the manager is now older? Perhaps the assessors, having sent the manager on a course, will simply assume that he must have benefited from it. Another possibility is that since the course began events have occurred which help the manager in his job.

The more specific the training, the easier validation becomes. If the management course referred to above had contained a course in accountancy, a test would show clearly whether this had been effective, in contrast with the more general parts of the course dealing with management principles, etc., which would be impossible to validate objectively.

11. Evaluation of training. By calculating the cost of training and comparing it with the financial benefits to the company from the improved performance of the trainees, validation may be extended to become evaluation. The ease and accuracy of evaluation vary a great deal.

(*a*) The cost of off-job training is much easier to ascertain than that of on-job training.

(*b*) The financial benefits of training are easier to estimate for manual than for non-manual workers.

(*c*) The costs of inadequate training can often be fairly easily measured, e.g. scrap material, spoiled work, customer complaints, overtime working to remedy mistakes.

(*d*) The benefits of training often go beyond an improvement in job performance (*see* **1**). It is, however, difficult to estimate to what extent relaxation of supervision and reductions in accidents and labour turnover are due to improved training. Expressing these benefits in financial terms is even more difficult.

TRAINING ADMINISTRATION

12. Industrial training boards. Between 1964 and 1970 the government established twenty-eight industrial training boards (ITBs) and an Industrial Training Committee to implement the Industrial Training Act 1964; it was decided in 1970, however, that no more boards should be created. An ITB consists of an independent chairman, members representing employers and employees within the industry and members from the education service. It has a permanent staff of training advisers and administrators.

Under the Act, an ITB may collect a levy from employers in its industry and make training grants to them if they train their employees in ways approved by the board. Two main interpretations of the levy–grant system appeared.

(*a*) Some boards fixed a high levy to provide a strong financial incentive to train. In order to claim grants, employers had to show in detail what training they had given over the past year. For example the Engineering Industry Training Board levied 2½ per cent of payroll and thereby collected £80–90 million a year.

(*b*) Other boards believed that a better approach was to fix the levy at 1 per cent or less of payroll and give grants either for specific kinds of training which the Board thought vital or for adopting the systematic approach to training (*see* **3**). They emphasised the consultancy role of the board, maintaining that large levies and grants could divert an employer's attention away from a careful consideration of his company's training needs.

During 1982 several ITBs were abolished and their industries asked to make voluntary arrangements to encourage training. It is too early to know what the results of this change will be. At the time of writing only seven ITBs remain, some of them dealing with a narrower range of employers than previously.

13. Employment and Training Act 1973. This Act showed that the government supported the second interpretation of the levy–grant system by laying down that the maximum levy should not be more than 1 per cent of payroll and that a company could be exempted entirely from levy if it could show that its training was adequate for its needs. The Act also set up (under the Manpower Services Commission) the Training Services Division to coordinate the work of the industrial training boards, to encourage training in industries not covered by boards and to administer the Training Opportunities Scheme (TOPS) for employees wishing to learn a new skill.

14. Responsibility for company training. Because training is so important in the utilisation and motivation of human resources it deserves the special attention of the senior management of the company. One of the advantages claimed for the high levy policy adopted by some ITBs was that it "brought training into the board room", the large amounts being paid to the training board forcing consideration at director level of possible ways of recovering the money. At a lower level, the line manager must regard the training of his subordinates as one of his responsibilities, since he is expected to use the resources at his disposal to the best advantage.

Some companies have training officers or departments which advise on policies and methods and may administer some of the training. Consultants are sometimes called in, particularly to give advice about unusual training problems, or to overhaul methods which are obviously inefficient. These various roles in training may be summed up as follows.

(*a*) Senior management determines a general training policy which is consistent with the objectives of the company. It may be derived from the company manpower plan (*see* XII) or based on an assessment of training needs to which junior levels of management have contributed.

(*b*) Line managers have a responsibility for training their subordinates and are often personally involved in giving it because training is always wholly or partly on-job (*see* **8**). In some cases they may design and supervise training programmes, while in others the training of their subordinates may be largely off-job, line managers being expected to provide the finishing touches when the employees begin productive work. In all cases it is the responsibility of line managers to ensure that the training which is given, by whatever means, is relevant to the needs of the department and is effective in its results.

(*c*) Training officers advise senior management on policy by applying their expert knowledge of training to the needs of the company. They frequently conduct surveys or are consulted when changes are proposed which will necessitate training or re-training. They design courses, administering them if they are off-job. They are expected to advise on external education and training facilities, maintaining contact with the ITB (where it exists), colleges, and various training organisations.

(*d*) Instructors are in direct contact with trainees, and in most cases are concerned with off-job training. They are not responsible for designing the course but they are expected to report any deficiencies it seems to contain. They are usually proficient workers who have taken a short course in training methods.

(*e*) Consultants tend to be called in when a company is facing unusual training problems, for example poor productivity or the consequences of reorganisation or technical change. They study needs, advise on appropriate methods and set up training procedures which the management of the company can then continue.

PROGRESS TEST 19

1. What benefits does a company hope to obtain when it trains its employees? **(1)**

2. Outline the systematic approach to training. **(3)**

3. Under what three headings should training requirements be considered? **(6)**

4. Compare on-job and off-job training. **(7, 8, 9)**

5. Define and distinguish between validation and evaluation of training. **(10, 11)**

6. What are the functions of the Training Services Division? **(13)**

7. Describe the place of line managers and training officers in company training. **(14)**

CHAPTER XX

Training Methods

TRAINING IN ATTITUDES

1. The importance of attitudes. The definition of an attitude (*see* VII, **12**) is as follows: "An individual's characteristic way of responding to an object or situation. It is based on his experience and leads to certain behaviour or the expression of certain opinions."

Attitudes determine the general approach of an employee to his work; for example the care that is taken to avoid mistakes, the way customers, clients or patients are dealt with or the degree of persistence shown in achieving work objectives. In some cases the appropriate attitude is already present when the employee enters the occupation in question—a nurse has probably chosen her career because she possesses attitudes favouring the care of the sick. In other cases the employee has not felt a vocation towards his job but has perhaps taken it up because it is convenient or respectable. A shop assistant, for example, may have an attitude towards customers which does not produce sales and may injure the reputation of the shop. Unless this attitude can be changed he will never be a successful employee. The importance of attitudes obviously varies according to the type of job; they are not particularly important when the work is highly structured because so long as the employee is at his work station he has little choice about the way he goes about his task. On the other hand, unstructured work, with its freedom of choice and its opportunity for self-regulation, cannot be carried out successfully unless the employee's attitudes are consistent with the purposes of the job.

2. Attitude training. Attitude training is difficult because many attitudes are deep-rooted and cannot easily be changed in a short time. The usual methods employed are as follows.

(*a*) *On-job experience within a group of employees* whose attitudes are thought to be appropriate. There is often no practical alternative to this method, but it is slow to produce an effect and will fail if the attitudes of the other employees are unsuitable. It is therefore unwise to put a new employee in a group of disgruntled workers.

(b) *On-job training by attaching the trainee to a senior employee* who has appropriate attitudes and the personal qualities likely to influence their acceptance. Coaching or a period as a personal assistant are examples of this method.

(c) *Off-job training* in which a group of employees discuss case studies designed to emphasise the relevant attitudes. Usually the group is divided into sub-groups or syndicates, each reporting back to the whole group through spokesmen. A discussion in a small group is thus reinforced by a discussion in a larger group. This method is useful because the case studies can be written with the particular background and needs of the trainees in mind. However sometimes discussion of imaginary incidents involving imaginary people fails to produce an emotional response. It is also possible for lazy trainees to make no contribution to the discussion and be completely detached from it.

(d) *Off-job role-playing exercises* in which a situation is described up to a certain point of crisis. Participants in the exercise are then asked to act out the parts of the people involved in the situation, extemporising the dialogue and behaving in the way they think is characteristic not of themselves but of the individuals whose roles they are playing. The group might act out situations concerning dismissal, a difficult customer or negotiations with trade unions. This method is usually enjoyed by the trainees, who show emotional involvement, sometimes intense. The training officer can make sure that lazy trainees are included by giving them roles to play. He can use audio or video tapes to record the role-playing so that the participants may discuss their performance afterwards. Non-participant critics may be asked to attempt roles themselves in a repetition of the exercise. It seems that attitudes are often modified by this method, though a great deal depends on the support which is given when the trainee returns to his normal job.

(e) *T-groups* are an off-job training method (the T stands for training) which has been in vogue in recent years. The group of trainees (not more than twelve in number) is told that its sole task is to examine and discuss its own behaviour. After a slow and awkward beginning, the group's discussion generally becomes somewhat emotional, even heated, with members criticising each other's attitudes or indulging in frank self-criticism. Group sessions often continue for several days, and are regarded by some as enjoyable and by others as unpleasant. The purpose of T-group training is partly to bring about a change in attitudes by showing individuals what others think of them, partly to demonstrate the importance of personal behaviour in group processes and partly to improve the social skills of the trainees. This form of training has never been clearly validated; its effects on some individuals have been quite harmful psychologically and many others have found it useless because they have been unable to practise their newly found social skills in an unsympathetic working environment.

TRAINING IN SKILL

3. Definition. The Department of Employment's *Glossary of Training Terms* gives the following definition of skill:

> An organised and co-ordinated pattern of mental and/or physical activity in relation to an object or other display of information, usually involving both receptor and effector processes. It is built up gradually in the course of repeated training or other experience. It is serial, each part from second to second is dependent on the last and influences the next. Skills may be described as perceptual motor, manual, intellectual, social, etc., according to the context or the most important aspect of the skill pattern.

(Receptor processes provide the sensory input and effector processes the output or response.)

More briefly, skill may be defined as a practised, expert way of perceiving a relevant stimulus and then responding to it (*see* I, **10** (*c*)). Skill training therefore comprises the following:

(*a*) recognition of stimuli, e.g. the sensation of the material feeling smooth;

(*b*) appropriate responses, e.g. the correct angle at which the carpenter should hold the chisel;

(*c*) establishing serial performance, each response providing a new stimulus which in turn evokes a new response and so on.

4. Methods of skill training. The traditional method of training in skill is usually known as "sitting next to Nellie", i.e. the trainee is told to watch and copy an experienced worker. If "Nellie" uses poor working methods, or if the job includes much that cannot be understood simply by observation, then the method is a bad one. If Nellie uses good methods and if the job is visible, i.e. it can readily be understood simply by observation, then the method can be effective and economical.

Since a very large number of jobs contain non-visible elements and many "Nellies" use poor methods of work, it is preferable on most occasions to use more organised means of training. Three typical methods of training will be described: training within industry (TWL); skills analysis; and the discovery method. Most skill training programmes are based on one of these methods or a compromise between them.

5. Training within industry (TWI). There are several TWI training programmes, among them a course which trains supervisors in the technique of instruction. Since the war many thousands of supervisors have attended Department of Employment TWI courses and the technique is therefore widely known.

(a) The supervisor performs the job himself and divides it into reasonably self-contained stages, each of which can be taught as a unit.

(b) He examines each stage to identify and describe "key points", e.g. special difficulties or dangers. An example of a TWI breakdown is given in Appendix III.

(c) He makes sure that the materials and equipment required for training are properly arranged.

(d) The supervisor talks to the trainee to find out what he already knows about the job and arouses his interest in learning it.

(e) The job is then demonstrated to the trainee in stages, explained slowly and carefully, with particular emphasis on the key points.

(f) The trainee performs the job, the supervisor observing to see that no mistakes are made and asking him questions to ensure that he has understood it. It may be necessary for the supervisor to repeat some of the instructions he has given in (e). The trainee repeats the job until the supervisor is satisfied that performance is adequate.

(g) The supervisor puts the trainee to work, watching him fairly closely at first but gradually relaxing supervision as the trainee gains confidence and skill.

The TWI method is cheap, and is suitable for small numbers of trainees. It begins by being off-job, though usually very near the

scene of production, but soon becomes on-job. A separate training department with specialist staff is not required. The analysis
of the job in (a) and (b) cannot go very deep, and the method
is therefore not appropriate for difficult skills, i.e. where the
stimulus–perception–response sequence is not obvious.

It is successful with "visible" jobs where everything of importance in the job can be observed, the mental processes being relatively unimportant; good examples would be packing or most
forms of assembly work. Jobs of this kind contain a low proportion of skill and a high proportion of procedural knowledge. In
the non-manual field, TWI is suitable for training in routine
clerical work.

6. Skills analysis. This method of training has been developed
for those jobs which require a high degree of dexterity and co-
ordination of senses and bodily movements. The actions of a
highly skilled worker are analysed in great detail to identify and
describe:

(a) what actions he performs with each finger, each hand and
each foot;

(b) how these actions are combined;

(c) the stimuli he recognises which give him the signals to begin
and end these actions;

(d) the senses by which these stimuli reach him;

(e) the possible faults that may occur in the article being
produced; these are classified, the reasons for them determined
and methods of rectifying and avoiding them analysed.

From this information is compiled a skills analysis breakdown
(see Appendix III) and a faults analysis. Exercises are developed
to train employees in the recognition of stimuli, the perfection of
difficult movements and the co-ordination of those movements.

Skills analysis training has been successful in reducing training
times and increasing proficiency. It claims to abolish the learning
plateau (see III, 7 (c)) because its carefully graded exercises allow
the trainee to make steady uninterrupted progress.

It is an off-job training method, for obvious reasons, and is
expensive and lengthy to prepare because a detailed job analysis
must be carried out by expert consultants. A company is only
justified in using it, therefore, when there is a large intake of trainees
and when training by simpler methods is fairly long, i.e. over one
month. In such cases the heavy initial outlay in consultants' fees,
special equipment and training premises may be amply justified.

7. The discovery method. This is a technique of skill training which has been developed in recent years and applied with particular success to the re-training of older workers. It is similar in many ways to the newer methods used in primary education.

Discovery learning occurs when the trainee finds out for himself the principles of the job and the correct method of performing it; it is claimed to be more motivating than other forms of training because it offers the trainee a challenge followed by the gratification of a discovered solution. The trainer is comparatively passive, giving little formal instruction or demonstration. Another advantage claimed for this method is that it is trainee-centred; it tries to approach training problems from the point of view of a worker who does not yet possess the skill rather than by taking an expert worker as a model, as in skills analysis. During a discovery training programme it becomes very obvious if a trainee does not understand, but when in contrast an instructor explains or demonstrates a task he can never be sure if the trainee has understood or not.

An illustration of discovery learning is the training scheme for menders of worsted cloth described in *Training the Adult Worker* by Eunice Belbin (HMSO). The trainees first learned the detailed patterns of the weaves by copying them using thick elastic instead of thread and then discovered how to mend faults which were introduced into the weaves. The size of the weaves was gradually reduced until it reached actual size; by then the trainees had reached in 12 weeks a standard of proficiency formerly attained in a year to 18 months.

The discovery method, like skills analysis, is an off-job training technique and requires a large intake of trainees if it is to be economically justifiable. It can be used quite successfully not only for skill but for knowledge training, by presenting the trainee with the opportunity to deduce for himself the answer to a problem, or indicating where he can find out necessary information.

TRAINING IN KNOWLEDGE

8. Knowledge requirements. No employee can work well without adequate job knowledge; in some cases it can be acquired in informal ways by experience in the job but usually it is imparted more quickly and accurately by formal training. Job analysis will show what knowledge is required, for example under the following headings:

(*a*) purpose—the function of the job within the total process;

(*b*) background information—the history, traditions and policies of the company, which may help the employee to understand the significance of his job;

(*c*) legal requirements;

(*d*) Quality standards—how accurate or how approximate the work should be;

(*e*) materials of work, e.g. for a salesman what goods are available, their prices and qualities, for a manual worker the physical properties of the materials he is using;

(*f*) tools and equipment;

(*g*) technical, e.g. accountancy, scientific or engineering knowledge;

(*h*) personal contacts—job relationships with other employees;

(*i*) procedures—the order in which things are done.

In contrast to attitudes and skills, knowledge may be imparted in many different ways, most of which are inexpensive and convenient. The most important methods of knowledge training are described below.

9. Coaching. This may vary from a rather casual "sitting next to Nellie" approach to formal regular sessions in which an experienced employee, usually a manager, explains the job, asks the trainee questions to test his knowledge and often exercises general supervision over him to check that he is making correct use of the knowledge. It is convenient, inexpensive and allows two-way communication, but depends very much on the ability of the coach and the time he is able to devote to training.

10. Formal lectures. When a company has a number of trainees in the same kind of work simultaneously, it may arrange for the group to have lectures on the subjects (*a*) to (*f*) in **8** by one of its senior employees. When this cannot be done, trainees may attend lectures outside the company, for example at a technical college, though the knowledge they learn here will be more general, and less specific to the company's needs.

Technical knowledge (*see* **8** (*g*)) is usually acquired outside the company. As in coaching, the effectiveness of formal lectures depends on their perceived relevance, the ability of the lecturer, the care with which the lectures are prepared, and the extent to which the trainees are encouraged to participate in discussions. Films and other visual aids can make the lecture more effective, and it is customary to give the trainee a hand-out covering the main points of the lecture.

11. Visits and tours. To help a trainee acquire knowledge under headings **8** (*a*), (*b*) and (*h*), arrangements may be made for him to visit other departments or establishments of the company and talk to employees with whom he would normally only deal by letter or telephone. The trainee often benefits by seeing the stages of work preliminary and subsequent to his own.

12. Manuals and charts. The trainee is sometimes given a detailed written description of his job, perhaps incorporating charts which show the route the work takes or explain the decisions the employee has to make. Many employees prefer to learn by this method instead of by personal contact, though it is still necessary for someone to be responsible for the trainee, introduce him to the work and check his progress.

13. Simulation. Instead of putting the trainee immediately to work, he may be asked to simulate the job using dummy materials or documents. A programme is devised which grades tasks from the easy and obvious to the more complex. This method often makes formal instruction unnecessary, because skilfully applied it can become very similar to discovery learning (*see* **7**).

14. In-tray. A special version of simulation is in-tray training, in which the trainee is asked to deal with a batch of miscellaneous documents which he is supposed to find in his in-tray. Decisions of various kinds have to be made, though not of course actually put into effect.

The value of this technique for training depends on the review which should follow, when the trainer discusses with the trainee the decisions he has made. It is used in management training and occasionally as a means of selecting managers, though the exercise is difficult to score objectively.

15. Auto-instruction. To benefit from this method, trainees need above-average intelligence and pertinacity. They are given a programme of assignments or tasks which take them to various parts of the company and require them to obtain information from departmental managers or from company files. The trainees are required to report back to their trainer periodically for a discussion and review.

Like the discovery method, auto-instruction is based on the

principle that knowledge gained by exploration and discovery is more likely to be permanent than knowledge imparted by instructors.

16. Programmed learning. This consists of a carefully ordered sequence of units or frames arranged so that the trainee masters each unit before proceeding to the next. It is individual instruction, each trainee working at his own pace, and can be presented as a teaching book, teaching machine or a visual display unit controlled by a computer which holds the programme.

Each frame contains some information; the trainee is then asked a question to test whether he has learned or understood it. If his answer is correct he moves on to the next frame. Programmed learning thus follows the principles of operant conditioning (*see* III, **5**) developed by B. F. Skinner, who has been mainly responsible for this method of instruction. The stimulus is the unit of information with its question, the response is the answer to the question, and the reinforcement is the immediate knowledge of results and in most cases the gratification of having made the correct answer.

(*a*) *Advantages.* Besides the advantages usually found in off-job training, programmed learning also offers the following.

(*i*) The trainee goes at his own pace.

(*ii*) The training can be decentralised, i.e. the teaching book or the teaching machine can be sent to the trainee instead of bringing him to a training school.

(*iii*) Most trainees find the method interesting; research has also shown that its effects are long-lasting.

(*iv*) It can be designed to meet specified performance standards and is continually being validated by the questions it contains.

(*v*) It is quicker than most other methods of knowledge training.

(*b*) *Disadvantages.* These are few but important.

(*i*) Learning programmes are expensive to produce and therefore are economically justifiable only when many trainees will use them.

(*ii*) If the subject is changing rapidly the investment in a learning programme will not be justified.

(*iii*) It is suitable above all for teaching facts and procedures; it is not appropriate for subjects where some discussion and flexibility of approach is desirable, e.g. literary criticism.

MANAGEMENT DEVELOPMENT

17. Definition. The *Glossary of Training Terms* gives the following definition of management development:

> A systematic process of development of effective managers at all levels to meet the requirements of an organisation, involving an analysis of the present and future management requirements, assessing the existing and potential skills of managers and devising the best means for their development to meet these requirements.

The definition shows that management development includes:

(*a*) manpower planning to assess the demand for managers (*see* XII);

(*b*) appraisal of managers' present abilities, sometimes using a management by objectives programme (*see* XVIII);

(*c*) appropriate development methods.

It is sometimes regarded as part of *organisation development*— a planned attempt to improve the effectiveness of a company by examining and reforming the way it is organised, its communications and its management style. The systematic approach (*see* XIX, **3**) cannot be applied to development, which aims to prepare for future jobs whereas training is concerned with improving performance in present jobs. Validation of a management development programme is therefore very difficult.

18. Development needs. These can be divided into three categories.

(*a*) Knowledge required to perform a manager's job in the company concerned, including:

(*i*) background of company, its organisation and practices;

(*ii*) company resources available;

(*iii*) company technology;

(*iv*) specialist management techniques, e.g. operational research;

(*v*) relevant law;

(*vi*) general, social and economic environment.

(*b*) Planning, analytical and creative skills, which include the following:

(*i*) recognising objectives and putting them in order of importance;

(*ii*) assessing the value of available resources, e.g. human, material, technological and financial;

(*iii*) formulating and administering plans, delegating as necessary;

(*iv*) discerning and solving day-to-day management problems.

(*c*) Social skills (sometimes called interpersonal or interactive skills), important because a manager may easily spend two-thirds of his time working with and trying to influence others. They include:

(*i*) communication upwards, downwards and laterally (*see* IX, **3**);

(*ii*) Co-ordination within a department or between departments.

(*iii*) Motivation of subordinates.

(*iv*) Awareness of others' needs, attitudes and perceptions.

19. Development methods. Needs may be met either by activities arranged within the company or by external courses. The latter appear to be losing favour because they are unable to take into account a company's particular systems, traditions or general management style. In-company programmes are growing in popularity, especially those which include a team of people who normally work together, or even a whole department. It is, however, often difficult in practice to release a whole team or department at the same time unless the programme is held outside normal working hours.

Development methods often used in management development fall into three areas.

(*a*) *Knowledge*. As in training, this is the easiest area to deal with. Company matters are dealt with by secondment, coaching or auto-instruction (*see* **15**), while outside courses (such as the Diploma in Management Studies) are appropriate for specialist techniques and the general environment.

(*b*) *Planning, analytical and creative skills*. This is the most difficult of the three categories. To a certain extent the acquisition of knowledge will help the manager by showing him the factors he must consider and the techniques he can use, but it seems that planning, analytical and creative skills can only be developed by practice, either in a real job or in a situation which attempts to simulate reality.

In the first case, the manager will feel fully responsible, will take genuine decisions and will deal with their consequences, though the mistakes of an inexpert manager can be disastrous.

In the second case, he may be more enterprising but he has little sense of responsibility; his behaviour in real life may be entirely different. A simulated situation, however carefully it is described, can never depict, for example, the personalities and organisational climate which are so important in management decision-making. Some simulated methods which are used to try to develop these skills are:

(*i*) *case studies and role-playing* (*see* **2**);

(*ii*) *in-tray exercises* (*see* **14**);

(*iii*) *business games* in which two or more teams attempt, for example, to market an imaginary product using the information supplied to them. The effects of their decisions are evaluated (usually by a computer) and fed back to them. The team which has made the largest profit will be the winner.

The following are real-life methods.

(*i*) *Projects*, i.e. special assignments given to managers, who must enquire into a company problem, make recommendations and sometimes put them into practice.

(*ii*) *Junior boards*, in which a group of young managers is given decisions of fairly low importance to make which have been delegated to the group by the main board.

(*iii*) *Action learning*, in which a fairly senior manager takes over a different job from his own, either within his company or outside it, for some months. The new circumstances are intended to stimulate his managerial skills by presenting him with completely different problems to solve. The department or company may in turn be stimulated by his new approach.

(*iv*) *Training companies*, usually small subsidiaries of a large group, which are intended to trade profitably, yet give opportunities for young managers to develop their skills in a somewhat protected environment.

(*v*) *Coaching* (*see* **9**) is often used and is frequently successful, but sometimes the experienced manager who is coaching may make his decisions so automatically that either he does not realise he has made them or he cannot explain his reasons for them.

(*c*) *Social skills*. These have received much attention in recent years and are always dealt with in special courses.

The main methods are as follows.

(*i*) *Attitude change*, e.g. by T-groups or role-playing (*see* **2**).

(*ii*) *Team-work and management-style courses*, usually given by consultants, in which groups are formed to carry out simple

tasks together and then discuss what lessons about their behaviour can be learned, e.g. Coverdale training and action-centred
leadership, or in which groups discuss their normal working behaviour in the light of a theoretical framework, e.g. managerial
grid (*see* VIII, **6**).

(*iii*) *Analysing individual behaviour* following a formal
system, sometimes with a theoretical basis, e.g. transactional analysis.

(*iv*) *Training in social techniques*. This is the reverse of
method (*i*) in which it is assumed that a change in attitudes will
modify behaviour. Instead, training is given in the techniques of
hand-shaking, smiling, eye contact, etc., in situations which are
as near to reality as possible, e.g. a simulated appraisal interview.
The trainee becomes aware of the benefits of his improved techniques in his social contacts, and thus modifies his basic attitudes.

(*v*) *Lectures* in the psychology of perception, motivation,
groups, etc., usually in conjunction with one of the above
methods.

PROGRESS TEST 20

1. What methods may be used for attitude training?   (**2**)
2. What are the disadvantages of the "sitting next to Nellie"
method of skill training?   (**4**)
3. Outline the TWI method of training.   (**5**)
4. Why does skills analysis training sometimes eliminate the
learning plateau?   (**6**)
5. What are the principles of the discovery method of training?   (**7**)
6. State three methods of knowledge training.   (**9–16**)
7. What are the advantages and disadvantages of programmed
learning?   (**16**)
8. What are a manager's main development needs?   (**18**)

CHAPTER XXI

Job Evaluation

THE BASIS OF JOB EVALUATION

1. Definition. Job evaluation is the process of placing jobs in order of their relative worth in order that employees may be paid fairly. It is concerned with the demands and conditions of the job and not with the personal qualities of the individual who is occupying the job. The first stage in job evaluation is usually to establish a rank-order for jobs and the second is to apply money values to it.

2. Importance of job evaluation. Payment for work can fulfil many functions (*see* II, **12**), from the provision of food and shelter to the recognition that an employee's job has a certain status and value, i.e. it can satisfy both lower and higher needs. Because pay is significant not only for what it will purchase but also for what it symbolises, a company's pay structure is very important to its employees, who will strongly resent what they perceive to be un-fairness or injustice. In some companies, for example, pay anomalies have appeared perhaps because of inconsistency of treatment in the past, a merger with another company, or high rates being offered to meet a temporary shortage of a certain type of employee. Sometimes no one can explain the anomalies. The purposes of job evaluation are therefore:

(*a*) to make pay administration easier by reducing the number of separate rates of pay;

(*b*) to harmonise internal rates of pay with those found in other companies;

(*c*) to provide a means by which a reasonable rate of pay can be fixed for new or changed jobs within the company;

(*d*) to protect the employee from arbitrary decisions by management.

In a small company these purposes can obviously be fulfilled without a formal system; no doubt some kind of intuitive evaluation takes place. Large companies, however, with their much more complex organisation and greater variety of occupations will find job evaluation almost essential unless their job structure is completely static, with pay relativities firmly established by tradition. Such firms are rare.

The Prices and Incomes Board reported in September 1968 that nearly 40 per cent of companies employing over 5,000 people used job evaluation, but only 6 per cent of companies employing less than 500. The Institute of Personnel Management found in February 1976 that out of 213 companies selected at random, 168 were using some kind of job evaluation.

3. Factors determining pay. A wage or salary is influenced by many different factors. Some of these affect the basic pay for the job and others the pay that individual employees receive.

(a) *Supply and demand*—eventually, when the supply of a particular type of labour is scarce its price, i.e. its wage or salary, will rise, and vice versa. The operation of this economic law is, however, affected by the following:

(i) people are often unwilling to move to another district;

(ii) pay is not the only reward gained from employment;

(iii) knowledge of the various rates of pay offered is not widespread;

(iv) training for a new occupation may take some years.

(b) *Difficulty of the job*—it is generally agreed that jobs which require a high level of intelligence, experience, knowledge or skill deserve a high rate of pay.

(c) *Unpleasant working conditions.*

(d) *Cost of living.*

(e) *Government intervention.*

(f) *Productivity, merit or length of service*—often determining the pay received by an individual over and above the basic rate.

4. Job rates and individual rates. Job evaluation establishes a basic rate by considering factors (a) to (d) in **3.** If it is thought desirable to reward differently the individuals who are doing the same job then additions may be made to their basic rate, perhaps on productivity (using payment by results—*see* XXII, **3–5**), merit (by appraisal—*see* XVIII) or length of service.

5. Introducing job evaluation. A new or altered job evaluation system is a change which must be very carefully introduced by management (*see* IX, **10–12**) because it affects the vital subject of pay. The method of evaluation must be clearly explained to employees and their representatives, some modifications perhaps being made at the employees' request. It is usual to guarantee that no employee at present employed by the company will receive a reduction in pay, though if his job is found to be overpaid his successors in it may be given a lower wage.

Some companies have found that the fairness of the scheme in the employees' eyes is increased if an appeals committee is set up to listen to complaints that jobs have not been given the value they deserve. Employee representatives, e.g. shop stewards, often sit on these committees.

6. Essential requirements. Any method of job evaluation requires two things.

(a) Job specifications for all jobs which are to be valued (*see* XIII, **5–6**).

(b) A committee to consider the job specifications and apply to them the particular technique of evaluation which it has been decided shall be used. The committee usually contains a few permanent members, e.g. the personnel officer, the work study officer, the organisation and methods officer together with other members drawn from a panel of managers who have all had training in the technique. Job evaluations carried out by an individual are not likely to be well received; using a committee will reduce the effects of bias and prejudice.

METHODS

7. Job evaluation methods. Three methods of job evaluation are in common use.

(a) *Ranking*, a non-analytical method because the job is valued as a whole, an impressionistic view being taken.

(b) *Grading*, a semi-analytical method in which the job specification is examined fairly closely but not exhaustively.

(c) *Points rating*, an analytical method which requires a very detailed examination of the job specification.

8. Ranking. In this method the committee judges each job as a whole and places the set of jobs in order of their worth. Sometimes this process is aided by using as points of reference one or two jobs whose place in the hierarchy is generally accepted.

(a) Advantages.
(i) It is quick and requires no complicated administration.
(ii) It is easily understood.

(*iii*) It is particularly suitable for fairly homogeneous jobs, e.g. all clerical, or where it is known that the pay structure is already reasonably satisfactory.

(*b*) Disadvantages.

(*i*) Although the method is easy to understand, its results are difficult to defend as they are based on impressionistic, almost intuitive judgments.

(*ii*) It is impracticable in large companies or in smaller companies in which jobs are very varied.

(*iii*) It does not indicate the spaces between positions in the rank order, i.e. job A may be judged to be worth more than job B, but the method will not show how much more.

A refinement of ranking is the *paired comparison* method, in which each job is ranked against every other job, taking a pair of jobs at a time. If N jobs are dealt with in this way then $N(N - 1)/2$ comparisons have to be made, i.e. to rank 20 jobs will require 190 comparisons. It is usual to distribute the pairs of jobs among several judges and collate the results on a computer. By showing how many times a job has been given first preference, not only may a rank order be prepared but spacing along the rank order will also be shown. The paired comparison method also enables jobs of different types to be evaluated.

The subjectivity of ranking is obvious, though experienced judges using this method very often achieve remarkable agreement.

9. Grading. This method provides a framework into which jobs can be fitted. It is decided in advance how many grades or classes of pay shall be created, and the jobs which should fall into each grade are defined. The lowest grade, for example, will be defined as containing those jobs which require little skill and are closely supervised. With each successive grade skills, knowledge and responsibilities increase. The committee then reads the specification for each job, matching it against the various grade definitions until an appropriate grade is found. Eventually every job in the company has been allotted to a grade.

(*a*) Advantages.

(*i*) It is relatively simple, quick and inexpensive.

(*ii*) The decisions of the committee can be supported by the definitions of the job grades.

(*b*) Disadvantages.

(*i*) Complex jobs are often difficult to fit into the system; a job may seem to have the characteristics of two or more grades.

Like ranking, the method is at its best when a fairly homogeneous family of jobs is being evaluated.

(*ii*) Because of the difficulty in (*i*) the original grades tend in time to be sub-divided into smaller grades, making the scheme more difficult to operate.

(*iii*) The method is less objective than appears at first sight. To a large extent jobs are valued before the specifications are examined because arbitrary decisions have been made that certain features of a job belong to certain grades. For example, an unscrupulous employer could attempt to depress the remuneration of his employees by defining the grades in such a way that the majority of jobs fell into the lower grades. On the other hand, this will not occur if the grade definitions have been prepared and published by an independent body, such as the Institute of Administrative Management, part of whose system of clerical workers' job grading is shown in Appendix IV.

10. Points rating. This is the most widely used method. A number of factors are first agreed against which jobs can be analysed. A very simple set of factors for manual jobs might be:

Skill
Effort
Responsibility
Working conditions

However it is usual to sub-divide each of the main factors into about three sub-factors, making about twelve altogether. For example, "skill" might be divided into education, experience and dexterity. Sometimes non-manual jobs are provided for by extending the factors to include, for example, complexity of duties, contacts with others or requirement to handle confidential information, or sometimes a special set of factors is used for a particular family of jobs.

Each factor carries a range of points; the committee analyses each job specification to decide how many points shall be awarded to the job for each factor. The total of points when set against other totals indicates the position of the job in the hierarchy. An example of a job evaluation scheme for manual workers is shown in Appendix IV.

11. Weighting. The factors chosen for job evaluation may not all have equal importance; skill, for example, may contain the three sub-factors training, experience and dexterity of which experience is thought to make the greatest contribution to the value of a job.

Weighting is the name given to the process by which some factors can be given greater emphasis than others. It can be carried out in two ways.

(a) A multiplier is introduced so that the points value given to a factor can be doubled, trebled, etc. Each factor carries the same range of points, e.g. 1 to 10, but the value given to, say, experience might be multiplied by 4 and that for training by 2.

(b) Factors judged to be more important have a wider range of points attached to them. This is the practice followed in the scheme shown in Appendix IV.

12. The choice of factors and weights. The choice of factors and weights is intuitive rather than objective. A company with no previous experience of job evaluation will probably begin by using a scheme borrowed from another company, or one which has appeared in a book. If the results of evaluating a few well-known jobs do not agree with commonsense or tradition the company will change the factors or weights until an acceptable set of relationships is obtained.

Different jobs require different factors; it is very unusual for a company to be able to evaluate all its jobs by the use of one scheme only. For example, factors for evaluating management jobs would be quite different from those shown in Appendix IV, consisting perhaps of:

Judgment
Qualifications and experience
Extent of decision-making
Control of staff
Contacts with others.

These factors would probably be sub-divided.

13. The subjectivity of points rating. The justification for the points rating system of job evaluation is that it works, not that it is objective or scientific. There are several subjective elements in the method, some of course being found in any job evaluation system.

(a) The job specification may reflect the bias of the job analyst.

(b) The members of the job evaluation committee, although guided by detailed job specifications and carefully-described factors, still make subjective judgments about the worth of a job.

(*c*) The selection of factors is based originally on imitation or conjecture and confirmed by intuition.

(*d*) Weights are selected according to the same principles.

In spite of its subjective elements points rating usually provides acceptable and consistent results if job specifications are well prepared and the committee is thoroughly familiar with the system.

14. Other methods. There are other methods of job evaluation which will not be described because their use is not widespread; among them are factor comparison, the time span of discretion, and the Paterson method of decision-making analysis.

JOB EVALUATION AND PAY

15. Grading jobs. After evaluation has been completed by the ranking or points rating method the jobs appear in an order of value. They are then divided into groups or grades, the object being to allot to each grade a particular basic pay rate or pay-range. If the grading system of job evaluation is used this division will have been done already.

16. Grades and pay. In very many cases it is found that most jobs contained in any grade are already paid at about the same rate; the few jobs for which pay is inconsistent are then brought into line.

Occasionally a job appears to be in one grade by job evaluation but in a considerably higher grade according to its present pay. If after checking the job specification and evaluation this difference remains it is usual to regard the discrepancy as being due to temporary abnormal market conditions; employees in that job are shown in the company's pay records as receiving the pay for their grade plus a special allowance to bring their total remuneration to the market rate.

17. Pay surveys. Some companies regularly make comparisons between their own rates of pay and those paid by other companies for similar jobs, e.g. rates are compared for the copy-typists, foremen or accountants employed in those companies. These rates are then applied to pay grades. This procedure can be misleading because:

(*a*) pay is not the only reward from a job—some companies may have low rates of pay but a high reputation for security (*see* II, **25**);

(*b*) the jobs compared may in fact be similar only in title; the duties and responsibilities may be different;

(*c*) it is not logical for a company to evaluate its jobs systematically and then base its pay structure on the wages or salaries paid by a company which may have made no attempt to bring order into its remuneration system.

PROGRESS TEST 21

1. What are the purposes of job evaluation? (**2**)

2. Name the most important factors determining levels of pay. (**3**)

3. What do all methods of job evaluation require? (**6**)

4. Describe briefly the ranking and grading methods of job evaluation. (**8, 9**)

5. How are factors and weights chosen in the points rating method? (**12**)

6. How are the results of job evaluation expressed in monetary terms? (**16, 17**)

CHAPTER XXII

Wages and Salaries

WAGE STRUCTURES

1. Definition. A wage is the payment made to manual workers. It is nearly always expressed as a rate per hour.

2. Wage structures. The foundation of a manual worker's earnings is his basic time wage, which is sometimes fixed by job evaluation but is subject in most industries to minimum rates agreed in national collective bargaining (*see* **XXV**, **7**) or laid down by wages councils (*see* **XXV**, **12**). He is paid the hourly rate for every hour he attends work, though he is frequently fined for lateness by quartering, i.e. for being five minutes late he will lose a quarter of an hour's pay.

In addition to the basic rate he will often receive other payments, the most common examples of which are as follows.

(*a*) *Overtime pay* for any work done beyond normal hours. It is usually paid at premium rates, i.e. at time and a quarter, time and a half, double time, etc., the rate varying according to the time or the day on which the overtime is worked. (*See* also **XXIII**, **11**.)

(*b*) *Shift pay* for employees who work unusual or changing hours, to compensate them for inconvenience and hardship. The amount of shift pay varies in different industries, but seems to range from about 10 to 20 per cent of the basic rate. (*See* also **XXIII**, **12**.)

(*c*) *Special additions*, e.g. danger money, dirty money or wet money which are paid to the employee during abnormal working conditions. Since the circumstances which justify these additions are hard to define, many employers find it preferable to allow for these contingencies in the job evaluated basic rate rather than give special extra payments which are often difficult to take away again.

(*d*) *Merit or length of service additions* to employees either on the results of appraisal (*see* **XVIII**) or on completion of a certain period of service. Merit payments are not very popular with wage-earners, who feel they are influenced by prejudice and subjective judgments. Length of service payments have an approximate relationship with merit, encourage employees to stay with the company, and can be precisely defined.

(*e*) *Cost of living allowances* are given quite commonly in response to a rise in the general price level or to employees who work in high-cost areas, e.g. London. In many cases they are eventually consolidated into the basic wage.

(*f*) *Policy allowances* cover miscellaneous extra payments, like the addition to the job evaluated rate for temporarily scarce employees (*see* XXI, **16**).

(*g*) *Payments by results bonus*, i.e. an extra payment based on the output of the worker or of the group to which he belongs (*see* **3**).

In private industry, about 70 per cent of a manual worker's total earnings are on the average accounted for by his basic wage and about 30 per cent by a selection from the additional payments shown above.

Total earnings have increased at a faster rate than basic wages (a phenomenon known as wages drift) because the additional payments have become proportionately larger. It should be noted that they are decided entirely within the company, often at a fairly low level of management, and are not easily influenced by government action.

PAYMENT BY RESULTS

3. Principles of PBR. In nearly all methods of payment by results the employee receives a basic rate to which is added a variable payment based on output. For each job a standard is set expressed either as the quantity produced per unit of time or as the time taken to do the job; bonus becomes payable when the employee exceeds this standard.

If a company installs a PBR system for the first time it therefore needs to take the following steps.

(*a*) The scheme is communicated to the employees with perhaps some modifications after consultation with representatives. Supervisors and managers are trained in its use.

(*b*) A standard rate of output is set for each job by measuring the reasonable time taken to do it and making allowances for rest periods and personal needs. There are various methods of setting standards, from intuitive judgment to detailed analysis of bodily movements.

(c) Administrative arrangements are made to record each employee's output, calculate his bonus, and add it to his basic wage.

The cost of running a PBR scheme, including work study, clerical work and dealing with disputes arising out of it, can be considerable. Some schemes are also rather complicated to compute and difficult to understand because the bonus does not increase proportionately with output but at a faster or slower rate, e.g. the accelerating premium system and the Rowan system.

4. Advantages of PBR. A well-designed and well-maintained scheme will increase productivity from the same number of employees and the same equipment and thus reduce unit costs. The work study which it requires may well show more efficient methods of production, and the supervisor need not control his subordinates so closely because the monetary incentive makes human control unnecessary.

The popularity of PBR is shown by the fact that about 40 per cent of manual workers are paid by this method. To operate at its best, however, it requires a steady flow of measurable work, the pace of which is within the control of the worker.

5. Disadvantages of PBR. There has been a reaction against PBR in recent years because the advantages described above are sometimes outweighed by the following disadvantages.

(a) A PBR system is exceptionally liable to decay; new methods and materials, introduced gradually, may slowly cause a standard to become loose so that workers can earn high bonuses very easily.

(b) It is a constant source of shopfloor conflict, both when a new rate is being fixed and when a worker is asked to move from a job where the rate is loose to another where the rate is tight.

(c) Supervisors are tempted to show favouritism in allocating jobs when it is easy to earn bonus in some but difficult in others.

(d) It is difficult to reward fairly the labourers and skilled setters or maintenance workers whose output cannot be measured although their work influences the output of others. Such workers are usually paid a lieu bonus, based on the average bonus earned by the PBR workers.

(*e*) Salaried supervisors sometimes earn less than their subordinates who are paid by PBR.

(*f*) Output norms are frequently found. A group of employees decides that no one shall exceed a certain level of output, on penalty of unofficial sanctions, e.g. ostracism, hiding or spoiling tools, damage to clothing. Output is restricted because:

(*i*) loose rates are not so obvious;

(*ii*) employment is safeguarded;

(*iii*) by reducing discrepancies in performance, the unity of the group is maintained (*see* VII, **8**).

(*g*) Earnings can fluctuate because an employee is not given a steady supply of work; at certain times therefore he is not able to earn bonus.

(*h*) Quality and safety may be adversely affected.

6. Group bonus schemes. In some forms of PBR the standard is based on the performance of a group rather than an individual. The bonus earned by the group is shared among its members sometimes equally, sometimes in proportion to basic pay. The advantages of group bonus schemes are:

(*a*) they can include indirect workers, e.g. labourers or maintenance men;

(*b*) they improve team spirit;

(*c*) they encourage flexibility, because individuals are more willing to move to other jobs within the group;

(*d*) they simplify clerical work;

(*e*) they are particularly suitable for jobs which are carried out by a team of men of various levels of skill, e.g. electric cable jointing.

Group bonuses tend to be unsatisfactory when the group becomes large, when its members constantly change or when it contains a mixture of very fast and very slow workers.

7. Plant-wide PBR. Some companies have PBR schemes which are virtually group bonus systems extended to cover a whole plant, bonus being payable according to the extent by which factory output exceeds a given standard.

Two other schemes are used in this country, though not widely, which do not require output standards to be fixed by work study methods; these are the Scanlon and the Rucker plans, both of American origin.

(a) *The Scanlon plan* first requires the following ratio to be calculated:

Sales value of production: Total payroll

A bonus becomes payable when in any month that ratio is exceeded, i.e. when payroll costs as a proportion of production value have decreased. It therefore becomes the aim of everyone to increase production and decrease manpower costs, e.g. by reducing overtime or allowing numbers to run down. A network of suggestion committees puts up ideas to improve efficiency.

(b) *The Rucker Plan* is similar except that the ratio is:

$$\frac{\text{Sales value of production} - \text{Value of bought-in materials}}{\text{Total payroll}}$$

This meets the objection that under the Scanlon plan employees can receive a bonus because prices have been increased to cover the increased cost of raw materials and components.

Both schemes work best when market conditions are favourable; if the company cannot sell its products bonus will be reduced or will disappear. They may eventually decay, the suggestion committees losing their impetus, particularly if the management of the company loses enthusiasm.

8. Measured daywork. This system is sometimes introduced as a substitute for a decayed conventional PBR scheme. It has several variations, but essentially it offers the employee a fixed weekly wage in return for an undertaking to produce to an agreed level of performance. Since the company is committed to paying high wages it will do its utmost to provide the employees with a steady supply of work, the scheme thus encouraging managerial efficiency. The employee is more ready to move to other work temporarily or accept changes of method because he does not have to consider such questions as tight and loose rates. Industrial relations, it is claimed, also improve because there are fewer causes for dispute.

The scheme gives a more responsible role to the supervisor, who is expected to interview employees who do not reach their agreed performance to find out the reasons and rectify them if possible. Difficulties have sometimes been reported when a large number of employees all fail to reach the output standards they have previously agreed to.

Levels of pay often have to be fixed at quite a high level when measured daywork is introduced because they must take account of pay anomalies and previous high individual bonus earnings. Some companies which have adopted the scheme say that the heavy financial commitment is justified by the improved attitudes that are found in management and employees; others have found that their measured daywork schemes have not been successful and have reverted to conventional PBR, though often on a group rather than an individual basis.

WAGES LAW

9. The Truck Acts. In the nineteenth century some employers paid their men partly in goods or in vouchers which could only be used in company-owned shops. To overcome this and other abuses Truck Acts were passed in 1831, 1887 and 1896 which state that, as regards manual workers:

(*a*) wages shall be paid in cash, in full and without deductions;
(*b*) the employer may not stipulate how a worker may spend any part of his wages.

Certain deductions are allowed, however, for medical attention, rent, food cooked and eaten on the employer's premises, and fines for bad work (if these are levied in accordance with the agreed terms of employment). It is also legal for an employer to deduct sums from the wages of an employee (with his written agreement) in order to hand them to a third party, e.g. trade union subscriptions. Statutory deductions, e.g. income tax payments, need no written agreement.

The practical effect of these Acts is that an employer should be very careful before making deductions from a manual worker's wages. If he supplies overalls to his employees for purchase by instalments, he must set up an overall club, deduct the instalments and pay them (by a book entry) to the club. It is also illegal to hold back final payment of wages to a leaving employee until all company property, e.g. tools, has been returned. These Acts apply only to manual workers, not to salaried staff.

10. Payment of Wages Act 1960. Under this Act the Truck Acts are amended to some extent to allow manual workers to be paid by cheque, banker's credit, money order or postal order instead of cash, if the employee agrees in writing. If he is absent from his usual place of work through illness or travelling on company business he may be paid by postal order or money order without his consent being necessary.

SALARY STRUCTURES

11. Definition. A salary is a fixed periodical payment to a non-manual employee. It is usually expressed in annual terms, implying a relatively permanent employment relationship, though normally paid at monthly intervals. In many ways it resembles a retaining fee. Salaried workers are usually termed staff.

12. Characteristics of salaries. A salary differs from a wage in many respects, reflecting the different attitudes traditionally held by an employer towards his non-manual compared with his manual employees.

(*a*) A salary is usually all-inclusive; there are no additional payments of danger money or productivity bonus, for example.

(*b*) A salary is progressive, in most cases increasing annually, whereas a wage-earner reaches the standard rate for the job early in adult life and does not receive annual increases.

(*c*) A salary is often regarded as personal to the individual, but a wage is the sum paid to all workers at a particular job.

(*d*) A salary is often confidential, but there is no secret about a wage.

(*e*) In the private sector of employment, salaries are less likely than wages to be the subject of trade union negotiations.

13. Salary administration. There are three typical ways in which a company can administer its salaries.

(*a*) *Ad hoc*, in which there is no attempt at any kind of job evaluation to assess a fair level of salary for a job. Increases in salary are given erratically, often at the demand of the employee rather than at the initiative of the company. In a small company this method is workable, but in a large company it can produce an illogical and unfair salary structure which will cause discontent and jealousy. For obvious reasons salaries paid by this system are intended to be confidential.

(*b*) *Merit review*, usually found in medium and large companies in the private sector. After job evaluation, a salary range is attached to every staff job. Employees are appraised and given personal merit increases each year which will move their salaries at varying speeds through the range. In this way individual effort and merit are rewarded. It is customary for salaries under this system to be kept confidential; in most cases the employees do not know the maximum salary it is possible to earn in their jobs.

(c) *Incremental scale*, found above all in the public sector, e.g. the civil service, local government and nationalised boards, though its use appears to be increasing in the private sector. All staff jobs are evaluated and graded, the salary range appearing as, for example, £8000 × £200–£9,000 indicating that there is a standard increment of salary each year of £200. Most schemes permit a manager to award a double increment for exceptional merit or withhold an increment for unsatisfactory work or conduct, but as a rule the standard increment is given automatically. In this system long service and loyalty are encouraged by regular salary increases and merit by the speed of promotion to a higher grade. It is customary for salaries in the incremental system to be non-confidential.

NOTE: Salary increases under the *ad hoc* and merit review methods may be limited in times of national pay restraint, but the standard increases under the incremental scale method have generally been given.

OTHER PAY LEGISLATION

14. Equal Pay Act 1970. This Act requires employers to give equal treatment regarding terms and conditions of employment to men and women if:

(a) they are employed on like work; or

(b) they are employed on work of equal value, e.g. as measured by job evaluation.

If a man or woman claims that terms and conditions are less favourable, an approach may be made to an industrial tribunal which, if it finds the claim justified, may award arrears of pay not further back than two years, or damages where non-financial terms are the subject of the claim. The Sex Discrimination Act 1975 (*see* Appendix V) forbids discrimination on the grounds of sex in employment matters other than pay.

15. Maternity pay. Under the Employment Protection (Consolidation) Act 1978, a woman who has had at least six months' service with an employer must not be dismissed because of her pregnancy unless she is unfit to do her normal job and suitable alternative work cannot be found. If she has had at least two years' service with the company, has continued at work up to the eleventh week before the baby is due and has given her employer at least three weeks' written notice of absence, she will receive for the first six weeks of her absence maternity pay, i.e. nine-tenths of her normal pay less social security maternity allowance. The company may claim back the pay from the Maternity Pay Fund to which all employers contribute.

If the woman is qualified to receive maternity pay she also has the right to return to her former job (or a similar one) if she informs the employer in writing of her wish to return at least three weeks before stopping work and exercises this right within twenty-nine weeks after the baby's birth. She must also, if requested by her employer not later than forty-nine days after confinement, confirm in writing that she intends to return, and whether requested or not a further confirmation twenty-one days before she proposes to return. Complaints about these provisions may be made to an industrial tribunal.

16. Guarantee payments. The Employment Protection (Consolidation) Act 1978 also gives employees, who have been laid off or put on short time because of a shortage of work, the right to continue to receive pay for a limited period, i.e. for up to five days in any period of three months. The amount per day is a normal day's pay or £9.15, whichever is greater. Many employers have made agreements with their employees which provide for guarantee payments more favourable than this.

17. Suspension on medical grounds. An employee who is suspended under certain health and safety regulations because his health is endangered is entitled under the Employment Protection (Consolidation) Act 1978 to receive a normal week's pay for every week he is suspended up to a maximum of twenty-six weeks. He will lose his right to this pay if he unreasonably refuses to do any suitable alternative work that his employer offers him.

PROGRESS TEST 22

1. Name possible extra payments a manual worker may receive in addition to his basic wage. (**2**)

2. What must a company do when it introduces a payment by results scheme for the first time? (**3**)

3. What are the main advantages and disadvantages of PBR? (**4, 5**)

4. For what kinds of job is a group bonus scheme particularly suitable? (**6**)

5. Define measured daywork and state why it is sometimes introduced to replace PBR. **(8)**

6. Summarise the Truck Acts. **(9)**

7. How does a salary differ from a wage? **(1, 2, 11, 12)**

8. What is an incremental salary scale? **(13)**

9. Summarise the Equal Pay Act 1970. **(14)**

CHAPTER XXIII

Safety and Conditions of Employment

SAFETY

1. Accidents at work. The Robens Committee on Safety and Health at Work reported in July 1972 that every year in Great Britain about 1,000 people were killed and half a million injured at work. About 23 million working days were lost each year through accidents and disease. As the report said, the cost of accidents at work is enormous, both in human suffering and in lost production, and the management of every company should give special attention to improving safety.

2. Safety programmes. As the concept of accident proneness is now largely discredited (*see* VI, **5–6**), safety programmes concentrate as far as possible on ensuring that the employee is suitable for his job and that he works in a safe environment. The following are often included in a safety programme.

(*a*) *Thorough investigation of all accidents*, to try to prevent the same accident occurring again. Therefore a system of reporting all accidents is required; in some companies near misses as well as actual accidents have to be reported.

(*b*) *Continuous review of accident prevention measures*, bringing them up to date particularly when there is a change in process or materials, and ensuring that machines are guarded, gangways kept clear, electrical equipment insulated, etc.

(*c*) *Careful selection of new employees* to eliminate those who are physically or mentally unsuitable.

(*d*) *Training which includes safety as an integral part* rather than as an afterthought.

(*e*) *Safety devices and clothing* which are acceptable to employees; if they hinder the performance of the job or make the wearer feel clumsy and conspicuous, they will not be worn. For example, female employees who object to goggles will often wear safety spectacles quite willingly.

(*f*) *Consideration of the possible effect of PBR schemes on safety*. If workers frequently remove safety guards or adopt dangerous practices in order to earn high bonuses it may be necessary to abandon PBR and pay time rates only if the company can find no way of making the process completely safe.

(*g*) *Propaganda campaigns*, e.g. posters, safety suggestion weeks, etc., are sometimes used, but there is general agreement that their effects are short-lived.

(*h*) *Provision of adequate first-aid and medical services* to mitigate the effects of any accidents which occur.

3. Safety officers. In 1969 a government report stated that one factory in eight employed a safety officer to carry out a safety programme similar to that described above. Safety officers are compulsory on construction sites above a certain size.

The effectiveness of a safety officer depends on the following:

(*a*) the speed and completeness of the accident reporting system;

(*b*) his relations with shopfloor workers and supervisors;

(*c*) his technical knowledge and training;

(*d*) above all, the extent to which he is supported by, and can influence, the senior management of the company.

4. Law regarding safety. The Health and Safety at Work, etc., Act 1974 covers not only all people at work (except domestic workers in private employment) but also the general public who might be affected by the work of others. It is mainly an enabling measure, laying down general principles of safety and providing the power to make detailed safety regulations. For the time being the previously existing safety legislation continue in force, in particular the Factories Act 1961 and the Offices, Shops and Railway Premises Act 1963 (*see* **7**).

The most important general duties laid down by the 1974 Act are as follows.

(*a*) Employers must maintain safe plant, safe systems of work and safe premises. They must also ensure adequate training and supervision in safety matters.

(*b*) A written company safety policy must be prepared and made known to all employees. Employers must let employees know the arrangements for putting that policy into effect.

(*c*) A company must be conducted in such a way that the health and safety of persons not in employment there are not affected.

(*d*) Manufacturers and suppliers of articles for use at work must ensure that they are safe when properly used.

(*e*) Employees have a duty to take reasonable care to avoid injury to themselves or to others, and they must co-operate with employers in meeting statutory requirements.

(*f*) Safety representatives from among the employees may be appointed by recognised trade unions. They must be consulted by the employer on health and safety matters, they may inspect the employer's premises, and they have the right to be informed by the safety inspectors of any matters found to affect health and safety. If at least two safety representatives require it, the employer must set up a safety committee.

NOTE: The Health and Safety Commission recommend that in companies where trade unions are not recognised, a safety committee should nevertheless be set up consisting of members drawn from management and employees. The employee representatives on such a committee would not have the rights of inspection and information described above.

5. The Health and Safety Commission. This was set up under the Act to develop health and safety policies. It consists of representatives of employers, employees, local government and appropriate professional bodies. The Commission's policies are operated by the Health and Safety Executive, which enforces the relevant legislation and inspects premises. The separate inspectorates, which previously existed under various safety acts, are now combined in one body under the Executive.

6. Enforcement. If an inspector discovers a contravention of the Act, one of the previous acts or a safety regulation he may do one of the following.

(*a*) *Issue a prohibition notice*, requiring the employer to stop a process which carries the risk of serious personal injury until remedial action has been taken.

(*b*) *Issue an improvement notice*, requiring the employer who contravenes a statutory provision to remedy matters within a certain time. Appeals against an improvement notice or a prohibition notice may be made to an industrial tribunal.

(*c*) *Seize, render harmless or destroy* any substance or article that he considers a cause of imminent danger or serious personal injury.

(*d*) *Prosecute* any person contravening a relevant statutory provision, in addition to or instead of serving a notice as in (*a*) and (*b*) above. For most offences the maximum fine is £1,000, but serious cases may be prosecuted on indictment in the Crown Court, with the possibility of an unlimited fine or imprisonment for up to two years. The powers given under the Act to prosecute a person rather than a company apply not only to a director or manager but also to any employee who does not co-operate in safety matters either for his own or for his colleagues' protection.

7. Previous legislation. The Factories Act 1961 and the Offices, Shops and Railway Premises Act 1963, the provisions of which together cover about 16½ million employees, still continue, except that they are enforced in the manner described in **6**. The table below compares the Acts.

Factories Act	Offices Act
Premises must be kept clean; walls washed and painted at prescribed intervals	Similar
400 cu. ft of space for each person employed, not counting space more than 14ft from floor	40 sq. ft floor space per person except where ceiling is lower than 10 ft
Temperature not less than 60°F after first hour—thermometers to be available	60·8°F (16°C)
Adequate ventilation and lighting	Similar
Separate conveniences for each sex	Similar
No one to lift excessive weights	Similar
Accidents causing death or more than three days absence to be notified to safety inspector	Similar
Machines to be guarded	Similar
Young persons not to work on any dangerous machines unless they have been trained	Similar, but applies to *all* persons
Hoists and lifts to be properly maintained, and also inspected every six months by a competent person	Not mentioned

Stairs and gangways to be soundly constructed and kept clear of obstructions	Similar
Fire escapes and fire alarms to be provided and certified satisfactory by fire authority. Fire fighting equipment to be provided	Similar
Drinking water, washing facilities and seats to be provided	Similar
Accommodation for clothing to be provided, with arrangements for drying	Similar
First aid box for each 150 employees, in the charge of a qualified person	Similar
Before beginning to use premises as a factory, inspector must be notified	Similar; usually notify local authority

Women and young persons:

Hours not earlier than 7 a.m. or later than 8 p.m.	Not mentioned
Maximum daily hours: 9 for 6-day or 10 for 5-day week	Not mentioned
Maximum weekly hours—48 (44 if under 16)	Not mentioned
Max. continuous spell of work—$4\frac{1}{2}$ hours	Not mentioned
Work beyond permitted 48 hours only with previous agreement of safety inspector	Not mentioned
Shift work (between 6 a.m. and 10 p.m., each shift not longer than 8 hours) allowed if a majority of workers have consented by secret ballot.	Not mentioned

To meet exceptional production requirements in a factory, an employer may ask for the restrictions on working hours for women and young persons to be relaxed. If he can show that adequate supervision and welfare arrangements will be provided, exemption may be given for not more than one year.

8. Compensation for accidents at work. An injured employee who considers his injury to be due to the negligence of his employer may bring an action for damages against him under common law. The employer is also held liable for accidents caused to his employees by the action of other employees, provided that this behaviour was in the course of their employment. If the employee's action is successful he will be awarded a lump sum depending mainly on the severity of the injury. The Employers Liability (Compulsory Insurance) Act 1969 requires employers to take out insurance against such claims.

Legal actions of this kind are independent of any action a health and safety inspector may bring against the employer, though of course if the inspector has taken action as in **6**, the claimant's case will be greatly strengthened.

WORKING CONDITIONS

9. The working environment. The principal requirements for a reasonable working environment were described in VI. Minimum standards covering space, lighting, heating, hygiene and ventilation are laid down in the Factories Act and the Offices, Shops and Railway Premises Act (*see* **7**).

10. Hours of work. Manual workers in most companies work longer hours than non-manual workers, partly because they are expected by custom to start earlier in the morning and partly because they do more overtime. Statistics published by the Department of Employment show that on average, male manual employees work about seven hours a week longer than male non-manual, and female manual employees about three hours a week more than female non-manual.

The hours worked by women and young persons in factories are closely regulated by the Factories Act (*see* **7**) but similar restrictions are not included in the Offices Act. The hours of work of male adult employees are regulated in only a few occupations, e.g. coalminers and lorry drivers.

11. Overtime. A company asks its employees to work overtime for the following reasons:

(*a*) to maintain production when there is a shortage of labour;

(*b*) to increase production temporarily or seasonally without increasing the number of employees;

(*c*) to enable maintenance to be carried out on plant and equipment while its users are not working.

Therefore, when properly managed, overtime can add considerably to the efficiency of the company. Research shows, however, that much overtime is worked not in response to one of the above needs but as a means of supplementing employees' incomes. It then becomes an inefficient practice because factory services have to be maintained beyond normal working hours for no gain in production.

Some companies have reduced or abolished overtime by negotiating with their employees a higher basic rate of pay so that earnings without overtime become approximately the same as total earnings were previously. A salaried worker is often not paid for overtime; when he is, the rate is usually plain time or a very low premium rate.

12. Shift work. During the last thirty years, no doubt because expensive capital equipment now being used must be continuously operated to cover its costs, there has been a steady increase in shift work, i.e. an arrangement in which one set of workers takes over from another to enable the production process to continue operating without a break.

It takes the form either of "double day shifts" in which there are two successive shifts but no night shift, or three shift working, in which the process continues for the twenty-four hours without a break.

Three shift working can bring the following problems.

(*a*) Supervisors require special training because management is not there to support them outside normal working hours.

(*b*) An incoming shift frequently blames an outgoing shift for bad work, an untidy workplace, etc.

(*c*) Canteens, first aid and security services must be provided.

(*d*) Machinery may break down more frequently because it is in constant use.

(*e*) Travelling to and from work by public transport is often difficult at shift change-over times.

13. Flexible working hours. A comparatively new development, sometimes called flextime or flexitime, allows employees to choose within limits what hours they work. Schemes differ in detail, but they frequently contain the following features.

(*a*) Employees must all be present during a certain part of the day, usually called coretime, e.g. from 10 a.m. to 12 noon and from 2 p.m. to 4 p.m.

(*b*) They may choose when they arrive or leave within limits set by the company, e.g. not before 8 a.m. or after 7 p.m.

(*c*) They may vary the length of the lunch break.

(*d*) Hours worked in excess of the standard total for the accounting period (usually a month) may be taken in whole or half-day holidays.

The advantages claimed for the system are that it improves employee satisfaction by giving considerable freedom for individuals to arrange their hours to suit their own circumstances, that it reduces absenteeism and that it enables the place of work to be manned outside the usual hours. On the other hand, lighting and heating will cost more, and those employees who attend early or late may not be able to work normally because other people on whom they depend are not there.

FRINGE BENEFITS

14. Definition. A fringe benefit is a reward to an employee apart from a wage or salary. It usually provides, at the expense of the employer, goods or services which the employee would otherwise have to pay for himself. The most important fringe benefits are described below.

15. Company pension schemes. The development of company (or occupational) pension schemes in this country has three main characteristics.

(*a*) Far more non-manual workers are covered than manual.

(*b*) Individual schemes vary widely in their contributions, conditions and benefits, manual workers' schemes in general being inferior to those for non-manual workers.

(*c*) On leaving one company and joining another it is difficult to transfer pension benefits to the new employment.

Under the Social Security Pensions Act 1975 it is hoped that these problems will become less serious. A much improved State pension scheme (effective from April 1978) provides benefits which will be adjusted to allow for inflation. Companies are allowed to contract out of part of the State scheme if their own schemes are comparable or superior, in particular if they provide a pension of at least one-eightieth of pensionable salary for each year of service, have pensionable ages of sixty-five for men and sixty for women, and preserve the pensions of employees with at least five years' service who leave their employment.

16. Sick pay. Most non-manual workers receive payment from their employers when they are absent from work through illness; a lower proportion of manual workers do so. In most cases the benefits provided by sick pay schemes for non-manual workers are superior to those for manual workers. There seems to be no difference in the amount of sickness absence between employees who are covered by a sick pay scheme and those who are not.

Employers' sick pay schemes are, of course, additional to the sickness benefits provided by the state.

17. Subsidised meals. A very large number of companies either provide meals on their premises at less than cost price or give their employees vouchers for full or part payment of meals in restaurants.

18. Company goods at a discount. Employees of companies which are either manufacturers or traders often have the opportunity to buy goods at reduced prices. A similar practice is the reduction in fares offered to their employees by railways and airlines.

19. Company cars. The use of a car is necessary in some jobs, e.g. sales representative, and when the company, as it often does, allows the employee to use the car for private purposes it adds considerably to the employee's real income, even though it is subject to income tax. The value and prestige of having a company car makes this fringe benefit probably the most highly prized of all.

20. Characteristics of fringe benefits. The following are the most important characteristics of fringe benefits.

(*a*) They are not related to merit but they often improve with status and length of service.

(*b*) They do not necessarily benefit all employees, e.g. the man who has good health or does not need company products.

(*c*) They are not established or amended after rational analysis but follow fashion or moral principles.

(*d*) They are not universal; large companies usually have a wide range of benefits while small companies tend to have very few.

(*e*) Once established they are difficult to abolish and become accepted by the employees as a normal condition of service rather than a benefit.

(*f*) There is no evidence that candidates are attracted to a company by its fringe benefits, but it is possible that fringe benefits discourage employees from leaving.

(*g*) They probably increase job satisfaction, but will certainly bring about dissatisfaction if they are inconsistently and carelessly administered, giving rise to accusations of favouritism, unfairness or meanness.

STAFF STATUS FOR MANUAL WORKERS

21. Equalising status. In recent years some companies have begun to employ manual workers on the same conditions of service as non-manual, showing that they regard them as having the same status. The most important effects on manual workers' conditions are as follows.

(*a*) Fringe benefits, particularly pensions and sick pay, are improved.

(*b*) Hours of work are shortened.

(*c*) Control becomes less strict; for example, manual workers are no longer required to clock on.

(*d*) A salary is paid instead of a wage, though often the employees prefer it to be paid weekly rather than monthly.

(*e*) Overtime is paid at a lower rate; the natural resistance to this change is often dealt with by a simultaneous productivity agreement which abolishes or greatly reduces the amount of overtime worked (*see* **11**).

22. Benefits. The following reasons are often given for equalising status.

(*a*) In many companies improvements in work methods have made the boundary between manual and non-manual employees much less distinct.

(*b*) Staff status will reduce labour turnover among manual workers.

(*c*) Jealousies between manual and non-manual workers will be reduced.

(*d*) Industrial relations within the company will be improved.

The last three reasons are hopes rather than certainties because deep-rooted attitudes cannot change rapidly. A much more important reason is the belief that it is morally wrong and logically indefensible to treat manual workers in an inferior way.

SUGGESTIONS

23. Procedure. Many companies have formal arrangements to encourage their employees to submit suggestions regarding efficiency, safety or welfare. It is usual to have a committee consisting of representatives of managers and employees to assess the suggestions and recommend whether they should be adopted, perhaps after taking expert advice. The originator of a successful suggestion receives an award.

24. Benefits of suggestion schemes.

(*a*) The company may be able to use more efficient methods.

(*b*) There may be fewer accidents.

(*c*) New uses may be found for scrap.

(*d*) Two-way communication is encouraged.

(*e*) Use is made of the employees' ingenuity and creativity.

(*f*) The recognition of these qualities will give the employees greater job satisfaction.

25. Problems of suggestion schemes. Interest in a suggestion scheme will flag unless the management of the company actively encourages it. Steps which may be taken are:

(*a*) publicity for every successful suggestion, perhaps with a circulated description and photograph of the formal presentation of the award;

(*b*) occasional suggestion campaigns asking for ideas to solve specific problems;

(*c*) generous awards, e.g. 25 per cent of annual savings;

(*d*) careful treatment of unsuccessful suggestors, i.e. full explanations of the reasons for rejection;

(*e*) a scrupulously fair procedure for assessing suggestions;

(*f*) a convenient channel through which suggestions can be submitted, e.g. a suggestions box.

Maintaining a lively suggestion scheme is expensive in time and money but many companies have found that the ideas which have come forward bring financial benefits which outweigh the expense many times.

JUSTICE

26. The importance of justice. Personnel policies and procedures designed to utilise, motivate and protect the human resources of a company will fail unless they are perceived by the employees to be just and fair in themselves and applied in a just and fair way. Justice in this context will provide:

(*a*) similar treatment to employees in similar circumstances;

(*b*) greater rewards to those who merit them or are particularly deserving;

(*c*) the opportunity to express an opinion which management will consider and possibly act on.

Job satisfaction is reduced and industrial relations deteriorate when employees perceive injustice and unfairness in company personnel policies and the way in which they are applied.

27. Fair procedures. Injustice will be minimised if the following conditions are observed.

(*a*) Job and personnel specifications are accurate and unbiased; performance standards, if set, are reasonable.

(*b*) New employees are not engaged at rates of pay higher than those received by present employees doing the same work, or offered exceptional privileges.

(*c*) Promotion, transfer, demotion and retirement policies are open and uniformly applied.

(*d*) Dismissal procedures (including those for redundancy) are clearly defined and if possible negotiated with employee representatives.

(*e*) Appraisal schemes give the employee the opportunity to discuss his progress with his manager.

(*f*) Selection for training is regarded as a reward rather than a punishment.

(*g*) Rates of pay are appropriate to the job and to the individual employee, i.e. they are based on job evaluation, with recognition to the individual by means of a well-maintained payment by results scheme, merit rating or length of service increments.

(*h*) Fringe benefits and working conditions are applied uniformly.

(*i*) Communications are two-way in all appropriate circumstances and participation is used where practicable.

(*j*) Disciplinary procedures are carefully applied, beginning with the disciplinary interview (*see* V, **16–17**). There are warnings and provisions for appeal, and penalties are not disproportionate to the offence or capriciously applied. The code of practice published by the Advisory, Conciliation and Arbitration Service gives useful guidance here.

Disparities between departments in the treatment of e.g. time-keeping, pay increases or leave of absence cause great resentment. Departmental managers have the difficult task of dealing with their subordinates in ways consistent with those elsewhere in the company yet responsive to the circumstances of individuals.

PROGRESS TEST 23

1. Outline a safety programme suitable for a manufacturing company. (**2**)

2. What duties regarding safety does an employer have under the Health and Safety at Work, etc., Act? (**4**)

3. What are the main similarities and differences between the Factories Act and the Offices Act? (**7**)

4. Name the benefits of overtime working to an employer. (**11**)

5. What problems are found in three shift working? (**12**)

6. Name the most important fringe benefits. (**14–19**)

7. In what ways do fringe benefits differ from wages and salaries? (**20**)

8. What benefits does a company hope to obtain from giving staff status to its manual workers? (**21–22**)

9. What are the benefits of suggestion schemes? (**24**)

10. Give some examples of the importance of justice in personnel procedures. (**26, 27**)

CHAPTER XXIV

Personnel Records and Statistics

PERSONNEL RECORDS

1. Purposes. Personnel records provide the following.

(*a*) A store of up-to-date and accurate information about the company's employees.

(*b*) A guide to the action to be taken regarding an employee, particularly by comparing him with other employees.

(*c*) A guide when recruiting a new employee, e.g. by showing the rates of pay received by comparable employees.

(*d*) A historical record of previous action taken regarding employees.

(*e*) The raw material for statistics which check and guide personnel policies.

(*f*) The means to comply with certain statutory requirements, e.g. the Contracts of Employment Act 1972 and the Redundancy Payments Act 1965.

2. Documents. An employee's personnel record begins with the application form which he completes when applying for a job (*see* XIV, **14**). To this is added the copy of the letter formally offering the job and the employee's acceptance. These papers are usually put into an envelope or folder which becomes the *personal file*. From time to time other documents are put into the personal file, e.g. appraisal reports, applications for promotion, sickness certificates, etc.

A summary of the information in the personal file is made on an *employee record*, which is set out in such a way that it is easily read and compared with other employee records. It is usually filed departmentally, unlike personal files, which are filed alphabetically.

3. The employee record. The essential details to be included in the employee record are as follows.

(*a*) Personal data:

(*i*) name, address and telephone number;

(ii) clock or company number (if any);

(iii) sex;

(iv) date of birth;

(v) marital status;

(vi) disablement registration number (if any).

(b) Company data:

    (i) date of joining company;

    (ii) past and present departments and dates;

    (iii) past and present job titles;

    (iv) past and present wage or salary;

    (v) reasons for changes;

    (vi) absence record;

    (vii) accident record;

    (viii) hours of work;

    (ix) holiday entitlement;

    (x) retirement date and pension scheme membership;

    (xi) disciplinary warnings.

(c) Qualifications and skills:

    (i) formal education;

    (ii) qualifications;

    (iii) training record;

    (iv) appraisals.

(d) On leaving the company:

    (i) date of leaving and reason;

    (ii) name of new employer (if known);

    (iii) suitability for re-employment.

Once included in the employee record, any information must be kept up to date, which in many cases is a considerable clerical task. Therefore before adding new items it is important to consider how often the information would be used, whether it could be obtained quickly from some other source, how easy it is to keep up to date and whether there is room to show it.

4. Manual employee records. In most companies employee records are kept in card indexes or loose-leaf binders. Many proprietary systems are available which provide quick identification of particular types of employees, e.g. the registered disabled, by attaching coloured signals to their records and are successful in showing all the information listed in **3** in quite a small space. In most circumstances manual records are quite satisfactory, being flexible, quickly amended, convenient and comparatively cheap.

5. Hand-punched cards. Some employee record systems on the market consist of cards which may be punched manually in certain places thus enabling various categories of employees to be quickly separated from the rest. These systems can be very useful for companies which have employees of many different kinds, e.g. occupations, locations, qualifications, etc., and wish to identify them easily and frequently. They also facilitate statistical analysis such as might be required in manpower planning.

It is unfortunately not possible for cards of this type to be filed in an overlapping arrangement to provide a visible index, an advantage which is nearly always found in the proprietary systems described in **4**.

6. Computer records. A computer can store many times more information than a card index system. It has the following advantages.

(*a*) In a modern system, information is immediately available either on a visual display unit or a printer.

(*b*) Lists of employees can be quickly produced according to a desired category, e.g. all over age sixty or disabled persons.

(*c*) Summaries, e.g. the number of employees in each category, and employee statistics can easily be produced.

(*d*) Ready-made programs may be purchased and personnel staff can easily be trained to interrogate the computer or insert new and changed information.

STATISTICS

7. Essential statistics. The following are the statistics which are essential.

(*a*) Statistics required by official bodies, e.g. Department of Employment.

(*b*) Total number of employees, subdivided as far as possible into departments, geographical location, age groups, male or female, etc., and showing the gain or loss over the previous period.

(*c*) Number of accidents reported to the health and safety inspector, analysed by department and cause.

(*d*) Labour turnover and stability rates (*see* XVII, **2**).

(*e*) Days lost through absence (expressed as a percentage of the total number of working days during the period) and the number of spells of sickness, both analysed departmentally.

These statistics are usually compiled at monthly intervals.

8. Optional statistics. The following provide useful information for management, but are not so necessary as those listed above.

(*a*) Numbers of employees in various wage or salary grades. It is not essential to compile these at monthly intervals but it is common practice to do so annually when remuneration is reviewed. Pay statistics are sometimes needed for a special purpose, e.g. if a trade union makes a claim for a wage increase.

(*b*) The accident frequency rate, a statistic which enables comparisons to be made between different companies and includes accidents which do not need to be reported to the health and safety inspector in the belief that every minor accident is potentially serious. The formula is:

$$\frac{\text{Number of lost-time accidents} \times 100,000}{\text{Total man-hours worked}}$$

A lost-time accident is one which causes absence on the day or shift following that on which the accident occurred. As a man works approximately 100,000 hours during his working life, the ratio expresses the number of accidents an employee would have, on average, during his working life if present trends are continued. It is usually found to be between two and three, and is calculated monthly, quarterly or annually. In order to obtain an indication of the industrial accident situation throughout the country, the Department of Employment collects the accident frequency rates of a number of representative companies.

(*c*) The figures described in XIV, **24** show efficiency in recruitment and selection.

(*d*) For manpower planning purposes, an analysis of employees by skill, training, place of residence, etc. If redundancy is expected, an analysis by length of service.

All personnel statistics carry much more weight if they are accompanied by a report which describes and explains them, and perhaps suggests future action.

PROGRESS TEST 24

1. What is contained in the personnel file? (**2**)
2. List the information which should appear in the employee record. (**3**)

3. What are the advantages of keeping employee records on a computer? **(6)**

4. Name the most important statistics relevant to personnel work. **(7)**

CHAPTER XXV

Industrial Relations

UNIONS AND EMPLOYERS

1. Trade unions. In 1981 there were 463 trade unions on the list held by the Certification Officer (*see* **20**), with a total membership of about 12,636,000—nearly half the working population.

Unions range from the very large, with a membership of over a million, to the small associations of fewer than a hundred members. In recent years amalgamations of unions have made the total number smaller and the average size larger. The twenty-five unions which each had a membership of over 100,000 together accounted for 81 per cent of the total trade union membership in 1981.

In a typical union a member is attached to a branch, usually in the nearest large town, which elects representatives to a district or regional committee. A national committee is elected to implement the policy of the union. There are permanent employees at district or regional level (called organisers or officers) and at headquarters (the general secretary and administrative, statistical and legal staff). The policy of the union is intended to be an expression of the views of its members rather than the decisions of its national committee or general secretary; it is a democratic rather than an authoritarian organisation, in contrast to a company.

Because a union caters for a particular type of worker, usually in a certain group of occupations, and a company includes workers of many different kinds, it is quite common for more than one union to be represented in a company. About 80 per cent of trade unionists work in multi-union companies.

2. Reasons for joining trade unions. An employee joins a union for the following reasons:

(*a*) to try to improve his working conditions;

(*b*) to gain some control over his working environment;

(*c*) in some cases, because of pressure from present union members or because a union membership agreement is in force (*see* **21**). He is less likely to join a union if he is an isolated worker, if he feels his status is high, or if he has a conscientious or religious objection.

3. Effects of unions on management. When a substantial number of its employees are members of trade unions the effects on the management of a company are that:

(*a*) decisions and policies are subject to challenge and negotiation;

(*b*) management powers are limited, and they may be used more cautiously;

(*c*) decision making may become centralised so that a unified company industrial relations policy can be formulated and practised;

(*d*) the management may be required to give certain information about the company to union representatives (*see* **24**).

The main subject-matter of industrial relations has traditionally been working conditions, especially pay, but in recent years it has grown to cover practically all the personnel management practices dealt with in XII to XXIII.

4. Trades Union Congress. The TUC is a voluntary association of over 100 unions, representing in all about $11\frac{1}{2}$ million workers. The unions which are not members are mostly very small. Its policy is decided by its constituent unions at the annual congress, usually lasting a week, when debates on industrial relations matters take place and the general council of thirty-eight members is elected.

The TUC has very few powers over its constituent unions, its chief functions being:

(*a*) to agree and express a policy for the trade union movement;

(*b*) to promote legislation to protect and benefit its members;

(*c*) to be consulted by the government;

(*d*) to deal with inter-union disputes.

5. Employers' associations. Employers within a certain industry usually form an association, partly for trade and information purposes and partly to negotiate on industrial relations matters for the industry. Some large companies prefer to remain outside the association for their industry while others, like the gas and electricity boards, cover the whole of their respective industries.

6. Confederation of British Industry. The CBI is in many ways the counterpart of the TUC, being a voluntary confederation of employers' associations. It was formed in 1965 by an amalgamation of some existing employers' federations. Unlike the TUC it deals with other matters besides industrial relations as its general purpose is to promote the prosperity of British industry.

COLLECTIVE BARGAINING

The system whereby an employee's terms of employment are settled, not by individual negotiation, but by agreements reached between representatives which apply equally to many employees, is called collective bargaining. In this country it is generally carried out at two levels, national and workplace.

7. National agreements. At national level, an employers' association negotiates with the trade unions which have members in the industry, sometimes forming a permanent body, meeting regularly, called a national joint industrial council. An agreement is made for the industry, confined often to the following basic terms of employment:

(a) minimum rates of pay for various categories of employee, often defined very loosely, e.g. semi-skilled;

(b) maximum length of the standard working week;

(c) overtime premium rate;

(d) minimum length of paid holiday.

A national agreement which included in detail a wide range of employment conditions would not be practicable in most industries because of the many differences in technology, size, profitability, etc., that are found among individual employers. The typical national agreement is therefore expressed in outline terms only and is intended to be supplemented by a further stage of bargaining at the workplace to determine the detailed application of the agreement to that particular company. The main functions of national agreements are to guarantee the employee minimum standards and to protect employers from competitors who might otherwise cut prices because they paid low wages.

National collective bargaining is sometimes restricted by government policies of pay restraint, which are either imposed by law or agreed with the TUC and CBI and then observed voluntarily by unions and employers. They usually contain an instruction or a pledge that pay increases shall be limited either to a fixed amount or to a certain percentage of present pay. There may also be a further restriction on the interval between pay claims, e.g. that not more than one increase shall be negotiated in a twelve-month period. Improvements in fringe benefits as a substitute for pay increases are not allowed, but employers are permitted to exceed the standard increases if they have concluded with their employees a self-financing productivity agreement through which improved methods of work (often including the abolition of restrictive practices) can be shown to produce savings at least as great as the total increased expenditure on pay.

8. Workplace agreements. The way in which national agreements are interpreted at company level depends partly on custom and practice, e.g. what categories of employees are to be regarded as skilled or semi-skilled, and partly on negotiations between managers and trade union representatives. In some cases the unions are represented by their full-time district officers, but often the management negotiates with the shop stewards, i.e. employees of the company who have been elected by groups of union members at the place of work to be their representatives and spokesmen.

The position of the shop steward is somewhat anomalous; though given little formal authority by his union constitution in fact he negotiates and concludes agreements on a wide range of subjects with his union's connivance. The reasons for his importance in industrial relations are as follows.

(*a*) He is immediately available, unlike the full-time officer, who is generally overworked.

(*b*) He knows the background of the company thoroughly, especially its payment system.

(*c*) As the elected representative of the employees, he is likely to express their point of view. Any agreement concluded with him will probably be accepted by his members and not repudiated.

(*d*) He is the channel of communication between the members and the union, since very few of them attend branch meetings.

(*e*) He is the appropriate person to express the employees' growing wish to participate in decisions about their work.

(*f*) Managers prefer to deal with someone they know and employ.

If authorised by his union, the shop steward will be the representative to whom the employer must disclose information under the provisions of the Employment Protection Act 1975 (*see* **24**).

DISPUTES PROCEDURES

9. National procedures. Besides making agreements about conditions of employment (*see* **7**) employers' associations and trade unions also negotiate a programme or procedure to be followed in an industry for settling a dispute at a place of work without resort to industrial action such as a strike. Procedures differ in detail, but the following is fairly typical.

(*a*) The aggrieved employee asks his shop steward or district officer to take up his case with the middle management of the company.

(*b*) Meeting between the district officer and senior management.

(*c*) Meeting between union officials and the regional committee of the employers' association.

(*d*) Meeting between national officials of the trade union and of the employers' association.

(*e*) In some industries, an independent arbitrator gives a final decision which both sides have agreed in advance to accept, although it is not legally binding.

Each stage of the procedure is used until agreement is reached; if the dispute is settled at stage (*b*), for example, the subsequent stages will not be used. The procedural agreement states that no industrial action shall take place until all stages have been used.

At present it is not generally the wish of either employers or unions that disputes procedures or the decisions which are reached from them shall be legally enforceable (*see* **24**).

10. Comments on national procedures. There are great variations in the effectiveness of national procedures. Some work quickly and appear to be respected by both sides. Others are slow, and are sometimes not used or only partly used.

In the later stages of a typical procedure the negotiators become more and more remote from the actual place where the dispute originated. It has been suggested that in order to reduce the large number of strikes which occur in defiance of national procedures, more attention should be paid to improving disputes procedures at the place of work.

11. Workplace procedures. In recent years the growing complexity of payment systems, the increasing rate of technical change and the wish of employees to take some share in decisions regarding their working conditions have led to more conflict between management and employees, sometimes expressed in industrial action.

For reasons described in **8** the shop steward is prominent in raising these matters and in negotiations to settle them. Sometimes an informal procedure for dealing locally with disputes is evolved between the management and the shop stewards, with the intention of using the official procedure only as a last resort. If in these negotiations a shop steward wishes to put pressure on management he has the following sanctions at his disposal.

(*a*) *Withdrawal of co-operation*, for example he will no longer help in solving disciplinary problems or interpreting national agreements.

(*b*) *Insistence on formal rights*, for example he may insist on raising with management grievances that he would normally consider too trivial to mention, or he may bring back strict demarcation between crafts.

(*c*) *Restrictions on output or overtime working*. He will organise a go-slow in which employees without breaking any terms of the employment contract reduce output by time-wasting methods, unnecessary journeys to stores, etc. They may also refuse to work overtime, or work it only on their own terms, a particularly useful tactic if the company relies on overtime working to meet its production and delivery commitments.

(*d*) *Withdrawal of labour*, quite frequently only for a few hours as a demonstration of solidarity or as a sign of impatience with the slow pace of negotiations. A strike called by a shop steward on his own authority is an unofficial strike because it has not been considered and authorised by his union. It is very unusual for a union to call an official strike unless a dispute remains unresolved after going through the complete national procedure or an employer is considered to have broken an agreement.

The sanctions at the disposal of a shop steward have their counterparts in possible action by the employer, who can also withdraw co-operation, insist on formal procedures being observed, refuse to allow employees to work overtime when they need it to augment their basic pay, or lock them out. These sanctions are seldom used by an employer, who relies instead on his power to refuse all or part of the demands made by the employees.

STATUTORY REGULATION OF WAGES
AND CONDITIONS

12. Wages councils. Under the Wages Councils Act 1959 (which succeeded earlier Acts of the same kind) and the Employment Protection Act 1975, statutory arrangements have been made to fix basic employment conditions for industries in which most individual places of work are too small and scattered for trade unions to become established. Examples of such industries are hairdressing, catering and retail distribution. About forty industries of this kind, including about 3 million employees, have wages councils comprising equal numbers of employer and employee representatives, with three independent members, one of whom is the chairman.

From time to time each council meets to consider a revision of the terms and conditions of employment in its industry. The proposed new terms are published, and after an interval during which any objections can be considered, the proposals (possibly amended) become legally enforceable. The council may also fix the date from which the change in the terms shall operate.

Wages inspectors, who have extensive powers of entry, search and interrogation, visit the premises of employers in wages council industries to check that they provide terms and conditions at least as good as those specified. An inspector may prosecute any employer who fails to do so, and a court may fine the employer and order him to compensate the employees affected.

13. Future developments. Government policy is to abolish wages councils where possible and encourage voluntary collective bargaining in their place. The Employment Protection Act 1975 lays down a two-stage procedure for this purpose.

(a) On application from either the unions or the employers in an industry, the Secretary of State for Employment may make an order converting a wages council into a statutory joint industrial council. This will have equal numbers of union and employers' association representatives but no independent members, and will have the same powers as the former wages council.

(b) When the Secretary of State believes that adequate voluntary collective bargaining has been developed to deal with pay and conditions of work, he may order the statutory joint industrial council to be abolished.

14. Fair Wages. The fair wages resolution of the House of

Commons states that a government contractor must observe the terms and conditions in his industry which have been established (usually by collective bargaining) in the district, or, if they have not been established, which are not less than the general level of the terms and conditions observed by other comparable employers.

This principle has generally been extended to contractors for local authorities and the nationalised industries. It encourages employers to observe collective agreements even though they were not a party to them.

STATUTORY BODIES

15. Industrial tribunals. These bodies were originally set up to deal with disputes arising from the Industrial Training Act 1964, but they now deal with an extremely wide variety of employment matters such as unfair dismissal, redundancy, discrimination, equal pay and safety.

They consist of an independent legally qualified chairman, an employers' representative and a trade union representative. Their proceedings are informal and it is not necessary for the parties in a case to be legally represented. Their purpose is to decide what is reasonable in all the circumstances of the case, and appeals from their decisions, which are heard by the Employment Appeals Tribunal (*see* **16**), can only be on points of law.

16. Employment Appeals Tribunal. This body, which is a court rather than a tribunal, consists of a judge and lay members representing both sides of industry and was set up by the Employment Protection Act 1975 in place of the National Industrial Relations Court.

It hears appeals on points of law from industrial tribunals and on decisions made by the Certification Officer (*see* **20**). Unlike the decisions of industrial tribunals, the decisions of the Employment Appeals Tribunal establish precedents.

17. Central Arbitration Committee. This body, also set up under the Employment Protection Act, comprises people experienced in industrial relations. It will arbitrate in disputes referred to it by the Advisory, Conciliation and Arbitration Service, ACAS (*see* **18**) and also adjudicate on claims that an employer has not disclosed to union representatives information requested for collective bargaining purposes (*see* **24**).

18. Advisory, Conciliation and Arbitration Service. This is an independent body governed by a Council which consists of members appointed after consultation with workers' and employers' organisations. It has the following powers and duties.

(*a*) The general duty of promoting the improvement of industrial relations and the extension of collective bargaining.

(*b*) Employers and trade unions can request its help in a possible or actual trade dispute.

(*c*) It may on its own initiative enquire into any industrial relations matter and publish its findings.

(*d*) It may enquire into a complaint by a recognised trade union that adequate information for collective bargaining purposes has not been disclosed (*see* **24**).

(*e*) It may prepare and publish codes of practice giving guidance for improving industrial relations.

INDUSTRIAL RELATIONS LAW

19. Definitions. The following are shortened versions of the definitions appearing in the Trade Union and Labour Relations Act 1974, as amended by the Employment Act 1982.

(*a*) *A trade dispute* means a dispute between workers and their own employer concerning terms and conditions of employment, engagement, non-engagement or dismissal of workers, allocation of work, a procedural agreement or trade union membership.

(*b*) *A trade union* is an organisation consisting wholly or mainly of workers, whose principal purposes include the regulation of relations between workers and employers or employers' associations. It is not a corporate body but has the power to make contracts and to sue or be sued in its own name.

(*c*) *An employers' association* is an organisation consisting wholly or mainly of employers or proprietors whose principal purposes include the regulation of relations between employers and workers or unions. It may be either a corporate body or an unincorporated association, in the latter case having the same powers as a trade union.

In all the definitions "worker" means any employee, manual or non-manual.

20. Independence and recognition. The Trade Union and Labour Relations Act 1974 defined an independent trade union as one which was not dominated by an employer and was not liable to interference by an employer because of the provision or withdrawal of financial or other support. A union is not independent, therefore, unless it is autonomous and financially self-supporting.

A Certification Officer was appointed under the Employment Protection Act 1975 to consider applications by trade unions for certificates of independence. A union certified as independent receives certain benefits under that Act.

A recognised union is one with which an employer negotiates with the object of reaching agreements. Very many companies have voluntarily recognised a union, or several unions, for a considerable time, but others have refused recognition. There are no statutory provisions for obtaining or enforcing recognition.

21. The closed shop. By the early 1970s nearly half the trade unionists in this country worked in a closed shop, i.e. a place of work where membership of a particular trade union was necessary in order to obtain or retain a job.

Closed shops have been brought about, usually by pressure from the unions, as a means of increasing their bargaining power and establishing their organisations within a company, but sometimes voluntarily by managements because a closed shop gave them an assurance that the unions with which they reached agreements represented all members of the appropriate class of worker. It is, of course, possible for a company to have a closed shop for some groups of its employees and an open shop for others.

The Trade Union and Labour Relations Act 1974 (amended by an Act of 1976) gave statutory authority to the closed shop, calling it a "union membership agreement" and defining it as an agreement which:

(a) is made between one or more *independent* trade unions and one or more employers or employers' associations;

(b) relates to employees of an identifiable class; and

(c) requires employees of that class to become members of the union or unions which are parties to the agreement, or another specified *independent* trade union.

The Act makes the closed shop legal but not compulsory and does not lay down a procedure for making a closed shop agreement.

However, it was amended by the Employment Act 1980 which states that it is fair to dismiss an employee who refuses to join an independent union with which the employer has a closed shop agreement unless:

(*a*) the employee has a genuine objection, based on conscience or a deeply-felt personal conviction, to joining any union or a particular union; or

(*b*) he was not a union member at the time the agreement was made; or

(*c*) in the case of an agreement made after the passing of the 1980 Act, if a secret ballot of those employees to be covered showed less than 80 per cent support for it;

(*d*) where the closed shop existed before the 1980 Act, if during the five years preceding the dismissal it had been supported in a ballot by 80 per cent of the employees covered or 85 per cent of those voting (a further amendment under the Employment Act 1982).

Where there is an agreement as defined in (*c*) and (*d*), an employee, when on company premises, only has the right to take part in the activities of a union specified in that agreement. This modifies the general right to be active in a union given under the Employment Protection (Consolidation) Act 1978 (*see* **23**).

A person who is, or seeks to be, employed in a closed shop may approach an industrial tribunal to claim that he has been unreasonably excluded or expelled from a trade union.

22. Legal immunities. When a lawful strike, as defined in **19**(*a*), takes place, the trade union, its officials or any workers concerned in the dispute are immune from legal action for:

(*a*) inducing or threatening a breach of contract, including a commercial contract or employment contract;

(*b*) interfering with, or threatening interference with, the performance of a contract;

(*c*) civil conspiracy, where two or more persons support non-tortious actions.

These immunities are contained in the Employment Act 1982, which, however, reduced the immunities given to trade unions under previous Acts. A union is now liable to pay damages (with an upper limit based on the size of its membership) where industrial action by its members or officials is unlawful.

The Employment Acts of 1980 and 1982 make unlawful "secondary action" to bring about a breach of a commercial contract. "Secondary action", defined as an inducement or threat to break a contract of employment with an employer outside the trade dispute, is only lawful when it is directed against a supplier or customer of the original employer with the aim of disrupting the flow of goods and services between them and is likely to achieve that purpose.

The 1980 Act also reduces the immunities hitherto given for picketing. Picketing a place of work in order to persuade someone to work or not to work carries legal immunity for actions in tort only if the pickets consist of:

(a) employees who normally work there;

(b) former employees, if the trade dispute concerns their dismissal, redundancy or resignation;

(c) employees who have no fixed place of work, or who cannot picket their own place of work—they may in these cases picket their employer's premises or the premises from which their work is administered;

(d) a trade union official accompanying a member of his union who is included in one of the above categories.

The picketing must be in contemplation or furtherance of a trade dispute.

It should be noted that picketing solely to obtain or communicate information does not involve possible breach of contract and is therefore free from the restrictions stated above. However, picketing can sometimes become a criminal offence if, for example, it is violent or causes obstruction of a public highway.

23. Legal rights of employees. Under the Employment Protection (Consolidation) Act 1978 it is unfair to dismiss an employee for trade union activity or for refusing to join a non-independent trade union. In certain circumstances (*see* **21**) he may be dismissed fairly for refusing to join an independent union where there is a closed shop.

If he is unfairly dismissed for refusing to join a union in a closed shop which does not satisfy the requirements of the Employment Act 1982 (*see* **21**(*d*)) he is eligible for compensation at a higher rate than normal. He may make the union party to the dismissal proceedings where he claims that the union put pressure on the employer to dismiss him.

The Employment Protection Act 1975 also gives an employee the right not to have any action short of dismissal taken against him:

(*a*) to prevent or deter him from joining or being active in an independent trade union (though this right is somewhat modified in a closed shop—*see* **21**);

(*b*) to compel him to join a trade union;

(*c*) to compel him to join any union where there is a closed shop if he has a genuine objection based on conscience or a deeply-felt personal conviction (*see* **21**).

The activities mentioned in (*a*) must take place either when the employee is not required to be working, e.g. lunch breaks, or at other times with the employer's permission. This protection is designed to help employees to organise where there is at present no recognised union or no union at all. However, once a union has been recognised its members must be given reasonable time off during working hours to take part in union activities.

Complaints that these rights have been infringed are made to an industrial tribunal, and a copy of the complaint sent to a conciliation officer in case the matter can be settled without a tribunal hearing. If the case is heard by a tribunal the onus will be on the employer to show that he has not infringed the employee's rights. If the decision is against him he may have to pay compensation to the employee, and the tribunal may make a "declaration" which will form the basis of the employer's future policy towards trade union activity.

The Trade Union and Labour Relations Act also gives a union member the right to resign from his union on giving reasonable notice and complying with any reasonable conditions. It will be seen that if he exercised this right while working in a closed shop he would be liable to dismissal without redress.

Under the Employment Act 1980 a person working, or seeking to work, in a closed shop has the right not to be unreasonably excluded or expelled from a trade union. Complaints are made to an industrial tribunal.

24. Law of collective bargaining. The Trade Union and Labour Relations Act 1974 states that a collective agreement is to be presumed not legally enforceable unless it clearly and in writing states otherwise.

Voluntary rather than legally enforceable agreements have always been preferred in this country, though the Industrial Relations Act 1971 tried unsuccessfully to change this attitude. The fair wages resolution (*see* **14**) does, however, provide a rather roundabout though very influential way of enforcing collective agreements.

The 1974 Act also states that a "no-strike" clause in an agreement can only be part of individual contracts of employment when the agreement:

(*a*) is in writing;

(*b*) expressly provides for the inclusion of the clause in individual contracts;

(*c*) is reasonably accessible to the employee at his place of work;

(*d*) is made with independent unions only.

The individual workers' contracts should include the no-strike clause either expressly or by implication.

The Employment Protection Act 1975 obliges an employer to disclose to representatives of an independent *recognised* trade union, on request, certain information for the purposes of collective bargaining. It includes information which should be disclosed in accordance with good industrial practice or which, if withheld, would impede the union representatives in bargaining. Union representatives are not, however, entitled to information which:

(*a*) would be against the interests of national security;

(*b*) would be illegal to disclose;

(*c*) had been obtained in confidence;

(*d*) related to an individual (unless he gave his consent);

(*e*) had been obtained for the purpose of legal proceedings;

(*f*) would be likely to cause substantial injury to the employer's undertaking.

The code of practice on this subject prepared by the Advisory, Conciliation and Arbitration Service recommends that the employer should disclose information on pay and benefits, conditions of service, manpower, performance, e.g. productivity, sales and orders, and financial matters. It suggests that unions should identify and request the information before negotiations begin, stating why they consider it relevant. Employers are advised to be as open as possible and to present the information promptly and clearly.

A union which believes it has not received adequate information may complain to the Central Arbitration Committee, which may then refer the matter to the Advisory, Conciliation and Arbitration Service. If conciliation fails, the Committee will hear the case and make a declaration on whether or not the complaint is well-founded.

The Committee in making its decision will consider to what extent the code of practice has been followed, although the recommendations in the code impose no legal obligations. If an employer refuses to comply with a declaration that certain information should be disclosed, the Committee may at the request of the trade union make an enforceable award of terms and conditions on behalf of the employees concerned.

It should be noted that the law affects national and workplace agreements equally, provided that recognised unions are involved.

25. Summary. The combined effect of the Trade Union and Labour Relations Act 1974, its amending Act of 1976, and the Employment Protection Act 1975 on industrial relations may be summarised as follows.

(a) Independent trade unions are encouraged rather than those which may be influenced by the employer, e.g. some company staff associations.

(b) Trade union activity is facilitated by penalising an employer who attempts to discourage it by dismissing or hindering employees.

(c) When an independent trade union is sufficiently strong it may press a company to give it recognition; its members are then entitled to reasonable time off for union activities.

(d) An independent trade union which has a substantial membership in a company (or section of a company) and has negotiated a union membership agreement, i.e. a closed shop agreement, has its position protected by the special provisions regarding dismissal and trade union activity.

(e) Strikers, who otherwise could be accused, for example, of inducing a breach of contract, are given considerable immunity against legal proceedings.

(f) Recognised unions have a right to information from the employer which will help them in collective bargaining.

(g) A collective agreement is presumed to be non-enforceable at law unless expressly stated otherwise.

PROGRESS TEST 25

1. Describe the organisation of a trade union. **(1)**

2. What are the effects on management of the existence of active trade unions in the company? **(3)**

3. Outline the scope of a typical national agreement. **(7)**

4. What is the relationship between national and workplace agreements? **(7, 8)**

5. What is a wages council and what are its powers? **(12)**

6. What are the main functions of an industrial tribunal, the Employment Appeals Tribunal and the Central Arbitration Committee? **(15–17)**

7. Define an independent trade union. **(20)**

8. Why do some employers encourage the closed shop? **(21)**

9. Define a union membership (or closed shop) agreement. **(21)**

10. In what respects is a union immune from legal action? **(22)**

11. Describe how trade union activity is protected within a company. **(23)**

12. Under what conditions must an employer give information to a trade union? **(24)**

Example of a Job Specification

JOB DESCRIPTION

Cement mixer operator   **XYZ Pre-cast Concrete Ltd**

Operates a cement mixing process which is largely automatic but requires checking to see that it is functioning correctly.

Manually adds colour to the mix when required.

Cleans interior of mixer at end of each day.

Keeps record of coloured mixes (normal mixes are recorded automatically).

Responsible to the plant foreman.

Not responsible for any other operators.

JOB SPECIFICATION

Major responsibilities. The operator is responsible for the production of satisfactory mixes and for the routine cleaning of the equipment. About 120 mixes should be produced per day, including colour mixes when required. He must be prepared to correct or stop the process manually if it is apparent that unsatisfactory mixes are being produced or if mechanical or electrical faults occur.

Routine duties. Starts process each day by operating controls.

By observing mixer control panel and appearance of mix, judges whether process is working correctly or if manual adjustments need to be made.

When instructed by foreman produces coloured mixes by adding colour from small pre-weighed bags. Enters details in record book daily.

Cleans equipment in last hour of the day.

Training (off-job, with an experienced operator) lasts two weeks. Should be able to work unsupervised after a further four weeks.

No unusual physical demands are made on the operator except

that cleaning the equipment necessitates some bending and stretching.

Non-routine or infrequent duties. During annual overhaul of plant assists for about a week in cleaning and dismantling.

May occasionally be required for general labouring duties, e.g. snow clearing.

Working conditions. A seat is provided by the mixer control panel but the operator frequently needs to stand or walk short distances to inspect the quality of the mix or to prepare coloured mixes.

There is some heating in winter from a hot water pipe running through the control area, which is under cover but draughty because of the entrance and exit points for the materials used in the process.

The work is occasionally dusty while the process is operating but very dusty while the equipment is being cleaned, necessitating the wearing of a mask.

There is a moderate noise and vibration, but it does not impede communication because the operator receives his instructions re coloured mixes in writing.

The work area is adequately lit.

Tools and materials used. The materials for the mix (except colour) are delivered and controlled automatically.

No tools are used except a hose, brushes and scrapers when cleaning.

Personal contacts. The operator is isolated except for very occasional visits from the foreman. He can see operators in other parts of the plant through the windows.

PERFORMANCE STANDARDS

120 mixes per day.
Colour mixes as required.
Satisfactory quality of mix.
No breakdowns due to inadequate cleaning.
Records of coloured mixes legible, accurate and up to date.

Example of an Appraisal Rating Scale

Name.................... Department................
Job .... How long in dept. ....
Date of birth............... How long in company ....
Please tick the ratings you think appropriate, after reading carefully the definitions of the factors and grades. You should add any general remarks in the space provided at the end of the form. Base your judgment on the requirements of the job and the employee's performance in the job.

---

1. KNOWLEDGE OF JOB
   (Present knowledge of job and of work related to it.)

   Knows only routine repetitive work. Will not learn ....
   Knows routine work and some parts of other jobs ....
   Knows most jobs but relies on others for special knowledge ....
   Good knowledge of practically all aspects of the work ....
   Complete grasp of all aspects of the work ....

2. ACCURACY
   (Standard of work compared with standard expected, degree to which work must be checked.)

   Work is inaccurate; requires constant checking ....
   Careless at times; requires frequent checking ....
   Usually accurate; requires occasional checking ....
   Accurate except on very difficult jobs ....
   Accurate on all jobs ....

3. SPEED OF WORK
   (Speed at which work is accomplished in relation to the standard expected in the job.)

   Very slow; always fails to meet requirements ....

Slow; often below requirements   . . . .
Average speed; meets requirements as a rule   . . . .
Above average speed; usually exceeds require-
ments   . . . .
Fast; always exceeds requirements   . . . .

4. CO-OPERATION
   (Ability to work with others at all levels; readiness
   to try out new ideas and methods; response when
   asked for a special effort.)

   Difficult to work with; often touchy and unco-
   operative   . . . .
   Occasionally difficult to work with   . . . .
   Normally co-operative; raises few difficulties   . . . .
   Always tries hard to co-operate; easy to work with   . . . .
   Co-operates extremely well with others at all levels   . . . .

5. INITIATIVE
   (Resourcefulness; ability to work without detailed
   instructions; readiness to offer ideas and suggestions about work.)

   Requires detailed supervision; waits to be told   . . . .
   Requires frequent supervision; asks for instruc-
   tions   . . . .
   Requires occasional supervision; sometimes offers
   ideas   . . . .
   Rarely requires supervision; resourceful, offers
   ideas   . . . .
   Never requires supervision; has many ideas, solves
   problems unaided   . . . .

TRAINING NEEDS
(Suggest any training courses or in-company experience which
might improve the employee's performance.)

PROMOTION POTENTIAL
The employee is an excellent promotion candidate because . . . .
The employee is a good promotion candidate because   . . . .
The employee is a border-line promotion candidate because . . . .
The employee is unlikely to be promoted because   . . . .

GENERAL REMARKS

GENERAL RATING

Assess employee's job performance in his *present* job:

Poor   Average   Excellent

Signed . . . .   Position . . . .   Date . . . . . .
Countersigned . . . .   Position . . . .   Date . . . . . .

Examples of Training Job Breakdowns

These job breakdowns are taken from *Recommendations for Training—Operatives* published by the Ceramics, Glass and Mineral Products Industry Training Board. The author is grateful to the Board for permission to reproduce them.

TWI JOB BREAKDOWN

Replacing tap washer

Element no.	Stage	Key points
1	Unscrew spindle cover (ferrule) to expose spindle assembly retaining nut	Turn in anti-clockwise direction
2	Support spindle cover (ferrule) in left hand, unscrew spindle assembly from tap body and lift out	Ensure correct size spanner, unscrew in anti-clockwise direction
3	Remove washer assembly and inspect valve seat	Ensure no ingress of foreign bodies
4	Unscrew washer retaining nut and remove—remove damaged washer	
5	Fit new washer replace retaining nut and tighten	Do not overtighten —might damage new washer
6	Replace washer assembly in tap	Ensure correct seating
7	Replace spindle assembly in tap body and tighten	Ensure washer assembly spindle is located in body of spindle assembly tighten clockwise direction
8	Replace spindle cover and tighten	Tighten in clockwise direction

Operation analysis sheet

Job: Linishing of television lenses
Element: Removing surface

Equipment—linishing belt

Left hand	Right hand	Vision	Other senses	Comments
AP to start grind	AP to start grind	Watch build up of ground glass appearing as a white curved line above point of contact with wheel. Density of line indicates amount being ground off. Red area shows point of contact	K to exert pressure and correct. Vibration of wheel indicates degree of pressure. Touch checks correct pressure being applied	Pressure exerted in a rocking motion to bring radius of face into even contact with belt
Hold	Hold	Check grind off of shear mark Check extend of grind up face ½ approx	K to reduce pressure in centre of screen	Extend grind to centre of screen holding elbows as grind reaches top half of screen Increase rate of locking across centre of screen
RG. Slide hand to bottom L/H side 3″ from corner	Hold	Follow white line	K to reduce pressure in L/H increase in R/H	
Push elbow away from body to assist rotation of screen	Pull screen towards body rotating screen through 180°	Follow white line to ensure smooth rotation		Weight of screen being taken by belt. Pivot for rotation of screen on belt at crown of screen face
RL and move	RG to top R/H corner, Th. inside touching angle of inside face and edge—1234 wrap over top edge	Follow white line to ensure smooth rotation	K & T to increase pressure in L/H group	
RG top L/H corner, Th. inside touching angle of inside face and edge—1234 wrap over edge	Hold	Follow white line to ensure smooth rotation		White line to be horizontal to belt—if at any other angle a cross cut grinding ridge may occur

AP—Apply pressure   RL—Release   K—Kinaesthesis   RG—Re-grasp   T—Touch   Th—Thumb

Examples of Job Evaluation Schemes

OFFICE JOB EVALUATION

The Institute of Administrative Management has developed a grading scheme for office staff which is described fully in its publication *Office Job Evaluation*. Extracts from the scheme are shown below, by kind permission of the Institute.

Eight job grades are defined as follows.

A. Tasks which require no previous clerical experience; each individual task is allotted and is either very simple or is closely directed.

B. Tasks which, because of their simplicity, are carried out in accordance with a limited number of well defined rules after a comparatively short period of training. These tasks are closely directed and checked, and are carried out in standard routine with short period control.

C. Tasks which are of a routine character and follow well defined rules, but which require either some experience (several weeks) or a special aptitude for the task, and which are carried out according to a standard routine and are subject to short period control.

D. Tasks which require considerable experience, but a limited degree of initiative, and which are carried out according to a predetermined procedure. The tasks are carried out according to a standard routine which may vary, but not enough to necessitate any considerable direction.

E. Tasks which may require one or more of the following:

(*a*) a basic level of professional or specialised knowledge, for example Part I or II of the ACMA examinations;

(*b*) performance or control of clerical or administrative work requiring mostly routine decisions, but occasional use of discretion and initiative;

(*c*) work supervision of a range normally of two to six clerical staff. The number supervised may vary according to the complexity or level of the work.

F. Tasks which may require one or more of the following:

(*a*) professional or specialised knowledge equivalent to an intermediate level examination of an appropriate professional association, for example Part II or III of ACMA examinations;

(*b*) performance or control of complex clerical or routine administrative work requiring occasional decisions of a non-routine type, and some use of judgment or initiative on routine matters;

(*c*) supervision of a range (normally five to twelve) of clerical staff in a section compact enough to enable full personal control to be directly maintained. The numbers supervised may vary according to the complexity or level of the work, and may include **E** grade assistants.

G. Tasks which may require one or more of the following:

(*a*) professional or specialised knowledge equivalent to a university first degree or to an advanced but not necessarily final qualification of an appropriate professional association, for example final years of ACA, the Institute's Diploma in Administrative Management or Part III or IV of ACMA;

(*b*) performance or control of work of wide complexity or importance requiring regular non-routine decisions and a regular use of judgment and initiative in the execution of predetermined policies;

(*c*) supervision of a range (normally nine to twenty) of clerical staff. Control of clerical work may be exercised through two or more grade **E** or **F** supervisors; or supervision of a smaller number of grade **E** or **F** professional or specialist staff. The numbers supervised may vary according to the complexity or level of the work.

H. Tasks which may require one or more of the following:

(*a*) professional or specialised knowledge equivalent to a university first degree with some experience or a final qualification of an appropriate professional association such as ACA, the Institute's Diploma in Administrative Management or ACMA;

(*b*) performance or control of work of significant complexity or importance requiring an extensive measure of judgment or initiative and responsibility for some contribution towards the development of departmental policies as well as for their execution;

(*c*) supervision of a range normally of twenty or more clerical staff. The numbers supervised may vary according to the complexity or level of the work, but control will normally require a deputy and two or more grade **E** or **F** supervisors; or supervision of a smaller number of grade **E**, **F** or **G** specialist staff.

The Institute gives examples of the application of the grading scheme to various types of office jobs. The following shows how computing jobs might be graded.

A. Stationery assistant. Fetching and distributing computer stationery, maintaining adequate stock at print units. Delivering tapes and disks to and from computer.

B. Trainee data preparation operator. Simple keyboard operation with no verifying.

C. Data preparation operator. Keyboard operating including verifying from a variety of source documents.

C. Computer output clerk. Receiving computer output and operating machines to trim, decollate, burst, guillotine, fold and envelope output.

D. Data preparation operator. Keyboard operating and verifying a variety of complex documents; operating equipment such as a punched card sorter where the sorting involves a complex coding system or a complicated analysis of information.

D. Computer operator. Trained computer operator.

E. Data preparation section leader. Directing the work of a small group of operators.

E. Programmer. Writing a variety of programs (typically with up to one year's experience).

E. Senior computer operator. Experienced member of operating team for computer with complex operating requirements.

F. Systems analyst. Responsible for systems design on small projects.

F. Senior programmer. Writing more complex programs (typically requiring one to three years' experience).

F. Chief operator. Responsible for a team of computer operators.

G. Senior systems analyst. Conducting complex systems surveys which may involve controlling the work of other analysts.

G. Programming team leader. Leading a small team of programmers and writing complex sets of programs.

H. Systems project leader. Responsible for leading a complex systems project requiring supervision of other specialist staff.

H. Chief programmer. Controlling complex projects with responsibility for programming section and possibly other systems staff.

The examples shown above are brief, and only provide a rough guide to the type or level of job in each grade. Fuller information may be found in the Institute's pamphlet *Office Job Evaluation*.

POINTS RATING SCHEME FOR MANUAL JOBS

The following is an example of a scheme used in industry for evaluating manual jobs. Note that the sub-factors under the heading working conditions are intended to cover outdoor as well as indoor jobs. A company in which nearly all manual jobs were under cover or free from contamination and noise would have a different set of sub-factors under this heading. The reader may wish to use this scheme to evaluate the job described in Appendix I.

	Max. points	
Skill and knowledge		
Education and training required	25	
Experience required	60	
Dexterity	15	
	——	100
Effort		
Energy and stamina required	60	
Working position	40	
	——	100
Responsibility and mental requirements		
For material and equipment	20	
For the work of others	25	
Concentration and alertness	20	
Need to act on own initiative	15	
Need to work steadily	20	
	——	100

Working conditions

Temperature and humidity	20
Exposure to climatic conditions	20
Atmospheric contamination (dust, dirt, smell, etc.)	25
Noise and vibration	15
Monotony and isolation	10
Nervous strain, hazards	10
	——
	100

Discrimination in Employment

1. Legal provisions. Two Acts, the Sex Discrimination Act 1975 and the Race Relations Act 1976, make it illegal to discriminate in all aspects of employment, e.g. job advertising, selection, terms of employment, promotion, training and dismissal. Discrimination means the less favourable treatment of a person by reason of sex, colour, race or ethnic or national origins.

An employer is liable if his subordinates discriminate unlawfully. Indirect discrimination is also unlawful, i.e. applying a condition or requirement which, although applied to both sexes or to all racial groups, is such that a considerably smaller proportion of one sex or of one racial group can comply with it, unless the employer can show the condition to be justifiable. An example would be a requirement for candidates for a senior clerical post to be at least six feet tall.

2. Exceptions. Employers may lawfully discriminate in the following cases.

(*a*) Where fewer than six people are employed.

(*b*) Employment in a private household.

(*c*) Employment carried out wholly or mainly outside Great Britain.

(*d*) For sex discrimination:

(*i*) where the job requires a person of a particular sex for reasons of physiology, e.g. modelling, authenticity, e.g. acting, or decency, e.g. lavatory attendant;

(*ii*) jobs in a single-sex establishment;

(*iii*) jobs which provide individuals with personal welfare or education services and those services can be most effectively provided by a person of a particular sex, e.g. probation officer;

(*iv*) jobs where there are legal restrictions on the employment of one sex, e.g. night work in a factory.

(*e*) For racial discrimination:

(*i*) where the job requires a person of a particular race for of physiology, authenticity or the provision of food and for consumption by the public in a special ambience, e.g. a Chinese restaurant;

(*ii*) jobs which provide persons of a certain racial group with personal services promoting their welfare and those services can most effectively be provided by a person of that racial group.

3. Complaints by individuals. A complaint of sex or racial discrimination in employment is made to an industrial tribunal within three months of the act complained of. A conciliation officer may be asked by both parties at this stage to settle the matter without a tribunal hearing, or he may intervene on his own initiative. If a settlement cannot be reached in this way a tribunal will hear the case and if it decides in favour of the complainant it may award the following:

(*a*) an order declaring the rights of both parties;

(*b*) an order requiring the respondent, i.e. the employer, to pay the complainant damages;

(*c*) a recommendation that the respondent should take a particular course of action within a specified time.

4. Enforcement through statutory bodies. The two Acts set up the Equal Opportunities Commission and the Commission for Racial Equality respectively. These bodies have a general duty to work towards the elimination of discrimination and promote equal opportunity between sexes and between racial groups. They may also investigate relevant matters, institute legal proceedings in cases of persistent discrimination and in exceptional cases help individual complainants.

If they find that an employer has contravened one of the legal provisions they may serve discrimination notices requiring the employer not to commit further unlawful acts. An employer may appeal against such notices to an industrial tribunal.

5. Implications for personnel management. Although discrimination in many areas of personnel management takes place constantly on the basis of personal qualities, experience, age and length of service, a company should be able to show that there has been no intention to discriminate unlawfully and that such discrimination has not taken place.

Job advertisements must not therefore state or imply that applicants of a particular race or sex will be favoured, and communications within a company regarding promotion, training or dismissal should obey the same rule. An employer should be able to show that the criteria for selection, promotion, etc., are fair, appropriate and without bias, and that candidates or employees are judged fairly against these criteria. As far as possible objective rather than subjective assessments should be made. Documentary evidence should be kept in case a candidate or employee makes a complaint.

Bibliography

INDUSTRIAL PSYCHOLOGY

Behavioural Sciences for Managers (R. L. Boot, A. G. Cowling and M. J. K. Stanworth) Arnold, 1977.

Industrial Psychology (E. J. McCormick and D. R. Ilgen) Allen & Unwin, 1981.

Job Satisfaction (ed. M. Weir) Fontana, 1976.

Personnel Selection Testing (R. F. Holdsworth) British Institute of Management, 1972.

Psychology and Work (D. R. Davies and V. J. Shackleton) Methuen, 1975.

The Psychology of Training (R. B. Stammers and J. Patrick) Methuen, 1975.

PERSONNEL MANAGEMENT

A Handbook of Personnel Management Practice (M. Armstrong) Kogan Page, 1979.

Employment Interviewing (J. Munro Fraser) Macdonald & Evans, 1978.

Manpower Training and Development (J. P. J. Kenny, E. L. Donnelly and M. Reid) Institute of Personnel Management, 1979.

Payment Systems (ed. T. Lupton) Penguin, 1972.

Personnel Management (D. Torrington and J. Chapman) Prentice-Hall, 1979.

Power, Innovation and Problem-solving in Personnel Management (K. Legge) McGraw-Hill, 1979.

Training in Industry and Commerce (E. J. Singer) Institute of Personnel Management, 1977.

Understanding Industrial Relations (D. Farnham and J. Pimlott) Cassell, 1979.

The publications of the Institute of Personnel Management and its monthly journal *Personnel Management* should also be consulted.

Examination Technique

1. Practice. Candidates who have not attempted an examination for some years, or who have not had recent experience in essay writing, often fail to do themselves justice in the examination room. Practice in answering previous questions, e.g. those in Appendix VIII, will add to self-confidence and give a better result.

2. Revision. If a long series of previous examination papers is available candidates may attempt to forecast what topics are likely to be included in the forthcoming examination; for example most examinations in this field contain questions about recruitment and remuneration, with other topics appearing in rotation. Quite often questions are set on subjects which have been discussed in recent articles in the relevant professional journal.

The progress tests at the end of each chapter of this book can be used to check that a student's revision has been thorough. Revision up to the last moment before an examination or late the previous night is not recommended; in the first case the student may remember clearly only those subjects he has just read and in the second he is too tired to think clearly. Students are often advised to stop revising three days before the examination and then relax completely, though few have been known to take this advice.

3. The question paper. Many candidates fail because they have not read the question paper thoroughly, perhaps producing good answers to questions which have not been set. The questions must be read carefully, then read again, noting particularly the following points.

(*a*) If a question asks for a comparison or a comment a mere description is not enough.

(*b*) When an examiner asks for a discussion of a quoted statement he expects some criticism, not complete approval of it.

(*c*) All parts of a question must be answered; if it asks for a description, a comparison and suggestions for improvement it is probable that each of these parts will be given approximately equal marks. Candidates should attempt them all.

(*d*) A question paper is a useful source of information. For example, a candidate faced with the question "What benefits would a company expect to gain from training its employees?" might well find that elsewhere in the paper there are questions on motivation, supervision, accidents and labour turnover which remind him of points to make.

4. Timing. After allowing about 10 minutes for settling down and reading the questions, the candidate can calculate how much time he should allot to each question, e.g. 170 minutes divided by five questions gives 34 minutes per question—half an hour of writing and 4 minutes for checking.

Although a candidate may feel that he could write for longer than half an hour he will lose marks if he does so; a quarter of an hour's extra work on a question may bring him two or three marks but the same time spent on a new question, even though it is difficult or uncongenial, can easily earn ten marks or more.

5. Planning the answers. Examiners do not have a high opinion of answers which consist of a number of disconnected and repetitive sentences apparently in random sequence. Candidates will avoid producing answers of this kind if they first spend a few minutes considering which topics they wish to deal with, and putting them in logical order, e.g. advantages, disadvantages, summing up, or description followed by discussion.

6. Irrelevant material. No marks will be given for parts of an answer which are not relevant to the question. Sometimes in response to a question asking for a discussion of one specific aspect of, say, training a candidate pours out all he knows about the whole subject of training, often failing to discuss adequately the particular point raised.

7. Illustrative examples. Examples to illustrate procedures or behaviour which have been taken from the candidate's own experience or from what he has read will add some individuality to an answer and show that the candidate understands the subject he is discussing. While preparing for an examination, therefore, a candidate is well advised to look out for and note any incidents or methods in his company which can be used as examination material.

8. Style and presentation. Illegible handwriting, poor spelling, complicated sentences and frequent corrections tend to irritate examiners, who are usually working under pressure. Submitting essays for criticism by others will help to remedy these faults, particularly if they have been written under mock examination conditions, i.e. without reference to books or notes and within a strict time limit.

The ideal examination answer is clearly written, expressed in short, direct and grammatical sentences which follow a logical order, illustrated by real-life examples and, of course, relevant to the question which has been asked.

Specimen Examination Questions

The following questions are included with the kind permission of the professional bodies listed below:

IAM Institute of Administrative Management
IMS Institute of Management Services
LCC London Chamber of Commerce and Industry, Private Secretary's Certificate
ICSA Institute of Chartered Secretaries and Administrators

1. (*a*) Describe the main features of two motivational theories developed during this century.

(*b*) Discuss the relevance of one of those theories in the light of the current economic climate in the UK.   (IMS)

2. Evaluate any major theory of motivation published since 1950, with special reference to the theory's practical applications, e.g. in your own organisation or in an organisation with which you are sufficiently familiar.   (ICSA)

3. Explain the importance of "motivation" and "job satisfaction" within the workplace.   (LCC)

4. Discuss the reasons why people work and the satisfactions that they may expect from working.   (IMS)

5. One result of technology has been to increase the number of boring jobs. What factors would you consider essential when looking at job design?   (IAM)

6. The interview can often be an inaccurate selection technique. How can its accuracy be increased, both by the improvement of the interview itself and by the use of additional techniques?   (IAM)

7. What characteristics should a work group possess in order to maximise its potential?   (IAM)

8. Explain the importance to the working group within industry and commerce of:

(*a*) attitudes;
(*b*) leadership;
(*c*) motivation. (LCC)

9. Why does an "informal organisation" come into existence within a formal structure? What implications does the "informal organisation" have for the personnel function? (ICSA)

10. "So far as an organisation is concerned, the attitudes of its employees are of no importance; it is their behaviour which counts." How far would you agree with this statement? What is the connection, if any, between attitudes and behaviour in a work context? (ICSA)

11. "Management in future must be by consent, not by authority." Discuss this statement. (IAM)

12. "Decisions which come as a surprise tend to be an unpleasant surprise." How can employees be involved in decision making? (IAM)

13. Why do individuals resist change at work and how best can such resistance be overcome? (IAM)

14. Discuss how attitudes to technological change are influenced by the social and economic environment. (IMS)

15. Describe the functions of the personnel department in a large company. (IMS)

16. Describe the main phases involved in carrying out a company manpower plan. (IAM)

17. You have been asked to recruit six additional technical clerks within the next two months. Describe the main stages of the recruitment process and indicate the problems most likely to arise and how they might be overcome. (IAM)

18. What is the difference between "recruitment" and "selection"? Illustrate your answer by reference to a named or specific category of employee, e.g. computer operators, sales representatives or secretaries. (ICSA)

19. If labour turnover is perceived to be a problem with any specific category of employees in an organisation, what steps should be taken to deal with the problem? (ICSA)

20. Discuss the possible causes of high labour turnover and the contribution of management services to its reduction. (IMS)

21. "Staff appraisal is a time-consuming administrative chore." How would you attempt to convince middle management of the true value of a suitable appraisal scheme? (IAM)

22. With reference to your own country, outline the role of government in encouraging training for work. (LCC)

23. What is the difference between "training" and "development"? To what extent can these processes occur through the medium of courses? (ICSA)

24. You are the training manager of an engineering company employing approximately 700 personnel. Produce for presentation to the management board a training and development programme for the supervisors and managers of the company. (IAM)

25. Discuss the merits and disadvantages of job evaluation as a means of determining an equitable distribution of wages and salaries. (ICSA)

26. What wage payment systems are currently to be found in use within industry and commerce in your own country? Choose one example and mention its particular advantages and disadvantages. (LCC)

27. In what ways can computers be utilised by personnel departments to enable them to perform their functions more effectively? (ICSA)

28. What are the advantages and disadvantages of a situation in which employees are represented by trade unions in an organisation? (ICSA)

29. Describe the role and functions of:

(*a*) the Trades Union Congress;
(*b*) the Confederation of British Industry;
(*c*) the Advisory, Conciliation and Arbitration Service. (IMS)

30. Describe the benefits, to a medium-sized business, in having:

(*a*) a formal grievance procedure;
(*b*) a formal disputes procedure;
(*c*) the availability of a public arbitration body such as ACAS.

(IMS)

31. Discuss the role of a shop steward regarding:

(*a*) working conditions;
(*b*) communications with management. (IMS)

32. What steps should an organisation take in order to ensure the absence of discrimination in its present policies (related to such areas as recruitment, selection, promotion and redundancy)? (ICSA)

Index

Details of some other Macdonald & Evans
publications on related subjects can be found
on the following pages.

For a full list of titles and prices write for the
FREE Macdonald & Evans Business Studies
catalogue and/or complete M & E Handbook
list, available from Department BP 1,
Macdonald & Evans Ltd., Estover Road,
Plymouth PL6 7PZ

EMPLOYMENT INTERVIEWING
JOHN MUNRO FRASER

This is one of the standard works on employment interviewing based on the five-fold method of assessing the individual and the work developed by John Munro Fraser. The author's approach is simple and straightforward and careful application of the method outlined will reduce the unavoidable margin of uncertainty in personnel selection to a minimum. Ideal for personnel officers and students of management, as well as for the employer who does his own staff recruitment.

EXECUTIVES IN ACTION
CAROL-LYNNE MOORE

The meaning and interpretation of movement has fascinated man throughout the ages, and present day research has confirmed that movement is not only related to both thought and action, but is a valuable means of communication in its own right. This realisation has now been given a tangible scientific basis through the Action Profile method devised by Warren Lamb. Thus, by application of this method, the movements of senior executives can be analysed and the result used to improve decision-making in management. Hence the subject of this book.

Executives in Action is a new and enlarged edition of the author's original book, *Action Profiling*, and describes how bodily movements and the forms of motion can be used to reveal an individual's inner needs and characteristics. Case studies in the form of movement portraits of managers are used to illustrate the various points, and the book includes sections on management action, decision-making, the nature of individual initiative, the relationship of non-verbal behaviour and motivation, and the methods of assessing this.

It will be suitable therefore for all those interested in industrial psychology, and personnel and human resources management by illustrating the role of movement awareness in improving management action and effectiveness.

HUMAN BEHAVIOUR IN ORGANISATIONS
IVAN T. ROBERTSON & CARY L. COOPER

This book is intended for students of management taking a first course in applied psychology. This includes students on BEC courses, undergraduates at polytechnics and universities, diploma students and others. It provides a straightforward but thorough introduction to many important psychological concepts and to their applications in work and organisational settings.

The book is divided into several sections. It covers fundamental topics such as human learning, attitudes, intelligence and personality. Other chapters describe group behaviour and focus on the characteristics of organisations *per se*. Topics of central importance to working life and organisational behaviour such as, the quality of working life, stress, personnel selection, training and behaviour modification are covered in detail. Emerging issues such as women at work also receive attention.

INTRODUCTION TO INDUSTRIAL RELATIONS
T.L. JOHNSTON

A working knowledge of the fundamental principles of industrial relations is crucial to any student of business studies, and whilst this book has been specifically written for students of the relevant BEC Option Module, it will also be useful to all those following courses in business studies, government, politics and social sciences, whether at "A" Level, BEC, or undergraduate level. The text adopts a multidisciplinary approach, and takes account of economic, historical, legal, political and social factors in the system of collective bargaining and disputes settlement, both at national and at workplace level.

A thorough study of the principles and practice of industrial relations in Britain is placed in its international context with the inclusion of significant features of several foreign systems.

LABOUR LAW
M. WRIGHT
This HANDBOOK is intended for all those preparing for examinations in labour law or industrial law, whether at university, polytechnic, college or professional level. It will also be useful to the general reader needing a concise statement of the main rules relating to employment and industrial relations. Contents include chapters on administration of labour law, the contract of employment, regulation of remuneration, trade unions, discrimination, termination of employment, safety and welfare, and the laws of collective bargaining and industrial conflict.

THE LAW ON HEALTH AND SAFETY AT WORK
M. DEWIS
This book, written in conjunction with the Institution of Industrial Safety Officers, is designed for safety officers preparing for the Institution's Associate and Full Membership examinations in law. It covers a range of topics which have seldom before been brought together in one publication, but which are all relevant and of particular interest to the safety professional. The book will also be most useful as a reference manual on health and safety legislation for practising safety officers, union safety representatives and those insurers, insurance brokers and liability assessors concerned with industrial safety. "The book is deep and detailed, it has an excellent chapter on fire and ought to be on every safety and fire officer's bookshelf." *Health and Social Service Journal*

OFFICE MANAGEMENT
J.C. DENYER, *revised by* JOSEPHINE SHAW
This book is invaluable to anyone concerned with office management, from the executive to the student preparing for a professional examination. The text takes account of factors such as the impact of employment legislation, the growing use of computers, the growth of white-collar unionism, and the increasing need of senior management for information for planning and decision-making, as well as the traditional aspects of the subject.

PERSONNEL MANAGEMENT
M.H. BOTTOMLEY

This book is written specifically for students taking higher level examinations in the subject, in particular those of the Institute of Personnel Management. It is also suitable for students of business studies in general and for personnel managers already in industry. It aims to present the subject as clearly and concisely as possible with the minimum of jargon and associated mystique which is so often a feature of textbooks on the subject. As well as the most recent research findings in the UK and USA, the contents include the work of the personnel department and the role of the manager, job analysis, description and specifications, manpower planning, job satisfaction, motivation, job enrichment, recruitment and selection of personnel, training and development, staff appraisals, discipline, grievance and dismissal procedures, salary and wages policy, industrial relations and the impact of the law on the personnel function.

The author, a former lecturer at the City of London Polytechnic, is currently Administration Manager at the Associated Octel Co. Ltd.

PERSONNEL MANAGEMENT
JANE BOYCE-MARTIN

Personnel management is that part of management which is concerned with people rather than with finished products. This book attempts to outline ways in which the main problems that prevent a company's human resources from being developed to the full can be overcome — if they are realised — or brought home to supervisors and managers if they have not yet been seen as a problem at all.